Managing the
Global Frontier

Managing the Global Frontier

Strategies for Developing Markets

PETER WILLIAMSON

with

Qionghua Hu

FINANCIAL TIMES

PITMAN PUBLISHING

PITMAN PUBLISHING
128 Long Acre, London WC2E 9AN

A Division of Longman Group UK Limited

First published in Great Britain 1994

A CIP catalogue record for this book can be obtained from the British Library.

ISBN 0 273 03969 5

Phototypeset in Linotron Times Roman
by Northern Phototypesetting Co. Ltd., Bolton
Printed and bound in Great Britain
by Biddles Ltd, Guildford and King's Lynn

The publisher's policy is to use paper manufactured from sustainable forests

CONTENTS

PREFACE

This book is about the next source of corporate growth: the extension of the multinational enterprise into great, untapped markets like China and eastern Europe. It picks up where traditional notions of globalisation leave off. Our task is to provide blueprints that senior management can use to succeed with geographic expansion into those few spaces on the boardroom map not already crowded with pins. The challenge is to get under the skin of strategy in action on today's global frontier – those regions where fundamental change is creating new opportunities in areas formerly so barren that world-class competitors are not yet entrenched.

The potential of these markets is widely appreciated. One cannot help noticing a huge economy like China, for example, after she has gone on notching up growth averaging almost nine per cent per year for more than a decade. To managers in North America and Europe where growth rates are struggling to reach two or three per cent, the attractions are obvious; especially so in a world where other sources of growth are hard to find. And it is proving difficult to squeeze more expansion out of diversification, product differentiation, increased variety and added service. In fact, the current trend to increased focus on a core businesses is, if anything, forcing companies to scale back. Yet shareholders and employees are still asking for double-digit growth, year after year.

But as we will quickly see, recognising this potential is not even the first step towards managing the global frontier. And simply cloning the kind of operation that has worked elsewhere isn't enough by far. Nor is having a big cheque book, teaming up with influential partners, or moving decisively to build a large scale operation – none of these, even in combination, can remotely provide a guarantee of success. The global frontier is littered with traps:

- the information void,
- brand ignorance,
- distribution systems that turn out to be 'black holes',
- organisations that never seem to be up to the job,
- structures that turn out to be undermining the strategy,
- locational deficiencies that put a drag on growth,

- new competitors that appear from nowhere,
- a cluster bomb of problems pulling managers in so many directions at once that they are unable to keep the business on track.

Despite this minefield it *is* possible to succeed, and in a way where the benefits are substantial enough to really make a difference to overall corporate results. In the quest to ensure managers ask the right questions before they leap and develop policies for frontier markets that will work on the ground, this book brings together strategic concepts with the lessons of practice. Throughout, the argument is illustrated with the experiences of numerous companies in Eastern Europe and the results of four months fieldwork in China involving face-to-face interviews with over 30 companies, among them many Japanese firms, who operate there.

In the chapters which follow we look at why expansion onto the global frontier is becoming a 'must' for more and more companies; the essential role of information as the raw material of strategy; cost-effective ways to find out what is going on in an opaque and rapidly changing part of the world; the role of two-way trade in providing a platform on which to build a frontier business, even where the ultimate goal is local production to serve the domestic market. We identify the routes to gaining locational advantage; the critical contribution that early investment in brands and innovative distribution strategies can make to frontier success; and the need to begin pre-empting future competition even before it arrives on the scene. We explain how companies have risen to the challenge of building a strong and capable frontier organisation in environments where skilled staff are scarce and difficult to retain; where workers are unfamiliar with even the basic systems on which modern business rests; and where risk-averse local managers have turned the avoidance of decisions into an artform.

As we proceed there comes the realisation that success in extending the global frontier requires dogma and heresy to live side by side. And in case after case, we see that winning strategies need the courage to turn conventional wisdom on its head; to flatly contradict the direction of management thinking in developed markets so that the peculiar challenges of the global frontier can be met. For those who are prepared for managing in a world turned upside down, the enormous potential for growth by extending the global frontier awaits.

Peter Williamson
London, September 1993.

ACKNOWLEDGEMENTS

Any book that draws as much of its inspiration from live case examples as this one does would not be possible without the co-operation and enthusiastic support of many practising managers. We would therefore like to thank the long list of people who contributed their scarce time away from managing the global frontier to answer our interminable questions and those put by our colleagues at *East Europe Business Focus*. Among those who deserve special mention are Xie Jinrong, Li Zhaoxi, Wu Xiaohong, Li Jianguo, Kimiaki Taira and Kajita Yukio in Beijing; Gábor Csaplár and Jenö Veér in Budapest; Yang Zhenqing and Ge Zhen in Dalian; Li Yijing in Guangzhou; Wu Jiufeng in Haikou; Weng Yonglin, Hu Dafu and Chen Ruifang in Hangzhou; Alex Sinyak in Kiev; Richard Jones, Tony Hales and Glen Steeves in Moscow; Ondrej Novak in Prague; Jin Zhongyuan, Fan Yongming and Su Shaohua in Shanghai; Zhao Wei and Sha Sha in Shenzhen; Ma Dongwen and Nie Yuhe in Tianjin; and Roman Dolczewski, Richard Lyon, Krysztof Suprowicz and Wojciech Trzcinski in Warsaw.

Particular thanks are also due to Michael Hay for his invaluable comments on earlier drafts of the entire manuscript. Any errors and misinterpretations that remain are, of course, entirely due to the intransigence of the authors.

1

GROWTH AND THE GLOBAL FRONTIER

Gazing at world maps is now a part of boardroom life. Faced with saturated markets and the economies of Europe and the US struggling to reach real growth rates of two or three per cent per year, top managements are looking elsewhere for expansion. They have little choice. Shareholders' demands for growth have not receded: they still expect double-digit increases in sales and profits, year after year. Satisfying the career aspirations of loyal employees also requires the flux of an expanding turnover and a flow of new challenges. 'More of the same' management, resting comfortably on existing products and familiar markets, is simply no longer good enough.

But many of these firms are already giants. To significantly alter their performance, big companies need to make moves consistent with their size. Yet, as they scan their lists of opportunities, what they see are only new market niches. At best, these new products and markets will provide icing on the corporate cake; an extra note in the annual accounts. At worst, they will provide little more than a management distraction; soaking up scarce management time and adding to complexity.

So when these top managers survey the horizon for growth potential, they are looking for something big; a new business that will make the kind of difference to the bottom line that most investment proposals can never even aspire to. On finding it, there is immense pressure to make a decisive move: a $100 million plant in China; an oil exploration lease on 18,000 square kilometres of the Volga valley. White elephants are all too often the result.

THE POTENTIAL AND PITFALLS OF FRONTIER GROWTH

We believe that by extending the global frontier, expanding into the world's great, untapped regions like China and Eastern Europe, companies can find the kind of significant growth potential they are looking for. Indeed, over the next decade it will become a necessity for more and more businesses to tap the global frontier for growth. But wringing that growth from frontier markets isn't easy. Without the right strategies, backed by the right capabilities on the ground, frontier markets can become a potential 'black hole' for scarce managerial resources and a trap for shareholders' cash.

The analogy of a gold rush is apt: among the crowd of ill-equipped and starry-eyed prospectors a handful will be lucky and stumble on a rich seam; quite a few will enjoy only a brief 'flash in the pan'; many more will return disappointed, having lost their shirts. When the dust settles, dabblers will have done little more than line the pockets of the people who sell the shovels (in this case the lawyers and advisers who collect their fees, whether or not the results of their handiwork survive). Only those who survey the terrain carefully, develop a strategy to set themselves apart from the sheep, and pursue this with determination and commitment, stand a good chance of building a substantial business capable of delivering the ongoing growth they need.

It may be fashionable to announce a major venture in a fast emerging market; it may even give the stock price a temporary kick. But the highways and byways of today's global frontier are more often paved with potholes than with gold for the taking. There are no free lunches. Perhaps more worrying still, a willingness to pour in investment cash is no guarantee of success. So resources need to be allocated with extreme care. The wide open 'steppes of opportunity' become crowded with jostling competitors at a frightening speed. So the strategic passes of the frontier terrain must be identified quickly and secured. The target is moving. So you need to have a clear picture of what you're aiming at. Seemingly powerful partners often fail to deliver; joint ventures can become a leaking bucket for technology and skills; early alliances can prove to be millstones as a previous order is turned on its head. So it is important to retain the bargaining initiative; giving too much away too early can leave you without enough bargaining chips later in the game. There is a 'chocolate factory of options' and too much to do. So prioritisation is essential. For all these reasons, a top quality **strategy**, not just resources and enthusiasm, is necessary to deliver profitable frontier growth.

Strategy in action

This book is about strategy in action on the global frontier. It provides a blueprint for managers to identify the hidden challenges, to begin securing long-term advantage from day one, and to build the local capabilities required for success. Equally important, it shows how parent companies need to change if their ventures on the global frontier are to become a significant part of the overall business. Throughout the book, we illustrate theory and concept with practical examples of what companies operating on the global frontier have actually done.

In the remainder of this chapter we show why it is becoming essential for companies to build positions in today's frontier markets despite the difficulties and challenges that lie in wait.

Chapter 2 tackles a problem that is endemic on the global frontier: lack of information on all aspects of business from customer needs to the availability of supplies. By constructing a fine edifice on a weak information base, numerous, well-capitalised projects have quickly begun to stumble. We therefore begin by focusing on strategies that will allow a company to learn what is really going on in its target market – as distinct from what regulatory tomes and glossy foreign investment promotions say it *should* be like. In Chapter 3 we then develop a framework to help companies build their frontier business in 'bite-sized' pieces; expanding their local capabilities step by step in a logical sequence to form a 'strategic staircase' to reach their long-term goals. The motto 'less haste, more speed' holds true.

One of the biggest nightmares of any frontier investor is of putting down deep roots in the wrong place. The ability to identify and exploit locational advantage brings the benefits of faster development and a stronger end result. As well as choosing a strategic location, the trick is to find ways to gain leverage from local customers, traditional skills, suppliers and service providers. Pulling this off is the topic of Chapter 4.

Faced with initial excess demand for their products in frontier markets, many companies wrongly fail to exploit the potential of pre-emptive marketing, brand building and innovative distribution strategies. In the early stages of their development, the communications channels available in frontier markets are relatively uncluttered with competing messages; customers are impressionable; distribution networks are being recast. Chapter 5 details strategies to make the most of these never-to-be-repeated opportunities.

The other side of this coin, of course, is that the uncluttered playing fields of developing markets, almost by definition, don't last. By the time competition heats up, it is too late to start looking for long-term, sustainable advantage. It is tempting to grab at deals as they come along. Frontier markets offer a deluge of attractive opportunities to anyone with cash.

Unfortunately the charms of most will prove ephemeral. The global frontier is littered with classic cash traps. Chapter 6 guides the investor through this minefield. It explains how successful ventures have laid the foundations of long-term advantage from day one.

Building an effective organisation is a keystone of long-term success; especially in the frontier environment where chronic skill shortages make it difficult to attract and then hold the right staff. In the drive to put physical capacity in place, organisational 'software' (staff, systems, skills, and style) often gets short shrift. The result can been disastrous: $150 million worth of shiny, new equipment spluttering to a halt because the organisation behind it is simply not up to the task. Chapter 7 tackles this issue head-on; using detailed case examples, it looks at how to build organisational capability on the global frontier. Chapter 8 follows up with an analysis of alternative organisational structures. The aim is deceptively simple: achieving a fit between strategy and structure. We look at why so many frontier businesses fail to achieve this fit. We suggest solutions: choosing an appropriate architecture between wholly-owned subsidiaries, various types of joint ventures and processing contracts; developing a workable organisation chart – one that provides the right kinds of group identity, co-ordination and informal as well as formal working relationships; putting suitable channels for communication with parent organisations in place.

Finally, Chapter 9 steps back from the detail. We draw together the threads of successful strategy for the global frontier around an essential and basic philosophy: managing an alliance, not a colony.

The list of pitfalls, problems and challenges looks formidable. Before setting out to meet them, we need to be clear why an increasing number of companies must embark on the treacherous voyage in search of frontier success.

STRATEGIC GROWTH: WHY FRONTIER MARKETS ARE BECOMING A 'MUST'

During the slump of the 1970s, diversification seemed to hold the key to breaking out of the strait-jacket of mature markets. In that decade the number of single-business firms within America's Fortune 500 reached a low of 14 per cent. But for many, this growth experiment turned sour. Throughout the 1980s, over 20 per cent of these same diversifiers substantially refocused their businesses.[1] As corporations decluttered their portfolios of businesses peripheral to their core skills, their turnovers shrank. When

Britain's BOC Group refocussed its portfolio in the early 1980s, for example, it had to unwind diversification into a range of industries from fish farming and pizzas to computers. Concentration back to its core gases businesses led to a substantial fall in total sales. The company had to look to international expansion halfway around the world to reverse this cut-back.

Short-term 'fixes'

During the 1980s, a massive increase in variety within each product line, along with waves of new product launches, helped stimulate sales in developed markets. But by the end of the decade these strategies left us with mind-boggling product proliferation: 26 varieties of disposable diapers from one producer, Procter & Gamble; and 205 brands of breakfast cereal on offer in the United States market, to quote just two examples. The resulting increase in operational complexity started to overwhelm our organisations and drive up costs. Consumers began to react against the latest products becoming obsolete soon after they left the shop.

In response, companies have begun to reverse their proliferation of product variety. They have scaled back the rate at which new models with little added value are being launched. There will still be an important role for new varieties in helping to squeeze higher growth out of existing markets. But their contribution will almost certainly be insufficient to close the gap between realistic growth rates in the developed world and the stretching goals that many corporations wish to meet.

Each new source of growth carries the seeds of its own demise because it sets in train processes which eventually make it uneconomic to squeeze more out of the same fruit. Growth through diversification eventually took companies too far away from a common set of core skills into businesses they had little idea how to manage and where the corporate value-added was close to nil. Increased variety and rapid-fire product launch began to get swamped in the complexity and truncated product life cycles it created. Each new plateau takes sales volume higher, but it is a plateau none the less. And so the search for a fundamentally new source of growth has to start again.

To see this cycle at work – and why corporations in the developed world must continually open up new product and market frontiers if they are to maintain their growth – one needs look no further than the experience of those postwar past-masters of high speed growth, the Japanese.

During the initial period of Japan's postwar expansion, much of the growth was achieved through relentless lowering of the costs of reliable, standardized products. Manufactured goods which had previously been the novelties of the rich became affordable to an ever increasing proportion of an expanding population. Today this is known in Japan as the 'product out' period.[2] The first oil crisis in 1973–4, combined with the beginnings of saturation of the local market, rendered this 'manufacturer push' strategy ineffective as an engine of further growth. For all their success, the quality circles, value engineering and zero defect systems, which had underpinned dramatic cost reductions and increased reliability, were no longer enough.

Recognising that new growth would come from convincing Japanese consumers they needed not just one home air-conditioner, but a different size, colour and specification for every room, for example, manufacturers began to add more variety to their product lines. Looking for overseas growth as a supplement, they added further models, with new gadgets, bells and whistles in order to differentiate their products as a way of wresting share from entrenched, local incumbents. This period, extending roughly from the mid 1970s through to the mid 1980s is known as 'market in'. While trying to lock in cost savings through component and process design, manufacturers added additional features to stimulate increased demand.

By the late 1980s, however, Japanese consumers were again reaching saturation, they not only had most types of products, they now had a range of each. Worse still, the gadgets, bells and whistles were losing their novelty. Quite simply, consumers were becoming bored. Manufacturers copied a trick the fashion industry had learnt a long time ago: if you want people to buy, keep changing what's on offer. Well before a product's technical life has run, ensure it's demonstrably out of date. Product life cycles were shortened, underpinned by simultaneous engineering and impressive reductions in product development times. Not only was the notoriously choosy Japanese customer offered a wide range of product varieties, new variations of each continually hit the market in the hope of exciting replacement demand.

Yet there was little time for congratulation; by the early 1990s business leaders were pointing out that the old ghost of **demand stagnation** was already beginning to reappear. Despite the past achievements, the task master of continuous growth was demanding to see a new trick. Given markets close to saturation and consumers who now regarded very wide choice, low cost, high quality and fast delivery as the norm, what could possibly add more value and continue to stimulate demand? Answer: the widest variety of all – to personalise the product for each customer. Firms started to **mass customise**: to produce suits, bicycles and golf clubs manufactured to fit the shapes and tastes of their future owners in a mass production plant. Now this principle is being extended to other products, from fishing rods to cosmetics.[3]

But the mass customisation growth strategy also has its limits. The Japanese cosmetics company Shiseido found itself trying to manufacture products with such complex, non-standard packaging in such short runs that it had to switch off some of its automated production lines and hire teams of people to finish each unit by hand. It has since reduced the total number of items by 36 per cent. So where are these Japanese firms looking for future growth? The answer: from the fruits of investment in geographic expansion.

Long-term strategies

In the first three years of the 1990s, overseas direct investment by Japanese firms exceeded $160 billion; almost doubling the existing stock of foreign non-financial assets. Their initial investments were primarily directed to the USA and later to the European Community. During 1992 and 1993, however, Asia became the destination for 44 per cent of the overseas direct investment planned by the top 115 Japanese firms.[4]

Similar trends are mirrored among corporations elsewhere. Since the late 1980s, both total world trade and foreign investment have been growing at almost twice the rate of output. Geographic expansion is back under the spotlight. World maps are going up on boardroom walls.

Corporate performance during the recession of the early 1990s seems to be confirming that companies who expanded outside the North Atlantic corridor are on the right track. Results released by the Anglo-Dutch food and consumer products group Unilever in 1993, for example, showed US operating profits down 8 per cent. European profits were down 1 per cent. In contrast, profits rose by 45 per cent in the geographic appendage that many companies, even Unilever, still describe as 'Rest of the World'. It is also telling that a substantial proportion of this profit increase came from Unilever's consolidation of its Brooke Bond and Lipton businesses in India and the £190 million acquisition of Cica, a tomato-based food business in Brazil.[5] Because corporate map gazers are finding that the obvious markets are already densely packed with pins – representing their own subsidiaries or those of competitors – their attention is turning to frontier markets. They are looking at previously uninviting territory partly because it has become more welcoming. But this new interest is partly because, although they know the going will be tough, most of the races for easy geographic expansion have already been run.

Like the other growth tonics before it, the potential for global expansion will reach its natural plateau too. Perhaps in ten years, maybe in twenty or thirty, the frontier of untapped markets will have pushed more or less as far as it can go. After that, it will provide the more modest growth of other well-developed markets, and corporations will have to rely on their ingenuity to find the next growth trick. But for now, the global frontier provides enormous potential for business growth.

THE POTENTIAL OF FRONTIER MARKETS

Reaching a precise understanding of frontier market potential is a formidable task for any serious investor. We will return to this successively in Chapters 2, 4, 5 and 6. But it is useful at the outset to prepare a thumbnail sketch of today's global frontier and where the major opportunities lie.

An identikit is a good place to start: how do you recognise a frontier market when you come across one? From the standpoint of corporate strategy, two essential features distinguish the global frontier. *First, frontier markets lie beyond the geographic line where world-class competitors are already entrenched.* On this criterion, for example, China would qualify, but for most types of business, Japan would not.

Second, to be a frontier market in the sense of this book, forces of change must be at work; forces that are creating new opportunities for multinational firms. These may include advances in technology that increase the viability of markets that were uneconomic to serve using previous methods. The use of new broadcasting technologies like cable and satellite by CNN or Star TV to supply customers across the Third World, where setting up a series of traditional TV stations would have been unprofitable, is a case in point. More usually, the changes that transform a region from simply being under-developed to become a frontier market, come from within. These include shifts in the stance of governments, deregulation, discoveries of new natural resources, or reaching the 'take-off' stage of economic growth. On this criterion Eastern Europe is part of today's global frontier, where most of sub-Saharan Africa is probably not.

Frontier markets are therefore those where new opportunities thrown up by change intersect with the absence of entrenched, world-class competition. Among the regions which satisfy this definition, of course, some are more attractive than others. Five factors comprise the initial, acid test of a frontier market's potential:

- its current size
- its projected growth rate
- its economic and human resource base

- the existing level of market saturation
- the strength of established competitors.

On today's global map, the China frontier stands out head and shoulders on the first two of these criteria, as illustrated in Fig. 1.1. A market comprising almost one fifth of the world's population is not be sneezed at. Even more important still, in the 14 years since China began the Deng Xiaoping reforms, its real growth in Gross Domestic Product (GDP) has averaged almost 9 per cent per year. At that rate of growth, its economy doubles in size every eight years.

To put that in a comparative context, this means China is generating the equivalent of a new economy about the total size of Malaysia each and every year.

Of course there are bound to be growth setbacks: overheating, inflation, political panics, stepping on the brakes. But if China hits its target of 10 per cent average growth through to the year 2000, a target it has so far exceeded in the early 1990s, it will have equalled the performance of Japan and Taiwan in the 23 years after 1950.[6] And for some in China, substantial disposable income is not just coming, it has arrived. Compare their situation with some of the South East Asian 'tigers': over 40 million people already have disposable income higher than the average Indonesian; a sizable proportion have more wealth than the average Thai.

Yet, as we will see, population, growth and income are incomplete measures of frontier potential. In 1991, the United Nations developed a more comprehensive indicator that combines national income with three other measures: adult literacy, life expectancy and average years of schooling – dubbed the 'Human Development Index'. This is plotted in the vertical axis of Fig. 1.2. We have combined this with a rough, but fairly representative, measure of consumer market saturation: the number of people per television set (the US is the closest to saturation – only 1.2 people, including babies, have to share each box). In China in 1990 it was one set between 100.7, suggesting there is room for a few more sales yet, before the market retreats to replacement demand. In fact, what this low saturation index signals, is that many modern products are virtually unknown to significant numbers of potential consumers.

On measures of economic and human resources then, the, China frontier is middle of the road: further along than India, for example, but well behind Latin America and Eastern Europe. The final piece of our rough jigsaw is the competitive strength of existing competitors. Here China scores well. State enterprises still accounted for over half of GDP in the early 1990s;

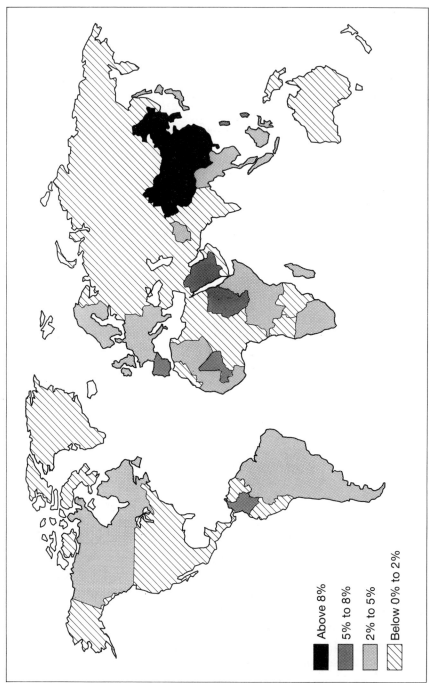

Figure 1.1　Worldwide economic growth

Source: The Economist, Pocket World in Figures, Century Business (1993)

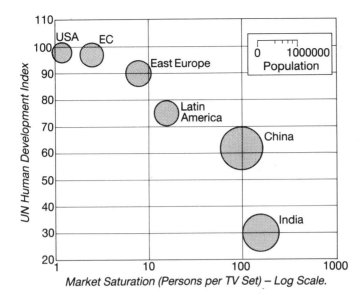

Figure 1.2   Market potential on the global frontier

Note: Circle size is log-proportional to population

Sources: United Nations, Human Development Report, Washington, 1992; The Economist Book of Vital World Statistics, Hutchinson, London 1992

many have productivity levels around one tenth of well-managed joint venture investments, sometimes considerably less. Around 37 per cent of output is accounted for by co-operative enterprises, mainly owned by local townships and neighbourhood enterprises. These generally have much better productivity, but limited resources. Lastly there are privately owned enterprises that account for 12 per cent of GDP.

Within the Chinese private sector there are strong locally-owned companies like the Stone Group, makers of computers and office equipment. China's largest private company, it has internationally comparable productivity levels with sales of over $350 million. But such competitors are few. There is also competition from over 17,000 foreign joint ventures and wholly-owned subsidiaries that have commenced operations (among 42,000 with approvals granted by 1992). They put some $23 billion of capacity in place by the end of 1991. In a few industries, as we will see in Chapter 6, this means that the playing field is already getting crowded. In most market areas, however, the foreign competition in this frontier market is still limbering up.

In Eastern Europe growth rates have been much less spectacular over the past decade: mostly below those of developed markets, and from a much smaller base. Since reforms and restructuring got under way, the majority of these economies have actually shrunk. But the potential of this part of the global frontier is not to be underestimated, especially as tough medicine begins to produce results. The current population of Eastern Europe exceeds 400 million.[7] And the region scores highly on latent economic and human resources, as demonstrated in Figure 1.2. Levels of education are generally high. The region's energy industry already produces more than eight tenths as much output as the entire OECD group of 24 developed nations combined.

The problem in Eastern Europe is certainly not a lack of resources, but what it does with them. If Russia could sell all the raw materials it produces at prevailing world prices, for example, it would earn twice as much as it could from selling the goods it produces with them. In other words, much of Russian industry actually destroys value, when measured by international standards: what it puts in is worth more than what it gets out. Large volumes of good quality inputs are used inefficiently to produce mediocre products and services. The same was true in the former East Germany. After unification it was found that the major exporter like The Karl Zeiss Jena Camera company had been importing DM30 worth of inputs for every DM8 of sales.[8] Reversing these nonsensical equations by improving efficiency and increasing value-added on a strong resource base, offers opportunities for foreign business on the East European frontier. As a now thriving exporter of plywood building panels from the former East Germany found, the basic materials and processing infrastructure was already there. But two critical elements were missing: selective investment in equipment to remove critical bottlenecks and quality failures in the product line; and modern management skills.

Our measure of market saturation in Fig. 1.2 has another interesting message: Eastern Europe is not quite as starved of goods like consumer durables as we sometimes think. The opportunity, as shown in Table 1.1, is only partly equivalent to that in China and India, where a large proportion of demand is from first-time buyers who have never had access to the generic product. A much higher proportion of east European families have a version of the product (although market penetration is still well below the saturation levels of many OECD countries). This means the frontier opportunity in Eastern Europe often involves pushing out poor quality goods and convincing consumers to trade up to a better offering. This has implications for the right strategy ranging from technology through to marketing.

Table 1.1   Measures of market saturation (1991)

	No. of persons per:			
	Car	TV	Telephone	Radio
OECD	2.6	2.0	2.5	2.1
Eastern Europe	21.7	7.8	9.4	4.4
China	1093.3	100.7	149.8	7.3
India	542.4	155.0	191.0	12.9
Latin America/Caribbean	45.9	15.7	16.5	4.1
Sub-Saharan Africa	357.0	695.7	345.1	10.3

Source: The Economist Book of Vital Statistics, Hutchinson, London, 1992.

Today then, China and Eastern Europe are the key areas where the global market frontiers are advancing afresh. Therefore it is from these markets that most of our case studies in the remainder of this book will be drawn. But many of the principles and strategies we outline will also find application in other markets that are beginning to show signs of a steady forward march.

India, looking jealously at China's growth at double its own rate, is rapidly deregulating. The restructuring which results will create the kind of opportunities unseen on the subcontinent for many decades. Despite these trends, many business people look at India's per capita income of only $336 and pass on. But when they point out that only 10–15 per cent of the population have money to spend, these observers forget that this middle-class niche alone comprises around 100 million people with substantial disposable income. Much of the local competition, both domestic and foreign owned, had become complacent, inefficient and reluctant to innovate or bring quality standards up to scratch during the long period of virtual autarchy. This provides a competitive opportunity while these incumbents struggle with the process of change necessary to improve both costs and product appeal. So this frontier now shows signs of life: in the year to June 1993, India attracted foreign investment proposals amounting to $2.2 billion, compared with an average of just $150 million p.a. over the previous decade.

The Latin American region, meanwhile, has a combined GDP of around $900 billion with a growing number of its economies returning to economic stability. On average, it falls in the very centre of the resources-saturation schema in Fig. 1.2, that is between eastern Europe and China: economic and human resources are substantial and saturation is a long way off. Of course the disparities between countries within the region are large: the Latin American region (including the Caribbean) covers a mix of economic saints and sinners. But even Mexico, recognised as a star performer since its reforms in the late 1980s, only managed real growth in GDP of 2.7 per cent in 1992 after a peak of 3.6 per cent in 1991. From 1982 to 1988, the economy did not grow at all; indeed, real income per capita fell by an average of 2 per cent per year. Maybe the remarkable period in Mexico's recent history, from 1950 to 1981, when real growth averaged 6.6 per cent per year (and a healthy 3.4 per cent p.a. per head) will return. Yet this frontier is not 'motoring' quite yet.

GETTING DOWN TO STRATEGY

Such macroeconomic sketches are a starting point; they give a sense of whether the 'game is likely to be worth the candle'; and whether any specific project is likely to get a fair economic wind. In an initial assessment of the global frontier, the five factors we detailed above are worth a careful look.

What is so surprising is that many strategies virtually stop there. To paraphrase one of these (that shall remain anonymous): 'We want to expand geographically; non-traditional markets are our key priority; of particular interest are populous markets where our product is virtually unknown; stop; now lets find partner and do a deal.' Veterans know better. They know, for example, that a strategy should mould the deal, not the other way around. On some parts of the global frontier, deals don't always turn out to mean what they might seem. It has been known, for example, for risk-averse officials who were not well versed in international practice, to sign letters of intent with a number of different foreign bidders for the same project.

It is easy to agree that sound strategy is essential for success, but strategy has to be based on **information**. And frontier markets are unfamiliar territory to most investors. Even for those with past experience, the rapid pace of change creates new uncertainties that quickly obsolete a good part of any stock of knowledge. Therein lies the first problem: how to fill the information void. Few databases or tidy market research reports exist here.

Some try to solve the problem with a war chest of cash, on the argument that on a global frontier where capital is scarce, the red carpet is bound to be rolled out, from the top of the country down. They are likely to be sorely disappointed. The fact that cash investment is no panacea, even when it attracts the attention of senior officials, is aptly demonstrated by the early history of Volkswagen's $300 million joint venture plant: Shanghai Volkswagen Automotive Company.

The deal, 50 per cent owned with four Chinese state enterprises, took seven years to negotiate. Three years after start-up it was producing 16,000 cars per year, compared with its capacity for 90,000 (and the plan had been to double that in 1991 with the acquisition of a neighbouring factory). The engine plant, designed to produce 340 engines per day was struggling to produce 70. And not for lack of labour: engineers estimated that only 800 workers were really needed in a plant with a payroll of 2,300 people. Fortunately, Volkswagen's financial exposure beyond the initial investment was limited by a clause in the contract that required the Chinese government to provide foreign currency for imported parts until the joint venture had produced 89,000 cars (a 'shake-down' period that in practice took more than five years).[9] The company is now back on the road, but Volkswagen was forced to mount a turnaround first.

Admittedly Volkswagen was one of the earlier pioneers on the China frontier in the 1980s. Many things have changed. And Volkswagen can hardly be accused of a 'shotgun wedding' – tales of these experiences are generally very much worse. But the example underlines an important point: even if you don't rush into a local alliance or joint venture deal, it is extremely difficult to develop a sound and detailed strategy and to look under all of the possible local 'stones' from many thousands of miles away. Trying to fill in the details after you have sunk a large investment on the ground means continually looking over you shoulder as the financing costs of an under-utilised facility mount up. Inadequate information is not a theoretical nicety; it translates into hard cash cost.

Yet, for all the problems associated with operating on the global frontier, there is no escaping the fact that its attractions are unique: opportunities created by favourable winds of change, where world-class competition has yet to become entrenched. For managers caught in the fork between saturated markets and demands of the organisation and its shareholders for ongoing growth, serious initiatives to crack frontier markets are fast becoming a 'must'. For today's corporate giants, few other initiatives offer the prospect of a new business so substantial that it can make a real difference to their global sales. Among the potential target markets, China and Eastern Europe stand out as offering the hottest prospects. Both these environments, however, present formidable risks. Even when joining the gold rush is accepted wisdom, there are few accolades to be gained placing big bets and coming home without your shirt. So managers face an immediate barrier: the lack of information necessary to give any investment acceptable odds. Chapter 2 develops the strategies to tackle this information void.

References

1 C. Markides, Corporate Refocusing, *Business Strategy Review*, Vol. 4, No. 1, Spring 1993.
2 See, for example, H. Yamashina, *Competitive Manufacturing and Subcontracting Systems*, Kyoto University, Mimeo, 1991.
3 See R. Westbrook and P.J. Williamson, Mass Customization: Japan's New Frontier, *European Management Journal*, Vol. 11, No. 1, 1993, pp. 38–45.
4 *Foreign Direct Investment Plans by Major Japanese Firms*, Export-Import Bank of Japan, Tokyo, 1992.
5 *The Financial Times*, 14/15 August 1993, p. 8.
6 The World in 1993, *The Economist*, London, p. 79.
7 Including the states of the former Soviet Union.
8 Russia's Value Gap, *The Economist*, 24 October 1992, p. 97.
9 Joint ventures in China: Inscrutable, *The Economist*, 17 March 1990, pp. 92–94.

2

WATCHING AND LEARNING

Strategy documents for the global frontier invariably start out upbeat. They paint on a broad canvas. The picture is of billions of people hungry for Western products from Coca-Cola to cars; markets where potential demand far outstrips available supply. Big opportunities are used to justify big moves and decisive investments. Chief executives jet in for a round of banquets, a visit to the Great Wall, an audience in the Kremlin. Confidence that market opportunity will be combined with government blessing from the top often appears sufficient justification for investment. With the benefits of modern technology and management systems, combined with low wage rates, success from shiny new factories seems assured.

We saw just this cycle of decision making during the 1980s as Western companies, led by US multinationals, rushed through China's newly opened doors. The race to build joint venture factories was on. With the benefit of hindsight, *The Economist* concluded simply : 'Almost without exception, American corporate leaders wasted their shareholders' money'.[1] They were not alone. Low productivity, poor quality and the burden of frittered welfare overhead undermined attractive financial projections which looked watertight at wages as little as 60¢ per hour. Even successful ventures found repatriation of local profits was hampered by scarcity of foreign exchange, reducing the real returns on hard currency investments. With the opening of Eastern Europe as we entered the 1990s most were initially more cautious. But as one chief executive put it: 'You quickly come to the point of "go" or "no go": without substantial investment there is not much you can do.'

ESTABLISHING WATCHING AND LEARNING POSTS

This doctrine of invest or abandon is commonplace. There is, however, another way. Scan the list of the top ten Sino-foreign joint venture investments published annually by China's *Economic Daily*, for example. Even as late as 1990, you would not have found a single venture backed by corporate Japan. Does this mean that Japanese companies are not interested in the commercial potential of their huge frontier neighbour?

If you look instead in the telephone directory of any city on the Chinese coastal frontier, from Dalian to Guangzhou, you will find literally hundreds of Japanese corporate representative offices, branch offices, industry association representations, Tokyo-headquartered consulting firms, banks research centres and Japanese government offices. These began to appear in the late 1970s. Already by 1985, some 75 per cent of all foreign offices in Beijing were Japanese. In 1991 Beijing had over 350 Japanese representative offices, still more than 50 per cent of the total of all foreign representative establishments. A recent survey in Dalian found that 33 of the 46 foreign offices were Japanese.[2] The Japanese trading house, Marubeni Corporation, alone has offices in 16 Chinese cities, more than it has in any other country. Its Beijing office employs a total staff of 80, including 20 Japanese. Capital investment is negligible. These individuals are not responsible for production facilities. They are prohibited by local government from direct involvement in trade. Instead, the network forms a powerful 'information vacuum cleaner'. These offices are busy: watching, listening, forming new relationships and strengthening existing ones. They conduct continuous and detailed investigation of development on the global frontier, emerging sources of supply, market conditions, the objectives of local communities and the shifting balances of power. These offices, and the detailed information they painstakingly gather, form the vital first stage of managing the global frontier.

The benefits of a permanent watching and learning post are, of course, not confined to the Chinese market frontier. The Japanese have successfully used this strategy before: in the USA in the 1960s and 1970s and in Europe in the 1970s and 1980s. First came the representative offices, then the distribution and service centres, so that by the early 1980s Japanese companies had invested a total of $34 billion in their American distribution and service operations – accounting for 40 per cent of the value all foreign-owned operations in wholesale trade.[3] Investment in manufacturing and R&D followed on later. Firms like Motorola, ICI and Kodak successfully entered the Japanese market by a similar route.[4] Today, British Petroleum (BP) is demonstrating the value of this same approach in the context of eastern Europe. BP has been engaged in trading operations in the former Soviet Union for many years. The core has been buying, and sometimes selling, crude oil. BP Nutrition has also imported large quantities of grain into Russia and over the past decade has built a significant business in buying and selling of chemicals. Until 1990 all of this trading activity was successfully conducted without a permanent presence. Why then, did the company struggle through a 12-month process of accreditation during 1989–90, to establish a representative office?

The answer lies in information and relationships. BP saw the possibility of involvement in exploration and production opening up. To access these opportunities, it needed to be seen locally as more than a trader. It needed to keep continuous tabs on what was going on. Initially, the local Moscow-based staff were primarily messengers. Their presence was a statement of future intent by the company. But other benefits quickly began to flow. BP already had good contacts with the relevant ministries. However, when in late 1990 the ministry of chemicals and oil refining virtually disappeared overnight and was reborn in a new incarnation, local contacts became more important – contacts with individual state governments, local associations, right down to grass roots level. Local representation made it possible to respond quickly to this fragmentation of decision making and to become involved in the new deals emerging as a result of complex and rapid change. It was also able to maintain continuity with key individuals as they moved.

Wellcome plc., the international pharmaceuticals group, is another example of the power of a local presence. Only around one per cent of its worldwide sales had been in Eastern Europe. Even these were often on the basis of agreements which would not have stood up in a free market.[5] Yet the company maintained representative offices in the Czech Republic, Hungary, Poland, Romania and Yugoslavia as well as the former Soviet Union. Through these offices it has built up a detailed knowledge of the medical infrastructure in these countries. Since all East European nations previously worked against a mandate to become self-sufficient in medical products, Wellcome's potential market was limited to specialised, high technology products which East European countries did not produce them-selves. Sales volumes, therefore, were sentenced to remain at low levels. But through continuing representation the company was able to build up many thousands of relationships with organisations and influential opinion setters in the East European medical professions without massive invest-ment. Now that markets to serve the medical needs of the 400 million people in Eastern Europe are opening up, Wellcome has an invaluable head start over competitors in the marketing, sales and distribution of its products.

THE POWER OF INFORMATION

In developed markets, superior information is increasingly viewed as a key source of competitive advantage.[6] On the global frontier, where communications infrastructure is severely lacking and secretive bureaucracies broke knowledge as the basis for power, information is gold dust. Yet, having satisfied themselves with an assessment of the broad panorama, many companies entering the global frontier leave the details to their local partners. They are wrong on two counts. First, the assumption that locals have the information is often simply incorrect. Second, even if they do have the necessary data, it will be passed on in a carefully filtered and selectively interpreted form.

The lack of independent information reduces a foreign participant's stock of bargaining chips. The opposite is also true; investment in information pays. As one Chinese general manager told us ruefully: 'It's really tough when I find myself negotiating with a foreign company with better information on national and local markets than I have myself. Its even worse when they are more informed about the latest political trends.'

In a banquet room of a hotel in Tianjin, Japan Airlines recently held a reception. It was to celebrate the 100th flight which just one senior representative of a Japanese pharmaceuticals company had taken in going to and from China over the previous two years. Gaining the information edge requires persistence. For most companies it requires a properly staffed representative office. One which is capable of untangling the complex web of power relationships which have been developed to an art form throughout much of the global frontier and of hosting the right people on the right occasions. Two other less obvious requirements, however, are also essential:

- the mindset, and systematic capability, to tackle the problem of unquestioned assumptions;
- the communication channels and the organisational structure necessary to secure the right responses from all levels back at headquarters.

Unquestioned assumptions

In our own markets we seldom question basic tenets of the way buyers behave, the status associations of familiar products, the practical implications of a legal document, the way stocks flow through the distribution pipeline, what motivates employees, or that the electricity will flow when we turn on a switch. Imagine, instead, that you walked into work one morning having shed all of the unquestioned assumptions you deploy daily in your job. Without this extensive base of 'givens' you wouldn't be ready to approve a major investment decision; in fact it would be difficult to take even minor decisions with any confidence at all. Yet this lack of 'givens' is close to the reality when we venture into a global market frontier. The terrain is a minefield, not because of malignant local forces, but as a result of the questions we never think to ask. Only sustained information collection, an extended period of watching and learning can sweep away those mines.

Take a simple example. Many negotiators on the global frontier spend countless hours perfecting the fine print of legal agreements. They are only satisfied when all of the verbal loopholes are finally closed and contingencies covered. The unquestioned assumption, of course, is that these legal rights could be enforced. The reality of the global frontier may be very different; as one official put it succinctly: 'Black and white is for printers. Here we negotiate the real laws.' A broader agreement with more time devoted to understanding the pressures on municipal authorities may have been much more effective.

Without a deep understanding of what makes a local market tick, we can also be deceived by numbers we find comfortably familiar. At the year end one company in our survey of frontier regions had celebrated its achievement of 50 per cent real increase in sales in a difficult market with rising inflationary uncertainty. Unconsciously it was making the reasonable assumption that what is sold is a good indicator of what is actually consumed. In fact, hoarding by distributors had been the source of the sales growth. Distributors had been building stock in a speculative attempt to profit from expected inflation. Two years later it was still struggling to manage the blocked distribution pipeline and associated sharply lower order flow.

The list of unquestioned assumptions that can trip investors up is almost infinite. Some of the most common ones we observed in our research are listed below. Which of these, or the many others, turn out to be most critical ones varies case by case. Rooting them out requires attention to the gritty detail, not just an open mind. So participation in the cocktail and banquet round is only a part of the watching and learning brief. Each time our Japan Airlines' revered, frequent traveller stepped off the aircraft in Tianjin, he came with a detailed list of questions; a mix of requests for hard facts and softer impressions.

Some of the unquestioned assumptions that have proved disastrously wrong on the global frontier have been:

- *Partnerships*
  - A majority shareholding confers control
  - Well-meaning, senior officials can deliver 'on the ground'
  - When officials needs one partner for a specific project, they will only issue a letter of intent to proceed
  - Joint ventures are the only stable form of partnership
  - Local partners don't have access to substantial cash to invest.

- *Supply*
  - Supplies can be purchased on the open market
  - Connection to water, electricity and gas means there is something to flow through these wires and pipes
  - Supply contracts are enforceable in the face of other demands or a better offer.

- *Operations*
  - Frontier markets are a good home for obsolete technology
  - Managers take decisions (their job may have been to avoid them)
  - A major city is the only viable location.

- *Marketing*
  - Frontier market consumers buy 'cheap and cheerful' products, not up-market brands
  - Advertising is a waste of money when you can't keep up with demand
  - A buyer who has the cash to purchase a piece of equipment also has money for the consumables they need to operate it.

- *Distribution*
  - What went into a distribution pipeline has been sold
  - Customers naturally look to distributors for information and service
  - Products consigned to one customer won't be allocated to another.

The questions to ask

By their very nature, unquestioned assumptions can only be unearthed through a systematic approach. Figure 2.1 outlines a framework which has

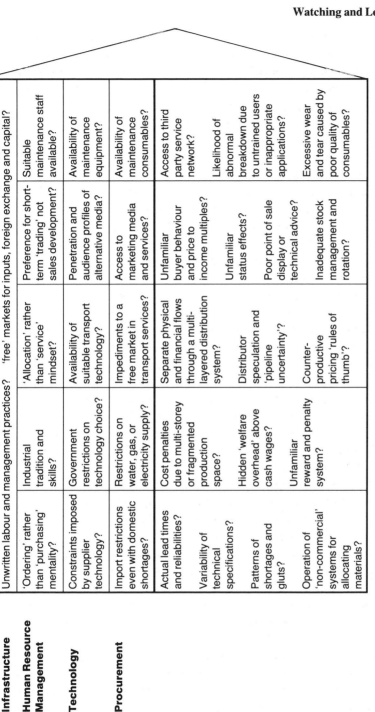

Figure 2.1   Systematic questioning for the global frontier

proven effective. It divides the chain of generic activities required to supply a product into five stages: inbound logistics, operations (including manufacturing and assembly), outbound logistics (distribution being the core), marketing and sales, and service (both before and after sale).[7] Lying along the top of the diagram are the primary functions necessary to support each of the operational activities: procurement, technology management, human resource management and commercial infrastructure.

The **inbound logistics** sector questions the practical lead times and reliability of various necessary input supplies, checks on constraints imposed by local suppliers' equipment and experience, and constraints on raw materials and component supply. The latter problems often persist even in the face of chronic domestic shortages on the global frontier due to government industry policies or restrictions on the use of foreign exchange.

In the **operations** area many joint ventures have paid insufficient attention to the predictable emergence of energy shortages in rapidly developing regions, early supply continuity often falters under the pressure of increased demand. In other cases the lure of low wages in greenfield areas has been undermined by the productivity penalty of lack of industrial heritage and absence of basic manufacturing skills among the workforce. As one production manager put it: 'It was only when it became clear most of my young workers had never actually used a screwdriver that I really understood the dangers of presumption.' Other local areas, by contrast, have manufacturing skills and ingenuity passed down through generations. Since old habits die hard, an understanding of traditional skills and mindsets can pay dividends. Likewise, in the race to minimise wages, other enemies of productivity such as the cost penalties of fragmented production sites or multistory facilities have often been under-researched.

For managers focused on getting their venture up and running, activities outside their factory gates risk receiving a lack of attention. But it is often in the areas of outbound logistics and **marketing** and sales, much of which occurs far from the venture itself, that a large number of the unseen issues arise. Long distribution pipelines combined with distributor speculation can introduce 'noise' into sales figures if not properly understood. It slows down the rate at which product changes or quality improvements flow through to final customers, forcing uninformed managers into a game of 'blind man's bluff'.

More than one professionally executed advertising campaign has faltered when it turned out that the prime customers didn't have television sets. One better researched marketing campaign ascertained that TV sets had a high penetration among the target group but failed to discover that the electricity to operate them was seldom available when their advertisement was screened due to the rationing schedule. The definition of a status symbol, meanwhile, changes rapidly on the global frontier.

Multi-layered, inefficient **distribution** and successive mark-ups through a chain of regional and local monopolies can fritter away the cost competitiveness of the base product.

Assumptions about the performance and reliability even of proven products need to be examined. Some companies have discovered that the poor performance of their standard products has been caused by use of low grade lubricants or other consumables. Lack of thorough research as to consumables locally available before launching the product meant early damage to their image – difficult to restore in markets where initial impressions count for a great deal. Research into the availability of appropriate maintenance equipment and skills may also be equally critical to building a quality image as having the right product.

Collecting the information necessary to raise the right questions and manage in an environment where unquestioned assumptions are a high risk takes time and commitment on the ground. Even then, this is not easy: frontier markets are often much less transparent than those we know at home; there are few requirements for disclosure and reporting conventions; few reliable statistics; little or no stock of market research; much of the information we need requires judgement and 'feel'; and accessing it requires getting behind doors that are normally shut.

If corporate espionage doesn't sound appealing, the good news is that there are other ways. And this doesn't necessarily mean immediately sinking capital into large scale manufacturing in the global frontier. In fact, the right sort of 'information vacuum cleaner' can even make a profit with minimum investment. An early focus on two of the ingredients most critically lacking on the global frontier: service and finance, suggest the way forward.

SERVICE INTELLIGENCE

One of the most effective sources of information about product demand and performance in any market comes from the records of after sales service. The service operation can help pinpoint sources of quality problems based on actual day-to-day usage in an unfamiliar environment. It can provide impetus for product or process improvement and innovation when more conventional sources of market research are unavailable. Assured availability of technically competent service and a reliable supply of parts also plays an important role in maintaining a recognition of brand quality over the life of machinery, vehicles, consumer electronics and other durable goods. The service network also offers a channel for educating customers in the proper use and maintenance of an unfamiliar product.

In frontier markets reliable, **third party service** is typically unavailable. The flow of information about field performance is generally non-existent. A quality image is easily undermined by poor maintenance, lack of spare parts and untrained operators. Early entry into the local servicing of imported product can therefore offer both a tangible (and probably profitable) way of watching and learning in a frontier market as well as laying the groundwork for subsequent expansion of exports and future local manufacture. The Shenzhen Huari Automobile Enterprise Ltd. (SHAE), the first Sino-Japanese joint management company in the city of Shenzhen, demonstrates many of the benefits.

Established in 1983, the company was formed as an alliance between a Japanese affiliate of Toyota, and two local entities: the Shenzhen Special Economic Zone Development Company and ACU Enterprise Ltd. It had three business objectives:

- to operate as a sole agent, authorised service centre for Toyota vehicles, including a breakdown service;
- to act as a sales and distribution centre for the supply of Toyota spare parts;
- to operate a taxi and transport service using Toyota vehicles in the region.

The commitment of fixed assets was limited: equivalent to under $500,000 with a further loan from Toyota in the form of cars and equipment valued at $1.5 million, to be repaid with interest over ten years. Toyota also provided an initial stock of spare parts and seconded technicians to provide on-the-job training. Without the need for construction of extensive specialised plant, progress was speedy: pilot operations in March 1984 reaching full capacity within a year.

The operating agreement for the taxi and transport service was established for a term of 5 years. At first sight, operating a taxi service may seem an unlikely activity for the giant Toyota Motors. Why would a company who manufactures 40 per cent of all cars sold in Japan want to run a modest Chinese taxi service? Doubly odd, some might say, since so much of their strength at home was built on the back of the Toyota Production System which pioneered the large scale use of Just-in-Time manufacturing. But consider the marketing impact in a global frontier market that lacks the barrage of media advertising for vehicles so familiar in the developed world.

When an official or senior manager from anywhere in China visits the go-ahead Shenzhen region, the taxi he or she travels in is a luxury Toyota Crown. This is as close as one can get to a fully paid for test drive. Not surprisingly senior visitors often leave with a determination to obtain one of these cars through their organisations back home. Moreover, as local people see their successful compatriots glide by in one of the 150 Toyotas which comprise the service, the marketing message is obvious: the new commercial elite ride in a Toyota. Since the service makes a profit, this advertising is free.

Few things are more destructive to the image of an imported product than to see it standing idle because it has broken down. Yet much of the global frontier is littered with machinery, vehicles, consumer goods and other equipment stalled because of lack of parts or maintenance expertise. Not so with Toyota cars and trucks. SHAE maintains an extensive range of parts in its Shenzhen stock. Stockouts are minimised by tight control and replenishment through a direct link with the parent computer system in Japan. The local sales and distribution system provides the customers with telephone ordering facilities and express delivery throughout almost every province in China. SHAE can obtain the scarce foreign exchange necessary for parts imports because the government wants to keep the country's stock of vehicles on the road. Levering off its systems, SHAE also exerts a degree of control over local substitute parts by parallel-stocking domestically-made items where technology is simpler or performance is less critical: parts like light covers and batteries, sold at considerably lower prices than the Toyota brand component. They also keep tabs on their major Japanese competitors by stocking a more limited selection of parts for their vehicles as well.

The local service extends to inspection, full maintenance and on-site breakdown repair supplied by SHAE's 290 staff. Again, for Toyota, the potential spin-offs are more critical to Toyota than this business itself: maintaining a quality image for its product, and collecting market intelligence. Quality assurance for repairs and cost and stock control are critical. As we discuss in Chapter 7, detailed Japanese repair procedures and checking routines are dominant, overseen by seconded technicians. The results are impressive: during the first half of 1990, for example, not a single vehicle was returned as a result of slipshod work. Computerised financial and stock systems impose rigorous cost and asset turn control. Nor does service stop with the customer – SHAE's own equipment is also subject to a 'Total Productive Maintenance' regime.

Organisations which have imported cars are usually willing to spend generously on maintenance and parts to protect their investment. Sales revenue at SHAE grew at an annual rate of 30 per cent over the first three years to exceed 20 million RMB (around £2.5 million) in 1990. Profits, which grew by 300 per cent over the same period, are split 70–30 per cent in favour of the Chinese partners. For Toyota, however, the real prize is not cash, but information.

In Japan Toyota's local dealers use their maintenance system to construct records of the sequence of cars purchased, the mileages clocked, vehicle performance and expenditure on repairs of every customer in their sales area. They even track household income and the ages of a buyer's children. On the global frontier this information system still has some way to go. But through SHAE Toyota can closely monitor the usage and performance of their own models, and those of competitors, as they run through the streets. This is the kind of information about the global frontier which money and market research cannot buy.

Rank Xerox came to a similar conclusion about the role of service in its Eastern European business. It had been trading in the region for over 25 years, setting up its East European Operations Unit as early as 1968 to establish and service markets for its products. While operating in the command economy brought a host of restrictions and other difficulties, it had at least one notable plus: the market could be accessed through a few large customer contacts. Prior to 1990, for example, 99 per cent of Rank Xerox's business in the former Soviet Union was conducted through a single buyer. By 1991, there were an estimated 30,000 individual buying organisations responsible for their own profits in Eastern Europe. Projections suggest this will rise to 450,000 such organisations in Russia alone by the year 2000. Rank Xerox concluded that these changes would inevitably mean a shift away from reliance on its direct sales operation into indirect selling though a network of distributors. For servicing of equipment, however, the company decided it wanted to move the other way: from indirect to direct responsibility for service. It recognised that its extensive marketing against increasingly aggressive rivals, primarily from Japan, would quickly have a hollow ring if its equipment was not properly installed. It was equally important that operators were well trained and the maintenance and repair service second to none. Through a network of new facilities it is exerting increasing control over the service operation. As it does so, Rank Xerox is finding that service, market research and sales overlap on the global frontier. The service system is a powerful way to build customer relationships, understand problems in the field and refine the marketing and training to solve them in the future.[8]

As well as these important spin-offs, early involvement in service can be a profitable business in its own right. The computer company ICL, for example, sees maintenance and service as playing much more than a supporting role. It is in the process of setting up a service organisation in every East European country with the goal of achieving 50 per cent of local revenues from services by 1995.[9]

LEARNING THROUGH LEASING

On the global frontier where information is scarce and scattered like gold dust, even a well-staffed representative office faces a basic problem in capturing information: it has little to offer in exchange. For some firms as we have seen, gathering specific market intelligence through a service operation is the solution. Others have used the powerful carrot of leasing to take them deep inside a myriad of different enterprises throughout the global frontier. The process of preparing feasibility studies for leases on everything from medical equipment to industrial and construction machinery opens up a mine of information. It allows the foreign lessor to build a detailed knowledge of the process of reform and plans for introduction of machinery and new technology. It also provides a unique opportunity to make firsthand comparisons of the technical and organisational capabilities of different local enterprises. The costs of all of this information gathering and corporate learning, meanwhile, are covered by the revenues from leasing and consultancy fees.

Leasing is also attractive to many local organisations on the global frontier. Governments, especially those prone to operate with the heavy hand of planning, closely regulate borrowing with quotas. But leasing generally shows up in the less regulated revenue and expenditure account – the finer points of contingent liability accounting are generally decades away.

The 'learning through leasing' strategy is perhaps best developed on the China frontier. Of the 25 leasing joint ventures we identified, 21 have Japanese partners. Their identities indicate the importance of information flow. International Union Leasing Company (IUL) links to the giant Mitsui *keiretsu* network of businesses from Toray Industries to Oji Paper and OSK Lines. The companies associated with this *keiretsu* jointly account for 10 per cent of Japanese GDP. Its closely associated companies also include the formidable financial institutions like Mitsui Bank and Mitsui Trust Company. The Industrial & Commercial International Leasing Co. (ICIL) acts as a prime information source for the networks of Tokai Bank Ltd. of Japan and Banque Indosuez of France. The Tokai link alone networks household name manufacturers like Suzuki and Ricoh and trading house Toyo Menka, part of the *keiretsu* shown in Fig. 2.2.

Local partners can also provide access to an extensive client base of the most progressive enterprises in frontier regions. IUL's partners, for example, the People's Construction Bank of China (with a 30 per cent shareholding) and China National Metals & Minerals Import & Export Corporation (20 per cent shareholding) between them bring a network of 3,618 offices across China.

The information collection role is reflected in staffing. IUL, for example has 23 staff, including 17 expatriates, for a mere $10 million of leasing business per year. Another leading firm, China Orient Leasing Co., maintains a staff of 97 to handle just under $100 million of lease contracts per annum. Procedures are designed to identify leading local companies in their fields and future export and import-replacement potential. Projects cover a wide range of businesses, including equipment for manufacturing, mining, construction, agricultural, environmental, medical, marine, power, scientific and measurement, transport, telecommunication and office applications. Rather than conducting purely 'arms-length' financial transactions, foreign leasing companies typically provide a portfolio for services which bring them close to their clients' businesses including vendor assessment, equipment purchase, import and associated consulting services.

Others have taken the financial entrée strategy of building dialogue and close involvement with local enterprises still further. Today, Sanwa Bank is widely renowned for its in-depth knowledge of Chinese commerce and industry – an undoubted benefit to its own *keiretsu* which includes Kobe Steel, Hitachi and Daihatsu Motors. In March 1963, even before the normalisation of the diplomatic relations between Japan and China, Sanwa established a correspondent banking relationship with the Bank of China. In June 1972 a Sanwa delegation visited Beijing to agree the extension of the agreement with the Bank of China to RMB-Yen exchange transactions. Sanwa opened its Beijing office in 1981 and subsequently in Shanghai, Tianjin, Guangzhou, Dalian and Shenzhen. In May 1986 the Shenzhen office was upgraded into a branch. Building on the resulting solid base of relationships, Sanwa has maintained its lead in major project loan syndication on the China frontier. It now has agency relationships with all of the Chinese banks and investment companies which have significant foreign currency business. This network, along with five joint ventures operating in trade, leasing and real estate development, gives it an unrivalled window on development opportunities across the China frontier.

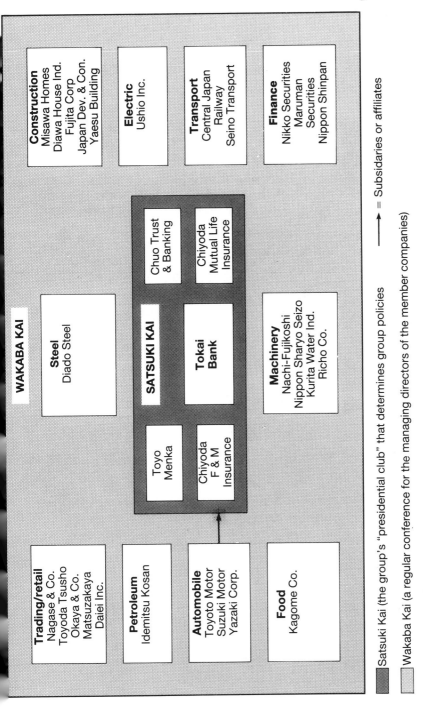

Figure 2.2   The Tokai group

Source: M. Eli, Japan Inc: Global strategies of Japanese trading corporations, McGraw Hill, London, 1990

RELIANCE ON INTERMEDIARIES OR GOING DIRECT

A time-honoured ruse of nondescript towns seeking a place on the tourist trail is to describe themselves as the gateway to a famous attraction or picturesque area. In some cases they prove to be a convenient base for touring; but we have all had the unhappy experience of finding that the gateway is actually many hours drive from where we want to be. Exactly the same can be true of **commercial gateways** to the global frontier.

Hong Kong, with its potential joint venture partners or established subsidiaries sits as a potentially attractive gateway to China. Austria, East Germany, Czechoslovakia or Poland are increasingly viewed as potential gateways to many areas of the former USSR. Use of gateway intermediaries offers obvious advantages: access to accumulated knowledge, established contacts and, in some cases, a way of narrowing the cultural divide. Computer peripheral maker Epson Engineering Ltd, for example, was able to use its Hong Kong subsidiary, which had 15 years of operating experience, to rapidly establish a wholly-owned printer assembly line in China. It is doubtful that it could have operated with the same speed, or even perhaps without a Chinese joint venture partner, had it chosen to manage this operation directly from Japan.

This route is most likely to be viable where operations are relatively self-contained – requiring only fairly simple links with other organisations and markets on the frontier. It needs to be recognised, however, that operating through what amounts to intermediaries in a gateway centre has several disadvantages, even if the intermediary is wholly owned.

1 Any intermediary brings its own **prejudices**. Since many of today's global frontiers have been effectively closed even to their neighbours for long periods, these prejudices are often poorly founded.
2 The frontier environment is almost certain to be undergoing substantial **change**. This, after all is usually one of the primary attractions. In such circumstances the benefits of an open mind may outweigh the disadvantages of familiarity with what went before.
3 Taking the line of least **resistance** by using an intermediary's existing contacts, which have probably been established for another purpose, may not be optimal in the longer run.
4 The intermediary or its staff may engender **resentment** on the part of those in frontier regions. Relationships between Hong Kong Chinese and those in the northern industrial cities, for example, are not always easy.

Potential strains are aggravated by the fact that many Cantonese-speaking Hong Kong staff have a poor command of spoken Mandarin. Eastern Europe, meanwhile, is criss-crossed with the undercurrents of historical ties and rivalries which go back for centuries.

5 Operating though an intermediary means a longer **chain of command** with the risk of reducing organisational responsiveness. And using a third-party intermediary means there is no internal advocate to help solicit support from headquarters or sister subsidiaries.

Additionally, but perhaps most important of all, accessing the frontier through a gateway intermediary may reduce the rate of corporate learning. Given our concern in this chapter with issues of accessing and internalising information, this effect is worth examining in some more detail. As we shall see, the standing of the intermediary within the overall corporate group is critical.

Intermediaries and corporate learning

In explaining the advantages enjoyed by successful firms, recent research work has pointed to the central role of capabilities and intangible assets which were accumulated through learning.[10] These range from the 3M Corporation's expertise in coating technologies through to McDonald's skills in developing reliable local suppliers and Unilever's detailed knowledge of local markets which underpins their success in selling detergents in widely differing environments around the globe.

Knowledge of how to successfully sell and service a product in an unfamiliar frontier market is another example of this kind of intangible asset. Like many other capabilities, it cannot easily be purchased on a free-standing basis. Some companies seek to gain access by means of acquiring a local firm. This is an increasingly popular option on the East European frontier. But when skills, knowledge and contacts are purchased packaged in the form of an acquired firm, these capabilities are often costly and difficult to integrate. They also come bundled with other strengths, weakness and culture which may be of dubious relevance. Many are also highly specific to the products, services and economic system of the past. For these reasons, the results of many **acquisitions** continue to be disappointing. In the final analysis, building local capabilities and contacts through direct experience is often the only real way forward. *Corporate learning on the global frontier can be a long and painful process. It is doubly difficult when information comes second-hand through an agent or distributor.*

The first potential problem associated with learning about a local market through a third party is what information theorists call **noise**. The more stages through which information must pass, the greater likelihood that it will be distorted or lost. This problem is aggravated if the mental maps of the market held by decision makers vary along the chain. Facts which might be highly pertinent to the manufacturer's marketing, product design or production management, might appear irrelevant to the local distributor. Even more common is the problem of information which local distributors take for granted or consider so self-evident that it does not warrant passing back to the manufacturer.

Investment in training of local distributors and systems to exchange information can help to reduce this problem. However, since organisational learning is strongly influenced by company culture and deep-seated assumptions which are difficult to change, the costs may be high and the pay-offs limited.

The second problem arises because the distributor or agent may lack the **incentive** to provide complete or high quality information to the manufacturer. In the absence of important economics of scope from sharing costs in distribution, the primary *raison d'être* for using a third party distributor often stems from access to his accumulated experience of the local market. If the manufacturer rapidly internalises this knowledge by learning from the distributor, the continuance of the relationship is likely to be threatened. At the very least, a well-informed manufacturer is likely to be in a more powerful bargaining position over distributor margins, especially if he has accumulated a detailed knowledge of local operating practices and costs. The distributor may therefore face a trade-off between the increase in sales which may flow from providing the manufacturer more information, versus the possible threat to his future margins or tenure.

Various devices might be employed to overcome this agency problem and assure the distributor that the flow of information back to the manufacturer would not put his future profits at risk. Long term **contracts** are one example. Yet this solution can bring its own problems: making it difficult for a manufacturer to terminate the relationship should the local agent's performance be judged inadequate; reducing the manufacturer's flexibility in the face of a changing market. Instead, establishment of a local presence in the market, possibly in parallel and undertaking largely complementary activities to those of the distributor, may be an attractive alternative for a manufacturer who wishes to ensure that potential for corporate learning is increased.

A final issue associated with learning through a third party concerns our old friend **receptivity**. Rightly or wrongly, how much notice we take of a piece of information often depends on where it comes from. For many organisations the 'not invented here' syndrome acts as a powerful hindrance to learning. The ability of a manufacturer to internalise and act upon learning about a new frontier market may therefore be greater if its own employees have discovered the market truths, rather than being told by a third party representative. Putting our people on the ground in local markets through partial or full forward integration, may therefore have a role in improving the effectiveness of organisational learning. It may also act as an important signal of commitment both to customers and suppliers as well as staff in the parent company.

Receptivity is also important with regard to the distributor itself. Conventional wisdom and well worn habits may impede the manufacturer in introducing innovations in local sales, distribution and service which have been found to work elsewhere.

In sum, while there are often advantages in using local intermediaries, as discussed in Chapter 5, the extra learning and control which comes from direct involvement in local sales, distribution and service should not be underestimated. Full or partial forward **integration**, reaching out to the final customer, has significant attractions.

SPECIAL ECONOMIC ZONES: A GOLDEN CAGE?

A final factor in a company's ability to watch and learn successfully is its location within the developing market. Special economic zones may seem like the obvious answer to the location problem, but they can become a proverbial golden cage.

Economic development zones are a growth industry on the global frontier. New acronyms like ETDZ (Economic & Technology Development Zone) or FEZ (Free Enterprise Zone) seem to sprout almost annually. Specifically targeted at foreign investors, these zones can offer a number of advantages:

- The availability of greenfield sites suitable for extensive, single-storey manufacturing facilities under one roof
- New or dedicated infrastructure including land transport and port facilities, power generation stations and water facilities
- Access to a fresh labour force of young people or former peasant workers

without the bad habits, entrenched work practices and historical baggage which can exist in older, hardbitten industrial communities
- Initial avoidance of head-to-head competition with entrenched rivals who are likely to protect their local bailiwicks with the resistance of a walled city.

Many joint ventures have initially prospered under these conditions. But taking the easy entry route can mean mortgaging the future. Indeed, it has often been early success itself which carried the seeds of growing problems.

Congestion in the fast lane

Judging by the pattern of foreign investment to date, the attractions of special economic zones must be real. The value of industrial output in the three special economic zones of the Pearl River delta (Shenzhen, Zhuhai and Shantou), for example, grew by 44 per cent in 1991. This followed average annual growth of 20 per cent over the decade of the 1980s. The driving force was foreign investment in manufacturing.

The results of this phenomenal growth are now obvious. Consumer durables like televisions, refrigerators, watches, electric fans and washing machines abound. GDP per person now exceeds $2000 a year. The town of Shenzhen had a population of less than 100,000 when it became a special economic zone in 1979. By the early 1990s, the population had exceeded 2 million.

There are clearly advantages for foreign investors in being associated with this success. The availability of both industrial supplies and backup services, for example, has improved dramatically. The downside, however, is that the infrastructure is failing to keep pace with the expansion. The road network is now heavily congested. Electricity and telecommunications capacity is stretched beyond its limits.

The result is rising costs. Electricity prices in Guangdong province, where Shenzhen is located, are now more than double those in neighbouring provinces like Hunan. The labour cost advantage, although still large compared with the West and Hong Kong, are being steadily eroded. The global frontier moves rapidly. What was an excellent springboard location in the early 1980s, may prove a costly base for further expansion a decade later. If one is to have a choice of location for subsequent expansion, it is necessary to extend the watching and learning net beyond the golden cage well before the need arises to begin a new operation.

Outside on the inside

The choice of where to locate the local operation arguably has more far-reaching implications than any other corporate decision. In theory it is possible for a business to relocate its main operating base. In practice few businesses do. They may extend their production and distribution networks but, having put down roots, the frictional costs of moving lock, stock and barrel are high. While special zones have undoubted benefits in the start-up phase, experience has shown that some important negatives can emerge for companies whose goals extend beyond operating largely self-sufficient, offshore processing or assembly plants.

The sub-tropical island of Hainan is a case in point. It is the largest Special Economic Zone in China with a provincial government actively promoting foreign investment. It has low levels of industrial development it has abundant land, agricultural and aquatic resources, and a potentially low cost workforce. Perhaps even more important, its corporate income tax rate is 15 per cent instead of 55 per cent on the mainland. However, the support of ancillary industries is largely absent; links to China's industrial base in cities like Shenyan, Dalian and Wuhan are hampered by distance and poor transport infrastructure, local sources of industrial raw materials are few, while labour force skills reflect an agricultural rather than industrial culture. Moreover, the island is divorced from the key domestic markets and commercial centres. It is easier to import goods into Hainan than to the mainland (although things have tightened up since 1985 when the governor was removed after Hainan had imported almost 100,000 foreign cars and countless container loads of electronic goods in a single year). This makes the island potentially attractive for assembly or processing operations based on imports or for resort and leisure development. As a base for industrial companies looking for broad access to the China frontier, however, the limitations are obvious. More generally, because of the Chinese government's desire to maintain policy differences between SEZs and other regions, companies are often faced with obstacles if they try to source supplies or labour from elsewhere in China itself.

Likewise for the Kemerovo Free Enterprise Zone in the Commonwealth of Independent States. It offers foreign companies the opportunity to invest directly in companies, banks, projects and equipment or indirectly through securities. Among the many advantages, companies are allowed to fix their own wage levels. Foreign investors are guaranteed 'full and unconditional protection by the state bodies and local government' and any discrimination against them is prohibited. Perhaps not surprisingly, however, interest in this free enterprise zone has been mainly limited to companies in the business of processing fuels and raw materials – Kemerovo is in Siberia.

The more general point is clear: access to potential suppliers and the mainstream market often means reaching out to the global frontier beyond special economic and export zones. Doing so also opens up new dimensions of corporate learning. Special economic zones can create a golden cage: protection from some of the harsh realities of the global frontier; but also limited development of the knowledge and capabilities required to fully access local markets, resource bases and production potential. Just as with more tangible location factors, the importance of these limitations depends on the long-term objectives of the operation. Many of those limitations may not show up until it's too late.

GETTING THE PARENT ORGANISATION TO RESPOND AND LEARN

No matter how good the information vacuum cleaner on the global frontier is, it will all be to no avail if the parent organisation ignores what it hears. To make a real difference local learning must also change behaviour back at home.

'When I arrived at their (the partner's) international corporate headquarters', said one local manager from a region on the global frontier, 'the staff knew exactly what kind of drink I usually prefer.' This is a tiny example of detailed communication and headquarters responsiveness. But the point is significant. Despite protestations of commitment from the those at the top, many of those charged with heading representative offices or even established ventures on the global frontier find the responsiveness of the layers of management 'back home' seriously lacking. Information disappears into a black hole. If requests for advice from the global frontier resurface at all, they are often reinterpreted to suit the headquarters. The HQ's organisational culture ensures that policies for the frontier do not upset plans for the replication of standard systems or contradict deeply held beliefs. Geographic distance, lack of immediate profit prospects or impact on the 'bottom line' performance measures ensures frontier managers' requests go to the end of the queue.

A second critical prerequisite for managing the corporate frontier is therefore increased corporate receptivity to the changes in conventional wisdom and well-oiled routines. Getting staff in the parent organisation to 'change their spots' is difficult. But this is what successful strategies in global frontier markets often demand. The 'but that's the way we do it here' syndrome or benign neglect need to be tackled, and tackled decisively.

While the idea of changing things on the global frontier is often viewed as the natural course of progress, making changes at the home end is generally regarded, at best, as inconvenient – the tail wagging the corporate dog. In other cases it is dealt with as a threat, especially where the prospect of lower cost final products, components or semi-finished goods threatens jobs.

Building corporate awareness of frontier needs

The problem of how to increase corporate receptivity has played a prominent role in discussions about how to manage joint ventures and alliances.[11] Many of the lessons can also be applied to the issue of soliciting sufficient headquarters flexibility and support to long-term ventures in developing markets. The key goal is to achieve the right mix of the pressure and participation. The local champion's zeal needs to be combined with people, incentives and systems which help achieve broad participation and shared responsibility back at headquarters. Obviously this is a conundrum, but following a number of guidelines can help.

1 *Make it clear why the venture matters strategically.* In many companies, people at the top know why entry into developing markets is important for long-term success, but for middle management it is just another distraction or a pipedream of the Board. Yet, the co-operation of middle management back at HQ is often essential to support day-to-day activities on the ground. At the implementation stage when a venture needs detailed, 'nitty-gritty' support, it must compete for time and energy with projects which are closer to home and seem to have more immediate pay-offs. Efforts to communicate the strategic importance of each venture in a developing market therefore need to reach well down into the organisation.

2 *Spell out the scope of the activities envisaged.* Most people in the parent organisation probably don't know much about developing markets on the global frontier. At least one thing they generally do know, however, is that wages in developing markets are much less than their own. As a result, rumours about exporting jobs and down-sizing at home often abound. If the intention is to supply the emerging domestic market on the global frontier, say so. If the venture is to supply components or semi-finished products to other subsidiaries, win over those who will gain. Whatever the likely impact on the home country operation, define its

limits and sell the benefits – growth potential, gaining a march on the competition, moving to higher value-added, etc.

3 *Involve and second*. Explaining the goals and the realities of operating on the global frontier can only achieve so much. Getting key individuals to experience the new market and its supporting operation firsthand is worth mountains of paper and tens of thousands of words. Seconding individuals to ventures on global frontiers, even for short periods, is often the fastest and most effective way for management and staff from the parent to learn. The benefits can also be lasting. When these people return home, they are in a much better position to understand and interpret requests for support. They know why products and procedures need to be adapted. If things have gone well, they may even become disciples for the cause inside the parent operation. All the better if they carry the clout of seniority (as, interestingly, we found most of those seconded to Sino-Japanese ventures did). The problem, of course, is cost. This means targeting key people for involvement and secondment: those from whom support and resources will be required and, perhaps, some of those who might otherwise ensure that the needs of frontier operations mysteriously kept finding their way to the back of the queue.

4 *Broaden 'ownership'*. Having a project champion is essential. But broadening the group of people back in the parent company who have a stake in the venture can also pay dividends. Too many ventures in developing markets are viewed as being the baby of a single director and few others. In order to tackle this problem and increase responsiveness throughout the parent organisation, some companies have successfully set up task forces or internal boards to broaden the feeling of ownership and build psychological commitment to the venture among those who control the resources and competencies it will require.

5 *Encourage internal 'contracting'*. In any large organisation, things that get measured get noticed. And things that get measured *and* rewarded, get done. If staff at headquarters or other subsidiaries continue to provide support to ventures in developing markets as a peripheral, almost extra-curricular activity, they are likely to get short shrift. To have the necessary bargaining power and status, ventures on the global frontier need to be able to purchase the services they need from other parts of their group on a quasi-commercial basis. Providing such a venture with the resources and systems to buy what they need internally may seem like an accounting nicety. It is unlikely to change the total cost to the group as a whole. But it

does act as an important signal to people in the parent organisation that responding to the needs of the global frontier is not an 'optional extra', or something to agree to only when they are having a good day. It does give managers on the global frontier increased bargaining power with resource holders back at home – especially if these peoples' bonuses depend, in part, on satisfying their internal contracts successfully.

Responding to corporate needs

These problems of securing support from the headquarters or sister subsidiaries are particularly acute when the frontier office has a watching and learning brief. In these circumstances, it has few favours to trade internally. And without a tangible payback, people up and down the company are bound to ask: 'What are those people out there achieving; where are the results?'

For this reason, frontier investments need particular management attention from the top during the watching and learning phase – no use shipping a group of people off out of sight and keeping fingers crossed. Traditional performance measures need to be adjusted to value outputs with less immediate benefit to the bottom line: like quality of information and an expanding knowledge base. But precisely because the benefits are less intangible, senior managers need to press hard to ensure progress is actually being achieved (especially since, in many frontier markets, it can be more comfortable to hide behind a desk).

There is no escaping the fact that a watching and learning phase sits uneasily with the performance criteria that permeate, at least in Western companies, from top to bottom. For impatient Chief Executives it is very tempting to find a short cut, a way to do something that demonstrates decisive management and reaps quick results. Unfortunately on the global frontier, those results are likely to be quick; they are also likely to be unpalatable, or little more than 'flashes in the pan'. And the decisive moves are likely to be decisively wrong. The insidious enemy, your own unquestioned assumptions, working in concert with the unusual lack of transparency that characterises frontier markets are powerful adversaries.

Like it not, filling the information void is essential. Without it, there can be no strategy, since information is its lifeblood. And filling the void takes time – both to ask the right questions and to find valid answers – in a frontier world where accepted wisdom often has to be turned on its head.

As we have demonstrated, there are ways, like service and leasing operations, to quickly get past the representative office phase. Trade deals, as we will see in the next chapter, provide a further information-gathering vehicle that can turn a profit. But to get the real payback on this learning phase, it needs to be part of something much more: the first step in a staircase with a substantial, and resilient business at its summit. Building that kind of business in a structured way where each step is followed by another step forward, rather than two steps back; and a way that can be communicated to those who ask 'What are those people in the representative office doing?', is the subject we tackle in Chapter 3.

References

1 *The Economist*, 13 January 1990, p. 99.
2 Xu Ming and Liu Hengrui, On Japanese Economic Structure and Adjustment and the Development Movement of its China Economic Policy, *World Economy and Politics*, July 1987, p. 1.
3 See P.J. Williamson and H. Yamawaki, Distribution: Japan's Hidden Advantage, *Business Strategy Review*, Spring 1991, pp. 85–105.
4 For a more detailed discussion of the role of investment in filling the Western knowledge gap in respect of Japan, see J-P. Lehmann. Japan 20: The West 1 – Reversing the Scorecard, *Business Strategy Review*, Summer 1993, pp. 59–92.
5 Wellcome to Eastern Europe, *East Europe Business Focus*, Issue 11, June 1991, p. 14.
6 See, for example, J. L. Badaracco, *The Knowledge Link*, Harvard Business School Press, Boston, 1991.
7 For a full description of this value chain framework and its application to developed markets see M.E. Porter, *Competitive Advantage*, Free Press, New York, 1985.
8 Rank Xerox: stickability and flexibility in eastern Europe, *East Europe Business Focus*, Issue 8, March 1991.
9 ICL – a flexible approach to East Europe, *East Europe Business Focus*, Issue 1, June 1990.
10 See, for example, R. M. Grant, The Resource-based Theory of Competitive Advantage: Implications for Strategy Formulations, *California Management Review*, Spring, 1991, pp. 119–35, I. Dierickx and K. Cool, Asset Stock Accumulation and Sustainability of Competitive Advantage, *Management Science*, December, 1989, pp. 1504–14.
11 See, for example, Rosabeth Moss Kantor, *When Giants Learn to Dance*, Touchstone Books, New York, 1989, Jordan D. Lews, *Partnerships for Profit: structuring and managing alliances*, Free Press, New York, 1990 and G. Hamel. Y.L. Doz and C.K. Prahalad, Collaborate with your competitors – and win, *Harvard Business Review*, 67, 1, Jan–Feb., 1989.

3

BUILDING FROM A BASE OF TRADE

Almost without exception, international trade is in the vanguard of the advancing global frontier. Yet the potential of a trading operation to provide a solid platform for future development, including local manufacturing, is often ignored. The reason is that many companies see trade and direct investment as alternative modes of entering a market rather than two elements in a sequence of development.

THE REALITY: TWO-WAY TRADE AT THE FRONTIER

When foreign companies think of trade, it is the potential of the global frontier as an export market that first comes to mind. To many business people frontier trade is synonymous with the foreign market sucking in imports. It comes as something of a surprise then, to learn that China, for example, has a trade *surplus* with Japan of over $5 billion per year – a position it has enjoyed for a fifth straight year. China also has a trade surplus with the United States which exceeded $18 billion in 1992. Poland's trading account, meanwhile, notched up a surplus with the rest of the world of $1 billion in the six months to January 1993, largely due to the growth of exports to Western Europe. Of course imports into developing markets are important, but trade within the global frontier is, in fact, two-way.

The total value of trade flows to and from frontier markets is also very significant. China is now Japan's second largest supplier, behind only the United States. Two-way trade between the the two countries exceeds $20 billion per annum. She is set to become the world's 10th largest trader in 1993. As we entered the 1990s, Eastern Europe already exported $75 billion worth of goods to the rest of the world, half of which was destined for Western industrial economies.

Nor is two-way trade simply based on export of primary products and raw materials from economies on the global frontier. China, for example, has supplied over 50 per cent of the total volume of Japan's huge imports of garments over the past few years. Perhaps even more surprising, China's exports to her neighbour now include a wide range of electrical machinery (including power generators, cassette tape recorders, radios and transformers) and other machinery and equipment. Hungary, meanwhile, is the world's fifth largest exporter of computer software.

Investment projects, rather than trade, usually steal the headlines. But as a rough point of comparison it is worth noting that total foreign direct investment in China for the entire decade of the 1980s from all countries was $19 billion – less than the current annual value of trade between China and Japan alone. The conclusion is simple: for companies seeking to do business on the global frontier, two-way trade is likely to be an excellent place to start. In this chapter we begin by discussing the benefits of building a base of trade and how to overcome some of the obstacles which new entrants are bound to meet. We then go on to outline the sequence of development, through equipment sales and technical advice, processing contracts and local production which logically follows.

DEVELOPING A PLATFORM OF TRADE

A favourite joke among Chinese traders concerns a piece of foreign sellers' logic known locally as the 'dollar-per-person hypothesis': making money in China must be easy, all you have to do is get each Chinese to purchase one dollar's worth of goods and over $1 billion of sales is yours. The reality, however, is rather different. The availability of foreign exchange for spending on imports is tightly guarded. There are quantitative import controls and secret trade regulations, the elimination of which some countries argue should be a condition of China's re-entry to the GATT. Punitive tariffs exist on many items. Affordability may be undermined by restrictions on the availability of foreign exchange, or administrative discretion over which of China's two official exchange rates is applied – an important distinction, since one rate is 50 per cent higher than the other. Trade regulations also vary haphazardly from province to province, reflecting the ability of provincial and municipal governments to spend the hard currency they, themselves earn. Personal relationships often intervene. For other types of goods like equipment, international tenders are the norm, often rendering margins razor thin.

In Eastern Europe the route for selling foreign imports is equally strewn with obstacles. The following extract from an interview with the sales manager of an American medical products manufacturer selling in Russia sums up some of the traps:

'Initially we believed knowledge of our product and demonstrating its advantages would win us the business. In a country like Russia, to be successful, of course you have to know what you offer, but you have to be a specialist on Russia even more than you have to be a specialist on your product. A large part of my job is to identify the right people, to talk to them in the right tone. One needs to identify who should be treated differently, because people are very sensitive to hierarchy. Many foreign sales people go around the market dreaming of millions. They come back and say 'There is plenty to do here and there', but the enquiries secured are unrealistic – Americans particularly, tend to take the Russians literally. They have not understood what the Russians really meant. Russians don't always expect to be taken literally.

One of our biggest problems is delivery. If you want to deliver something in Russia, you may think that you've delivered it and three months later it is still not there. But your contract to supply it is there with your guarantee of the date. In Russia you are obliged to use a local transport service. As a monopoly they charge an awful lot. When the order is delayed you try to contact the customer, but you can't because the telephone communication is bad or a telex goes astray.

The sale itself can be either slow (often) or is very quick (rarely). Some of our deals have taken two years for something to materialise. It can be quick, but this is generally when they want to buy from you to weaken the power of your competition.

Machine performance is also often outside our control. For example, we delivered a machine with disposables where I knew the supply of disposables would quickly run out. Given the lead times, I knew the machine would be idle for three to six months. We do our best in such situations, but without an order you can't ship anything. If you do, chances are you will be asked to ship a second lot when the paperwork comes through.'

Obviously there are many examples of companies, like this one, successfully selling imported goods on the global frontier despite the obstacles. If this were not the case, billions of dollars of imports wouldn't be flowing into these markets each year. The French telecommunications company, Alcatel, for example, has installed three million lines in China, with orders for another 10 million more. But to build a solid base of trade requires a stock of local knowledge, contacts and ways over the many hurdles accumulated step by step. The managing director of Morgan Crucible's East European subsidiary summed it up this way:

'Its very nice to get a one-off opportunity and nice profits on deals, but it doesn't give you continued reliability and stability, so it's really the long-term possibilities which we need to seek and will support.'[1]

As with any new market, however, the problem is how to get started on the road to building a customer base.

Buy imports first, sell exports later?

In most parts of the world, its easier to enter a market as a buyer rather than a seller. Markets on the global frontier are no exception. In developed markets, the organisations you are likely to buy from are often unrelated to those you might want to sell to. Unless you're lucky, relationships and knowledge built up by buying generally don't provide a platform from which to sell. But in developing markets, especially those emerging from a regime of central command, this is not the case: the organisations you might buy from and your potential customers are often one and the same. Unlike the West, players like ministries, provincial and local governments, and trading institutions often control the buying and selling sides of an industry. Buying imports, therefore, can establish powerful relationships that can be used to smooth future entry into the market as a seller.

Take the example of British Petroleum. It began by building up its purchases of crude oil from the former Soviet Union. Over a number of years it reached the point where BP was taking between 7–8 per cent of the Soviet Union's exportable crude. This established strong links with a number of ministries: the oil and gas ministry, the geology ministry, and the ministry of chemicals and oil refining. Relationships with the latter paved the way for the sale of chemicals into the former USSR where the ministry of chemicals and oil refining was also a key actor. Through its subsequent work in agricultural chemicals it was exposed to the agricultural sector. These entrées led to BP providing up to 10 per cent of the country's total imports of chemicals and grain. Total two-way trade handled by the company in 1991 was approximately $1 billion. BP is reportedly now actively considering expansion into the supply of local consumer markets as well as major oil production and exploration projects already mentioned in Chapter 2.

The history of Tessek, one of the very first joint ventures to be set up in what is now the Czech Republic, is an interesting case of a buying arrangement providing the seed corn for a much broader set of activities. A Danish research firm, Senetek, entered the Czech market as a buyer of laboratory equipment and associated biochemicals from a state-run organisation, Telsa

VHJ. The Danes became one of Telsa's long-term customers. Ever closer interaction concerning users' needs and new products ultimately led to the establishment of the Tessek joint venture with R&D and production facilities in the Czech Republic, a research and production facility in Denmark, a trading company in West Germany and a sales bureau in Byelorussia.

The equity is shared 49 per cent to Senetek, 39 per cent to Telsa and a further 6 per cent with each of a Czech chemical producer and a local machinery works. In addition to its base chromatography products and 'interferon', the venture has developed products for testing the levels of heavy metals in foods and computer packages for managing laboratory equipment. The Czech partners have obtained a source of cash, access to new marketing opportunities outside their traditional markets and an international network which will soon include a US operation. The Danish firm has gained access to additional know-how, production facilities, a highly skilled workforce and a valuable position in Eastern European markets – Tessek is the principal supplier of chromatography products to the Russia Academy, Poland, East Germany and Hungary, as well as enjoying a 90 per cent share of their home market.

Purchasing has also been used successfully by Japanese companies as an entry route into China. In 1972 the Japanese fashion house Ishii began importing wool and rabbit hair garments through the China National Garment Import and Export Corporation. Today it holds a 33 per cent share in the Wanle Garment Company in Tianjin, a joint venture which exports to Europe (East and West) and Russia as well as selling into the Chinese market and supplying quality garments for sale by Ishii in Japan. Drawing originally from locally available raw materials and designs, Wanle now sources fashions, and even wool, from around the world to supply its international customers.

Hard currency shortage and two-way trade

The shortage of hard currency on the global frontier is another major reason for developing trade on the basis of two-way flows. Until very recently, for example, this was almost a 'must' in China due to lack of international convertibility of the Renminbi and regulations which effectively required each individual company to balance their expenditure of foreign currency with hard currency earnings. The government demanded that, at a minimum, foreign affiliated ventures be foreign exchange neutral. The chronic shortages of hard currency which have characterised Eastern Europe can also be expected to continue for some years. Local companies must buy equipment, technology and components, stretching foreign currency reserves, before they can establish a currency inflow by selling goods in Western markets.

The availability of hard currency during the initial start-up phase can engender dangerous complacency. The honeymoon often proves temporary. In addition, lending by organisations like the IMF combined with a less than perfect financial system, can lead to temporary booms and busts in the availability of foreign exchange. In this environment, it is essential to ensure that a trade or joint ventures are underpinned by flows of hard currency from a sustainable source. The source, *par excellence*, is revenue from hard currency sales.

Barter trade in unrelated goods

Sometimes unusual commercial acrobatics are necessary in order to get the currency balance right. Computer manufacturer ICL, for example, has a thriving joint venture with the Polish furniture trade. Why furniture? is an obvious question for a computer manufacturer. ICL explain the rationale as follows:

> 'A collaboration evolved with the furniture industry in the area of countertrade, where we saw an opportunity to export furniture products from Poland to generate currency which we hoped would be able to be linked to other users' requirements for the purpose of computer systems. The concept evolved into a fully fledged joint venture. We saw the opportunity to generate currency. We added to that concept the ability to bring in computer kits that we could assemble locally – which represented transfer of technology, and therefore was of special interest to the Polish state. So we had a number of things: we had a mechanism for generating convertible currency through Polish furniture exports; a mechanism for transferring technology, whereby we could become a local manufacturer or assembler of equipment; and added to that we had an organisation which could help establish an effective network of distribution and sales outlets. It was the marrying up of all those things that made sense then, and still does.'[2]

From the Polish partners' perspective, the venture would provide new opportunities to expand their sales, gain a share of the additional foreign currency generated, and lever off their existing skills in managing local assembly and sales operations to share in the growth market for electronics.

The resulting Furnel joint venture was set up in 1987. At the end of its first full year of operation, hard currency exports of furniture and wooden products totalled $12.5 million within its total turnover of $50 million. By 1990, the joint venture employed 6,500 people in 12 plants and eight branches, with an annual output of $100 million and over $17 million of hard currency earnings.

Even now that the Polish Zloty has become convertible, ICL still sees benefits in the arrangement: being a local manufacturer greatly enhances its image in Poland, the joint venture's sales force has been merged with ICL's direct sales operation, and the company's export earnings provide an insurance policy for ensuring ICL can obtain the foreign currency it needs.

As frontier markets develop, the foreign currency problem slowly recedes. An active market for exchange of Renminbi for foreign currencies has now developed in China, for example. With access and liquidity regulated by central government intervention, the estimated volume of swap transactions totalled $18 billion in 1991. Meanwhile, the cost penalty associated with obtaining foreign currency through the swap market, compared with restricted sources of foreign exchange through the banking system, is now less than 20 per cent as illustrated in Fig. 3.1. As a result the swap market is becoming a viable source of exchange for companies who cannot balance their two-way trade, rather than the costly option of a last resort. It should be added, however, that this situation depends on continuation of a

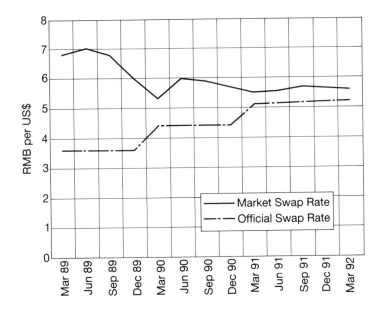

Figure 3.1   Development of China's market in foreign exchange swaps
Source: China Business Review.

surplus on China's international trading account. For this reason alone, a two-way balance of trade must be preferred.

Clearing away the obstacles back at home

The final hurdle to successful, two-way trade is sometimes overlooked. Goods from the global frontier are often first in the firing line of Western import controls. The Belgian shoe chain, Brantano discovered this to its cost. It successfully contracted with a Chinese producer for a supply of shoes. Production was completed on time; the quality standards had been met. Delivery of the shoes, however, was blocked. Chinese shoes are on a list of hundreds of items (including bicycles, television sets and tableware) whose entry is restricted by one or more European Community states.

Had the shoes come to a port in Germany, the Netherlands or the UK, they would have sailed through. Belgium, France and Italy, however, interpret the current state of the regulations differently; one of the many loose ends which introduction of the Single European Market on 1 January 1993 hasn't tied up. Even then, EC-wide quotas on these goods are the likely result. In the meantime, Brantano's shoes remain impounded. Many other shipments, including products from Eastern Europe, are caught up in a debate over the process for setting anti-dumping duties into the EC.[3] In the United States too, frictions over goods supplied from the global frontier continue, especially in the face of the growing trade deficit with China.

The overall message is clear: even if the long-term aim is local production, one of the best ways to enter a developing market is on the back of trade. From the standpoint of developing the right relationships, bargaining power, and currency balance, two-way trade is the ideal. Even if the future goal is export sales, finding a way to establish relationships first as a buyer has attractions. The calling card of the buyer often opens more of the right doors: it most easily establishes a relationship with clear benefits on both sides. But accessing trade potential requires both careful planning and creativity to clear away the obstacles at both ends of the exchange, especially for companies whose core business is local manufacturing and sales, rather than international trade.

CLIMBING THE FRONTIER STAIRCASE

Trade deals may offer a good way to start. For a company whose long-term aim is local production of substantial export sales on the global frontier, however, trade's role as a stepping-stone must be kept in perspective. The best trade deals to help build the platform for a future manufacturing operation or develop an export market, are not necessarily the same ones a pure trader would choose. The long-term mission, therefore, needs to be clear from the outset.

In setting out to achieve this mission, however, even the most motivated market champion generally faces three sorts of problems.

1 The long-term goal looks dispiritingly distant and impossibly unlike what exists at present. There are too many things to do at once, and no one to do them.
2 Familiar corporate planning systems are based on projecting the past. In the frontier market, however, there is no past history to project. In a completely new environment it is also dangerous simply to duplicate what we already know how to do, but doing something different is often frowned on as 'risky'.
3 The twists and turns involved in learning about a new and changing market can look to head office like inconsistency of purpose – a directionless enterprise buffeted by events.

The next sections examine how these problems can be overcome: by planning backwards from future goals, by breaking the daunting gaps into manageable steps, and by ensuring the strategy has room to learn as experience accumulates.

Planning backwards from goals

When expanding into a frontier market it is all too easy to convince ourselves that the lowest risk option is to repeat the business formulae which have served us well in the past. Our products, technologies, procedures, information systems, job descriptions and organisational structures are set up to do just this. And, we would argue, there are enough uncertainties without changing our basic business formulae.

With this mindset, our first reaction to a business environment that contradicts our beliefs is to deny that the differences we see around us are anything more than superficial. Once the evidence of differences in the demands on the business becomes indisputable, then we tend to argue that they don't require a fundamental shift in what we are doing.

Overstated or not, there is some of this fundamental conservatism in every company when it faces the uncertain and fluid markets on the global frontier. The root cause goes back to the simple fact that when we know how to do something, it's a nuisance when the new market asks us to do something different. It is not surprising, therefore, that we are most comfortable with planning systems which re-create a clone of the parent operation. At worst, we start by replicating a scaled down version of a familiar business unit, pretend we can forecast the future, and then make a few adjustments well chosen to ensure they aren't too disruptive. Of course in frontier markets we make allowance for the fact that you need to invest for a few years of losses before profits start to flow. Familiar sales and profit 'hockey sticks' are the result.

In fact, one of the most basic features of the global frontier is that the past is an exceptionally poor guide to the future. As we noted in Chapter 1, one of the very characteristics that distinguishes frontier markets from simply under-developed ones, is the presence of fundamental, structural change, because of the opportunities it creates. In this environment, if nowhere else, straight-line projections are bound to be wrong. Worse still, as we argued in Chapter 2, a strategy based on projecting growth forward from a replica of the kind of operations we have elsewhere – with bags of unquestioned assumptions built in – is unlikely to work at all.

So in the unfamilar and erratic environment of the global frontier our tidy plans are quickly thown off course. The danger then, is that we keep on throwing switches and pulling levers in an attempt to bring us back to the mythical world of the hockey stick plan. Forever fighting fires, sometimes more a product of the plans than reality, we never build the capabilities required for success. In consequence our original mission floats by like the

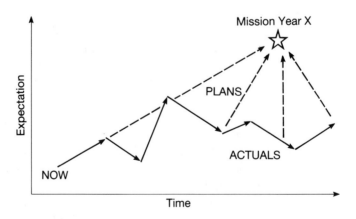

Figure 3.2   Fire-fighting and its effect on achieving the frontier mission

star in Fig. 3.2. Before long, the original mission loses credibility. We have failed before we have really begun.

In order to build a business effectively in the rough and tumble of the global frontier, the lack of capacity to deliver quality goods and services on time is generally the biggest problem. So the planning process must do an 'about face'. It must start from the mission and derive it's milestones from working back towards the present.

Figure 3.3 depicts this process of working back. Its starts from our mission and asks: 'if we are to achieve that mission 5 years out', for example, 'where do we have to be by year 4?' So far, so good. But to have reached that point by year 4 – it could be a sales target of $100 million, with a certain product range, requiring three local plants and a sales and service network of 16 centres – we need to ask another question: 'If we are to achieve that where do we realistically have to be by year 3?' And so on. By working back in this way we quickly come to ask the question of immediate concern: 'Then to meet this corporate building plan, what do we need to be doing now?' This may sound like a simple ruse, but it has far-reaching implications.

The three stages of working backwards

The first implication concerns the specification of the mission itself. Take the example of the Beijing Stone Office Equipment Technology Company (SOTEC), a joint venture with Mitsui of Japan which is discussed in more detail below. In setting out to achieve its mission 'to become a major

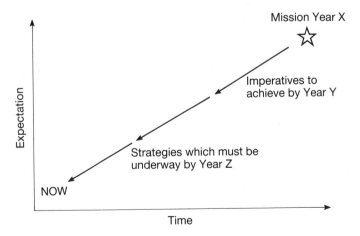

Figure 3.3   Strategy needs to 'face the other way'

international supplier of electronic office equipment', it must begin with an identikit of what success might look like. Does this imply that it must be significant in the US domestic market or is it more important to concentrate on Chinese-speaking populations in other parts of Asia? Which segments of its target markets will it seek to compete in? What will be its key sources of competitive advantage versus other Chinese and international players: cost, Chinese-character software, rate of product introduction, branding?

The second stage involves considering the supply side. To ask what the organisation capable of delivering SOTEC's vision of success would need to look like in terms of scale, production technology, resources, staff skills, organisational structure, brand image, etc? More specifically, is it important to have hardware development capability, or will its approach be to assemble different models using standard components and bundle this with specialist software, what role will branding play, how will it distribute products inside and outside China? Rather than forecasting demand and sales, working backwards from the venture's long-term goals emphasises prediction of the capabilities necessary to deliver a future definition of success.

As with any forecasting, this 'supply-side' prediction is far from being free of uncertainty. Rather than assuming it away, uncertainty must be fed into the process. The greater the uncertainty about the exact type of capability required to support future success, the more flexible must be the means of building it. The bounds of uncertainty around how much capacity SOTEC needs to deliver it's mission, for example, must be reflected in the extra land it holds in reserve for expansion at existing sites and the lines of credit it has on standby. Thus capacity for stretch and flexibility may become objectives in their own right at certain stages of the plan.

Stage three involves projecting our supply-side prediction back in time to ask the question 'What milestones must we have reached (say) two years prior if we are going to be on track to get the resources, skills, capacity, brand preference, and structure that we need to achieve this supply-side goal, given realistic lead times involved?'

Successive application of this planning procedure allows management to work back to what actions must be taken now to build the future capabilities required. This amounts to defining the mission in terms of the **supply-side imperatives** to achieve it and planning the critical paths to constructing them. It is analogous to defining the frontier mission, goals and strategy like a civil engineering project with plans for its completion.

Getting the sequence right

Putting together a clear, supply-side plan is one thing. But filling the gaping holes which become apparent relative to most firms' current capabilities on the global frontier is quite another. Focusing on the overall gap between the local capabilities it has now and those it must develop to support the achievement of its mission, the gulf often looks daunting, even for a company already successfully involved in trade. Management and staff approach the task resigned to failure. Attempting to fix everything at once is beyond the total capacity of current resources. There are too many things to do at once and no one qualified to do them. Indeed, most managers charged with growing the business in frontier markets will probably recognise Rosabeth Moss Kanter's classic characterisation of executives overloaded with too many, often contradictory tasks:[4]

- 'Think strategically and invest in the future – but keep the numbers up today.
- Be entrepreneurial and take risks – but don't cost the business anything by failing.
- Know every detail of your business – but delegate more responsibility to others.
- Speak up, be a leader, set the direction – but be participative, listen well, co-operate.
- Continue to do everything you are currently doing even better – and spend more time communicating with employees, serving on teams, and launching new projects.'

The answer to these problems lies in breaking up the overall requirement to close a capabilities gap into bite-sized pieces: tasks which employees can focus on, which they can believe are realistic rather than overwhelming. These can then be sequenced to take account of the complementarity between the capabilities and the order in which they must be deployed in the market.

Just as in any construction project, getting the sequence right is critical for two reasons.

First, the customer's buying decision often works in steps. If your product doesn't qualify at the initial hurdle (the right size for example) it's disqualified from the race. Whatever other qualities it may have, they won't even be looked at. Nor is the customer's purchase hierarchy of needs always obvious. When Allami Biztosita, Hungary's largest insurance company, went to update their computer system, finding equipment that could interface with small satellite dishes was a prerequisite. Those Western vendors who offered old technology at cut prices were surprised when they were excluded. The reason for satellite compatability as overriding criterion: bypassing unreliable Hungarian telephone lines.[5] The answer was to use state-of-the-art technology to overcome the shortcomings of existing infrastructure. Underdevelopment meant that the frontier required more advanced technology, not less.

Once they are satisfied that there is little difference in two competitors' ability to satisfy these primary characteristics, the basis of their decision switches to other criteria like maintenance service or technical support. If both competitors offer very similar levels of this, some other criterion, like price, then becomes decisive. The same is true of many other products. When we purchase a watch these days, we expect it to keep time with a high degree of accuracy; once this is satisfied, we switch our focus to the design of the case, price and so on.

Customers on the global frontier often have a strong hierarchy of purchase criteria. They are quite uncompromising on an attribute, until they find themselves in the position where there is little to choose between competitors. Then some previously unimportant factor becomes the dominant driver of the purchase decision.

This has important consequences for the sequencing of an entry strategy. It says that unless you develop your competitive capabilities to deliver in a sequence which parallels the customers' **hierarchy of buying criteria** you will get nowhere. You will be investing in being able to deliver secondary attributes at a stage when many buyers are not even willing to consider your offering.

The second reason for a critical role of sequencing is internal to the organisation. The successful development and exploitation of some capabilities must build on the base of other skills. Excellent marketing skills which stoke up customer expectations could be a definite liability if deployed before having the capabilities to deliver. A sophisticated product is of little use if you can't supply the training, technical support and maintenance to keep it running smoothly. Similarly, it may be impossible to recruit and motivate a sales force before you have a suitable local product which they can believe in.[6]

Climbing the frontier staircase step by step

Obviously the appropriate staircase for the global frontier will differ for every individual organisation. Different businesses and even functional departments will need their own staircase plans. An overarching problem for companies extending the global frontier, however, lies in finding the right sequence through which to increase its level of involvement. Establishing a huge, fully-integrated manufacturing capacity before developing other capabilities through a series of incremental commitments which extend a company's knowledge base and network of relationships in preparation, is a game of Russian roulette.

Figure 3.4 illustrates this kind of sequential development which has underpinned the operations of a number of the global frontier's most successful companies. It begins with the types of information gathering and service networks discussed in Chapter 2. The next step is the development of a two-way trade platform as described above. In beginning to make the transition from trade to production, a number of successful companies have taken the route of exporting plant and equipment to a local organisation with whom they are considering a future joint venture. This equipment is purchased by the recipient along with a contract for technical support. This raises the technological capability of the potential partner and provides direct experience of working together before either side commits to substantial investment in a joint venture. We discuss some case study examples of this approach below.

The fourth step in the sequence might take the form of a processing

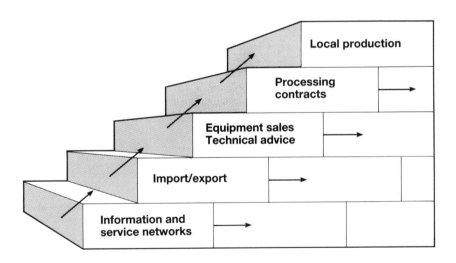

Figure 3.4   The frontier staircase: a step-by-step approach to the next phase of global expansion

contract. The local organisation, now with improved technical and organisational capabilities, contracts with the foreign firm to undertake a discrete part of a manufacturing process – such as the assembly of a product module or component. The overseas partner supplies the inputs and takes the finished output, paying the local firm a unit processing fee. In many cases such contracts make provision for certain local management functions, like quality assurance, to be taken over by the foreign partner. Again, we discuss some case study examples below.

Each step is consolidated by the introduction of procedures, routines and management systems into the local enterprise (denoted by the horizontal arrows in Fig. 3.4) as a closer relationship develops through the sequence. The final stage is a joint venture investment in a larger scale operation with more sophisticated technology, often designed with the aim of serving the local market as well as export trade. By laying the groundwork and gradually extending both the relationship and the capabilities of both partners in this way, the probability of a profitable and joint venture operation on the global frontier is greatly enhanced. Taking the time to lay solid foundations often means that the final joint venture is capable of remarkably rapid growth once established.

SOTEC: a case study in sequential development

The evolution of SOTEC, whose parent Stone Group is now the largest private company in China, provides an instructive example of the incremental, step-by-step approach to successful business development on the global frontier.

What is today SOTEC, the Beijing Stone Office Equipment Technology Company, began in 1984 through co-operation between a Chinese enterprise, Beijing Stone Group, and the Japanese trading house, Mitsui. The Mitsui Corporation already had a well-established network of representation in China through which it tracked changing market conditions and identified trading opportunities. The market for computer printers appeared promising, but incompatibility with Chinese computer protocols limited the sale of Japanese printers to the niche of imported systems.

After extensive discussions with the Stone Group, a trade agreement was signed whereby Stone would import standard printers from Japan, insert a card to allow existing Chinese computer equipment to drive them, and then handle the sale to local customers through its existing channels. The trade link was consolidated through exchange of technical information to assist Stone in the design of the card and a long-term pricing contract.

The next step took the form of a full-blown technical co-operation agreement for the development of a personal computer (PC) package, including exchange of staff. During 1986 and 1987 this co-operation led to the launch of a PC system based on hardware provided by Mitsui and software written by Stone. This activity built on Stone's strong capabilities in software development and links with leading universities, research institutes and the Chinese Academy of Sciences. The Mitsui hardware filled an important gap in Stone's capability to meet the market requirements – held back in the hardware area by weaknesses in some of China's basic industries on which hardware depends. During this period Stone also strengthened its marketing and distribution to form a network of 19 sales subsidiaries in key markets around China as well developing its relationships with national distribution channels.

The new PC package sold well and links between the two companies strengthened. Experience in the market indicated that many applications used only the word processing functions. Latent demand could be unlocked by selling a dedicated word processing machine. Focus would allow more competitive pricing and also the development of improved software to enable conversion between old and new Chinese character sets along with capabilities to handle foreign languages. In response, an assembly operation was set up to support the launch of a dedicated word processor, the MS-2401.

The SOTEC assembly joint venture in Beijing began in 1987 with a total investment of $4 million, 25 per cent in cash from Mitsui. The Stone Group capitalised $1.2 million of software into the venture as well as allocating land, buildings and ancillary equipment to support the line. This operation began by limited assembly of large, prefabricated base modules. As SOTEC accumulated experience and installed quality and manufacturing control systems under the guidance of Mitsui staff, the assembly operation gradually migrated upstream towards sub-assemblies and eventually basic components. This built improved technical capabilities within the company and reduced its costs.

During the latter half of 1988, Mitsui staff in China conducted a feasibility study into establishment of a fully-integrated manufacturing facility based on a mix of imported basic components and locally supplied inputs. As a result, in April 1989, SOTEC expanded its operations to full local manufacturing, bringing on-stream a new plant in the Shenzhen with an initial production capacity of 70,000 word processors per year, plus a further capacity of 30,000 machines per year on the Beijing site. One of the three deputy general managers at the new plant was seconded from Mitsui where he had been responsible for component supply to the earlier assembly operation.

Since that time, SOTEC has continued to develop its operations with a series of new product introductions and new production lines. It began earning hard currency by building knowledge of new types of customers by developing the market among Chinese export organisations and foreign joint ventures. By 1991 it was exporting 10 per cent of its expanded output to Hong Kong and South East Asia. New efforts are now focused on the launch of products specifically designed for international markets.

Learning along the way

Perhaps somewhat paradoxically, a tightly defined supply-side strategy based on the strategic staircase can open up more options for flexible response to unexpected market developments than the more traditional planning dominated by demand-side estimates of market growth and sales.

Rather than trying to second-guess the twists and turns in the market from quarter to quarter or year to year, supply-side strategy emphasises a planned approach to the capabilities which will be required to succeed long term. The responsiveness to uncertain conditions comes, instead, from how these capabilities are applied to the emerging frontier market during any short-term period. Here opportunism and unplanned, bottom-up strategy is to be encouraged as a route to increased market responsiveness. In a nutshell, what we propose is a very systematic development of the mission an individual must achieve to build each step in the staircase, combined with considerable flexibility and individual responsibility as to how that step is taken.

The plan supports investment in key capabilities. It should not attempt, however, to over-determine the actions of each individual. Armed with a mission and a clear perspective as to the sequence of priorities and corresponding capabilities the firm is developing, each member of staff must become the proverbial 'gardener'. Observing day-to-day developments in the market in their area of responsibility, no matter how narrow, individuals must be able to identify 'weeds' (unexpected occurrences which divert the company from its strategic course), and make the necessary corrections to arrest growth of these undesirables. Likewise, recognising a 'flower' (an unexpected development which, nevertheless, fits well with the firm's strategy) staff should take the initiative to use the company's capabilities to promote it. In this way the organisation gains as they respond flexibly to market conditions at the level of each individual.

Consider Henry Mintzberg's famous characterisation of emergent strategy:

> 'Out in the field a salesman visits a customer. The product isn't quite right, and together they work out some modifications. The salesman returns to his company and puts the changes through; after 2 or 3 more rounds they finally get it right. A new product emerges, which eventually opens up a new market. The company has changed its strategic course.'[7]

In the quotation above numerous people are making strategic decisions from the salesman, through to the R&D and marketing staff, manufacturing and top management. Strategy is working well when they are not simply responding to every suggestion any customer makes. Rather, their decision to expend their scarce resources on a new project reflects the fact that, although not planned, it fits well with the staircase the company is trying to build.

The deliberate, sequential, internal development of capabilities and skills, combined with enhanced awareness throughout the organisation of market-driven opportunities to deploy these capabilities, provides the basic building blocks of this approach. The strategic staircase provides the instrument to bridge the gap between the present and the hypothetical aim in the future, and the framework that directs the choice of what skills are developed and when. At one level this framework is a powerful organising idea around which the strategy development process can be undertaken. It also has another, vital function. It provides an effective device for presenting, communicating and, indeed, selling strategy within an organisation. A good communication tool is especially necessary, given that business on the global frontier remains largely a mystery to many, even senior, people. Without it, responsiveness to rapidly changing local conditions within the framework of a planned sequence of development might be interpreted as lack of direction – misinterpreted as an enterprise simply buffeted by events.

CONSOLIDATING A TRADE PLATFORM

Rapid, sometimes erratic change on the global frontier also necessitates action on another front: initiatives to consolidate established trading links. Without this consolidation, trade is unlikely to provide a firm platform for future development. Past investments in relationship-building are at risk of disappearing in shifting sands.

The Morgan-Trans case study: consolidating trade

In this context the establishment in 1991 of a new trading company, Morgan Trans, provides particular food for thought. From its first sales of crucibles in Hungary in 1907 and establishment of a factory in Lenin(Petro)grad at about the same time, Morgan Crucible has maintained its relationships in Eastern Europe through good and bad. In Hungary, for example, it has been involved in import/export business, switch deals and barter trade with the same partner, Transelektro, for 40 years. As stable a trading relationship as one might hope to get.

During this period Transelektro had already set up direct links to other markets, including Western Europe, through a network of offices across East Europe, in Vienna, and in France and Germany. But in 1990 it began an even more fundamental transformation: from what was effectively a traditional Eastern European foreign trade organisation to a Japanese-style trading house and joint stock company. Privatisation would be the next step. In the face of these changes Morgan and Transelecktro decided it made sense to consolidate their trading relationship by forming a joint venture trading company. The aim was both security and assured cash availability which could only come from a formal, long-term commitment by the partners. The result was Morgan Trans with a 51 per cent shareholding by Morgan UK and 49 per cent by a Transelektro subsidiary based in Munich. The new company formally linked a network of activities in the 33 countries where Morgan operates with those in which Transelektro was already established. Overlapping contacts were integrated, resulting, for example, in joint development of trading in China.

Initially, the activities of Morgan Trans were purely in trading. But it also put a platform for other activities in place. Morgan's first manufacturing joint venture in Hungary was with a large motor manufacturer which had been a Transelektro customer for decades. This venture will now take over production of the carbon brushes originally supplied by Morgan through Transelektro. The benefits of consolidating a trading relationship into the right platform for future development, therefore, are already becoming clear. It takes little imagination to realise that such projects would hardly be possible on the basis of a trading relationship that was only as good as the last deal.

Zhejiang Sanmei Tea: locking in supply

The transfer of technology and equipment to a trade partner is another means of consolidating trading links. This mechanism has been especially popular among Japanese companies as a means of developing business in China. It has played a role in industries as diverse as soya beans and miniature electric motors, case studies which we discuss in later chapters. The concept is also neatly illustrated in the evolution of Zhejiang Sanmei Tea.

While China is synonymous with tea, most of its modern production is not the green tea most prized in Japan. Although the processing technology for steamed green tea dates back to the Chinese Tang Dynasty about 1400 years ago, its mechanisation and reliability has been achieved by the Japanese. Seeing a potential new source of supply, the Japanese sent five pilot steaming machines used in the setting of green tea to Zhejiang province and Hangzhou Tea Testing Farm in 1973. From this base, trade in green tea developed.

Seeking to consolidate its position and further develop this trade, the Japanese beverage company Sanmei established a joint venture company in 1986 with the Tea Import and Export Corp. of China, the Zhejiang Tea Company and several other growers in the region. The investment from Sanmei of $400,000 was represented by two sets of tea processing equipment, matched by transfer of land and buildings of equivalent value by the Chinese partners. Processing capacity was expanded in 1988 with further Chinese investment of $1 million. The venture's products include bulk green tea, high quality branded tea and tea bags, sold in Japan, USA, Canada, Germany and Hong Kong. From a base of $460,000 sales in the first year of operations, turnover had grown to $1.6 million by 1990.

The Japanese partner remains the major, although not exclusive, customer for the venture's output, its off-take fluctuating with market conditions. Moreover, the Japanese have only limited involvement in the management of the company, sending technical staff to supervise the manufacturing process and quality control during the Spring picking and production season. Parts and maintenance support for the machinery is also supplied from Japan. As with many similar arrangements, however, the venture remains a loose partnership aimed at consolidating a trade source, following the Japanese practice of investing limited capital and technical know-how in their suppliers to cement the relationship and increase control.

FROM TRADE TO PROCESSING CONTRACTS

We have already mentioned the benefits of developing trade with the global frontier on the basis of two-way flows. Seeking to improve the quality and consistency of imports supplied by developing markets, companies like Sanmei have provided equipment and technical advice to their suppliers. In exchange, they also share in the margins earned on sales to third parties. Other companies restricted trade to the sale and purchase of equipment, sometimes exporting whole plants to the global frontier, without linking this trade to a continued flow of product.

Processing contracts, often known as co-operative joint ventures in China, take the integration of the frontier operation with the foreign partner one stage further. Yet they stop short of a full equity joint venture. Typically, a processing contract commits the foreign partner to supply components or materials (retaining ownership of these inputs), 'lend' equipment to the local partner, to provide technical advice and to accept 100 per cent of the output of the venture. The frontier partner provides labour, buildings and supporting infrastructure in exchange for a piece rate, processing fee. Processing contracts on the global frontier involve products ranging from suits and medical equipment in China to animated cartoons in Poland. Prior to 1986, almost 50 per cent of foreign 'joint ventures' in China were, in fact, processing contracts. Even in the 1990s, these arrangements still account for 20 per cent of the total.

The Omron processing contract

The Japanese electronics firm, Omron, for example, has had electronic blood pressure and body temperature meters assembled by the Dalian Recorder Factory since 1988. Like many state-owned organisations, Dalian Recorder lacked the capital, technology, parts supply and sales channels to support such a business. It did, however, have a trained workforce and the infrastructure to support it – both under-utilised because of falling sales in its core consumer electronics business as imports flooded in.

A number of foreign firms had proposed sourcing deals to the Dalian Municipal Government to access these idle pools of skilled labour. The stumbling block, however, was an unwillingness of the Chinese authorities to take the risk of purchasing specialised equipment to supply a processing service with an uncertain future. Omron overcame the problem by lending the equipment to Dalian Recorder at no cost, initially for a period of 2 years. Two Japanese technicians were also seconded to Dalian Recorder to handle the logistics of supply and shipping as well as quality control. $50,000 was invested by Omron to refurbish the buildings allocated to the project by the Chinese partner.

In exchange, Omron was able to negotiate an attractive piece rate for the work. Dalian Recorder selected some of its best, young operators to work on the line. Their average income was considerably higher than colleagues working in the core Dalian business provided they could meet the productivity challenge. Some returned to their original jobs. Those who stayed achieved results – defect rates 66 per cent below comparative Chinese operations, continual increases in productivity and an ever-expanding skill base. After 2 years the line was handling double the volume originally envisaged; from three initial product types, the operation had developed the capability to handle 10 different models.

The processing contract has been successful for both sides. For the Chinese it has brought in cash, absorbed idle labour, expanded the skill base of its workers, and introduced new manufacturing systems, procedures and disciplines – many of which can be applied to existing and future operations. Omron, meanwhile, have gained cost-efficient assembly capacity, up and running quickly, with little commitment of capital and personnel. At the same time, the arrangement has limits: the partners are frustrated by reliance on poor logistics and support services which, within the bounds of a processing contract, they cannot own or even control. Working within the personnel policies of state organisation also imposes constraints, especially in respect of flexibility of staffing. Looking to the future, therefore, Omron is exploring the benefits of establishing a wholly-owned subsidiary as a possible next step.

Hanna-Barbera: developing a business in Poland

Trade and local 'processing' have also combined in underpinning the development of Hanna-Barbera's operations in Poland. Its joint venture, with Polskie Kino Animowane (Polish Animated Films) began operations by selling Hanna-Barbera video cassettes in Poland. In its second full year it sold some 650,000 tapes, a figure which astonished even the American partner. But the driving force for Hanna-Barbera was the quality of Polish animators – a highly developed profession in the country – at competitive costs. In parallel to video sales, therefore, the venture built a suitable studio to fulfill contracts for the US parent. Starting with 24 animators, it had a staff of over 200 within 3 years.

The next stage for Hanna-Barbera, and the final step in Figure 3.4, will by a fully-integrated local business: as well as trade and processing contracts, it will develop and produce and market films locally. We will return to discuss the issues of how to structure, manage and grow this type of independent, local subsidiary in Chapters 7 and 8. The important lesson here is that rather than rushing into a major investment, there are distinct advantages in climbing the strategic staircase step-by-step.

SETTING THE PACE

We began this chapter with a discussion of trade and the role of trading activity, not as a substitute for direct investment, but as a step in the development of a full-fledged frontier business. The rapid growth of trading potential in the early development of a frontier market and the relatively low costs of getting up and running, make trade deals an attractive way to enter, and to learn. And, contrary to the initial instinct of many, it has proved easiest to enter a frontier market as an importer of local goods – as buyer, not a seller. Paradoxically, because doors opened more readily for buyers, and the sale of local goods overseas could help provide an ongoing source of foreign exchange, buying could be the most effective way of laying the groundwork for an integrated operation designed to serve the local market. Exports, equipment sales, processing contracts and finally, local production could follow – each step building on the information base, contacts, and trust laid down in the preceding stage.

Throughout, however, one point must never be forgotten: the kind of trade deal (or equipment sale, or processing contract) that makes best sense as an end in itself is not necessarily the same one that will provide the best launching pad for a further step towards a full-fledged business. So the mission needs to be clear from the outset, and with it the staircase that follows logically from working back along the critical path. Only then is it possible to assess whether today's trade supplier might make a future joint venture partner; only then will investment beyond the one-off deal make sense.

Approaching development of a frontier business as a strategic staircase has three major advantages. First, it allows the formidable task of succeeding on the global frontier to be broken down into bite-sized pieces. At each stage it focuses management on the key things it needs to achieve in order to move forward – and to do those things well. Priorities are clear, a godsend in an environment where there is constantly too much to do and too few resources to do it. Second, since each step is part of a staircase, preparations can be made to help support each new initiative before the 'start button' is pressed. Staff, for example, can be trained in company systems in advance using the existing business; and the new activity can draw on the support infrastructure already in place. And the homework has been completed, the information void has already been bridged. Third, the staircase provides management and staff with a vision of the future. As we will see in Chapter 7, in the face of the uncertainty and change which characterises the global frontier, the necessity to build confidence in the future is essential to motivate and retain that most scarce of all assets in frontier markets: skilled staff.

The argument often given against this staircase approach is our old friend speed: 'we need growth now, we haven't got time for all that'. This is a powerful argument, but on the global frontier, it's often untrue. The case histories in this chapter demonstrated that each step need not be a long, drawn-out affair. How fast you move through the sequence depends on how quickly the capabilities necessary to succeed can be put in place. Most of them you need to build anyway – and it's much more difficult when you try to develop them at once. At each step effort is focused on a narrow target, not dissipated across a broad front: tunnelling through the obstacles rather than trying to push them out of the way. And on a staircase you don't waste time taking one step forward and two steps back; its the traction of a bulldozer, not the Formula 1 racer on a mud slide. Less haste, as they say, and more speed.

References

1 Morgan Trans – a new Morgan Crucible vehicle for trading and beyond in eastern Europe, *East Europe Business Focus*, Issue 8, March 1991, p. 12.
2 ICL – a flexible approach in East Europe', *East Europe Business Focus*, Issue 1, June 1990.
3 EC Trade Policy Proves to Be a Bad Fit For Belgian Firm Importing Chinese Shoes', *The Wall Street Journal*, 12 February 1993.
4 Rosabeth Moss Kanter, *When Giants Learn to Dance*, Touchstone Books, New York, 1989, p. 20.
5 Hungary's mother of invention, *The Times*, 15 January 1993.
6 For a fuller discussion of the strategic staircase as a planning tool, see M. Hay and P. Williamson: Strategic Staircases: Planning the Capabilities Required for Success, *Long Range Planning*, Vol 24, No. 41, 1991, pp. 36–43.
7 Mintzberg, Crafting Strategy, *Harvard Business Review*, July–Aug., 1987, p. 68.

4

GAINING LOCATIONAL ADVANTAGE

Most people know the old adage about the three success factors in retailing: location, location and location. The same might be said of business on the global frontier. The problem is that frontier markets are a sea of shifting sands. And an investor's worst nightmare is to put down deep roots in a location where it will be forever handicapped relative to competitors. The major city in any frontier market might seem like the safest bet. But as we shall see, it is not always the best horse to back.

CHOOSING A LOCATION

Once a location decision is made, it has potentially far-reaching consequences. Ask any company to explain the location of its international headquarters. Why is Ford headquartered in Detroit? Why is Stuttgart the home of Daimler Benz, Basel the headquarters of all three Swiss pharmaceutical giants, or Boeing still overwhelmingly located in Seattle? Sometimes the answer lies in historical accident. More often than not, a business is attracted by the early advantages of a particular location. As the firm develops it becomes 'locked in' to this base.[1] There are exceptions: Pilkington plc moved the centre of its European glass business from St Helens, in the north west of England to Brussels. But few firms uproot their headquarters, lock, stock and barrel and move to a new location.

By and large, the pattern is the same for overseas subsidiaries: once the national or regional headquarters is established in a particular town or city it tends to be difficult to move. This kind of 'stickiness' can present particular problems for businesses operating on the global frontier. Developing markets are inevitably in a state of flux; as the market environment changes, so does the attractiveness of a particular location relative to the alternatives.

Without a careful, forward looking strategy for gaining locational advantage frontier ventures can easily find themselves marooned as the rivers of commerce change their course.

Choosing a location that reflects the long-term, competitive fundamentals is one, albeit critically important, element of a strategy for gaining locational advantage. But it would be wrong to see locational strategy for the global frontier as a one-off, largely passive decision. The ability to *create* new, locational advantages through various types of interaction with the local environment is paramount to competitive advantage in the long run.[2] In developing markets which are so often plagued by input shortages, lack of ancillary services and inadequate infrastructure, three proactive approaches to location strategy play key roles:

- securing control over local supplies;
- developing local content;
- exploiting 'cluster' economies.

The first task of this chapter is to set out the factors which need special emphasis when choosing a location in rapidly changing frontier market environments. Each alternative location will inevitably have pros and cons for different parts of the organisation. Our second topic, therefore, is how much a business should compromise by concentrating its activities in a single location. Alternatively, should the organisation be 'decoupled', enabling (say) manufacturing to be located in one place and sales to set up in some more suitable location elsewhere? (As we saw from the networks of representative offices in Chapter 2, the forces for decentralisation are often strong in frontier markets.) We then go on to outline some of the positive strategies frontier businesses can use to build upon the initial advantages their chosen location(s) have to offer.

Locational magnets

In choosing a location we need to do more than simply pinpoint 'magnets' like the abundance of inputs, skilled labour, ancillary services and customers. These factors are obviously important in frontier markets where the ability to overcome shortages and poor transport and communication links can make or break a business. But in any market, 'abundance' must be assessed relative to demand. The attractiveness of a pool of labour with specialist skills or a concentration of customers in a particular city depends on how many competitors are also casting their nets in the same pond. In the long run it may prove cheaper to fish elsewhere, even if this means investing to expand the supply of a particular local resource or skill base. Ultimately, advantage comes from differentiating a business from its competitors rather simply following the pack. Depending on the intensity of local competition for a similar set of resources and customers, locational magnets not only attract, they can also repel.

Five factors stand out among the familiar location considerations as being particularly important to businesses operating the global frontier:

- Avoiding rival's 'walled cities' and early head-to-head competition
- Pre-empting key raw material supplies
- Levering off traditional skill bases
- Benefiting from proximity to customers
- Accessing ancillary industries.

Each of these factors merits discussion in turn.

Avoiding 'walled cities' and early head-to-head competition

Even in developing markets, a new entrant is likely to face competitors who are already well dug in. They may be local champions, foreign firms with historical roots, or 'first-movers' in a new phase of frontier expansion. Over time, these businesses have often created a network of barriers which impede new entry and help entrench their position. They may have pre-emptive rights over local raw material sources, exclusivity agreements with suppliers or major distributors, occupation of prime sites, alliances with local schools and technical colleges, and well-developed brand loyalty. Perhaps most important of all, in frontier markets local incumbents' links with municipal and regional authorities are likely to run very deep. For an outsider, such a network of relationships is not only hard to break into, it is even difficult to understand: only the results of these relationships are observable, not the links themselves. Its like walking around in the dark: until you bump into the web, you don't know exactly where it extends.

A company's local, home field market, meanwhile, often occupies a special place in the corporate psyche. It will fight to retain its established, local customers from competitive attack at almost any cost, even beyond the bounds of strict economic rationality. History and pride, not only sales revenues, are at stake.

Together these protective networks can form virtual 'walled cities' around established competitors. They may be fertile bases if a partner invites you in. Indeed, as we will see in Chapter 8, access to a walled city may add to the attractiveness of a prospective partner. Alternatively, it may be possible for a business to lay siege to such protected markets once it is firmly established elsewhere. But, unless the case for unique access to customers or suppliers is overwhelming, an entry point which avoids head-to-head competition must be preferred. Discretion is often the better part of valour. It is no accident, for example, that when Otis Elevator, the world's largest company in its sector, entered China it chose Tianjin. An important transport and trading centre since 1368, Tianjin is China's third largest city and second largest manufacturing centre. The potential partner, Tianjin Elevator Company was established by the Chinese central government in 1956, but managed by the City of Tianjin. The number two global competitor, Schindler of Switzerland, already had established a successful joint venture with the Beijing Elevator Company.[3] The third major, world player Mitsubishi, which dominated the Pacific region, had long-standing trading links with the major elevator manufacturer in Shanghai. Tianjin offered an attractive, but 'unclaimed' location for establishing a base from which Otis has subsequently expanded its operations into other key regions of the country.

Even in the absence of a 'walled-city' competitor, the downsides of locations which will attract head-to-head rivalry need to be considered. Two opposing sets of forces tend to be at work when competitors concentrate in a location. On one hand, competition for specialised inputs and skills tends to bid up local prices. Likewise there is an ever-present danger of price warfare as a number of sellers vie for each customer. On the other hand, a growing industry concentration may attract skilled labour, input suppliers or providers of ancillary services from elsewhere. With a diversified local customer base, suppliers may be more willing to accept the risks of committing to expand their capacity. Meanwhile, the availability of large volume of product combined with a barrage of marketing information as multiple brands compete in one location may help overcome initial buyer resistance more quickly, allowing the product category to reach the critical mass required for demand to take off.

Which of these opposing sets of forces proves dominant depends on:

1 whether or not the supply of required inputs is elastic; in other words will a concentration of competing users attract a larger supply base, or is the local availability of resources, skills and support services essentially fixed – in the latter case, concentrations of competitors will simply drive up input prices;

2 whether customers are more likely to buy the product when they see their neighbours adopting it, which may be because the product benefits from

'network economies' (as in the case of a telephone service, which generally becomes more useful the larger the number of local subscribers) or may be the result of a 'demonstration effect' – few buy the product until it becomes a fashion.

Given the nature of their products, the concentration of some types of frontier ventures in major centres looks convincing. Others go to a national capital or major city by default, just as the early investors in Britain or the USA gravitated to gateways like London or New York. But since one of the greatest attractions of many frontier markets is unsatisfied demand and weak local competition, the choice of a location that is plagued by head-to-head competition may render the whole strategy self-defeating. More and more leading companies are choosing a less crowded gateway to enter frontier markets; a solid base for future expansion, yet removed away from the home base of entrenched competition and sheltered from a possible flood of imports. Take the example of Kobayashi Takashi Co. Ltd., the No. 3 Japanese toiletry products manufacturer. Even back in 1986, it concluded that two of the most obvious sites were already becoming overcrowded. Shanghai already had two joint ventures in the cosmetics field, while Guangzhou was awash with imported cosmetics and toiletries. Instead the company established base in Hangzhou, the capital of the coastal Zhejiang province. As one of the most densely populated parts of China, Zhejiang provides a market of 40 million people in its own right. Nor can the location's image do a cosmetics and toiletries company any harm: the city Marco Polo described as 'the most distinguished and beautiful in the world', Hangzhou has been associated with fine silken clothing since ancient times.[4] From this base the company's products have since been rolled out nationwide.

Pre-empting local raw material supplies or sites

Frontier markets can offer unparalleled, and never to be repeated, opportunities for first movers to secure control of local raw material supplies and prime sites. When the British Ready Mix Concrete company acquired former state-owned Rüdersdorfer Zement in 1991, for example, one of the major attractions was its well located material reserves. An important lime manufacturer, Rüdersdorfer enjoyed 50 years worth of raw material reserves close to the expanding Berlin market.

A strategy of tying up quality raw material supplies in an emerging market is, of course, fine in theory. But in practice, governments on the global frontier are increasingly well aware of the hard currency earning potential of these assets. The oil majors, for example, have found the former Soviet republics extremely protective of foreign exploitation of their oil reserves. Taxes and participation fees have been high. Poland has been wary of foreign investment in its huge coal industry. And so the list goes on. The danger is that in buying access to raw materials investors will be forced to pay a full, or even premium, price.

There are still profitable opportunities to be had by pre-empting key raw material supplies on today's global frontier. But cash buying power is not enough. To succeed with this strategy, joint ventures must first look for new types of benefits to bring to the party. Take the example of Dalian Nisshin Oil Mills, a Sino-Japanese joint venture in soya bean products. Soya beans are subject to export controls in China and prices are set with an eye to production costs in the USA and Brazil, the other major world producers. However, through a joint venture with Mitsubishi Trading Co., Nomura China Investment Corporation and a carefully selected group of Chinese partners (discussed below), Nisshin has secured access to a consistent flow of 1,000 tonnes of raw soya beans per day at highly competitive prices, an exportable flow of soya bean meal to meet the needs of its Japanese operations, and participation in the Chinese domestic market for cooking and salad oils, where demand for better quality products is booming.

From the Chinese perspective, the key to unlocking this deal lay in provision of world-class processing technology and a $25 million investment in new plant – a significant, but hardly crippling cash input for a venture that earned $20 million of hard currency revenues during its first year of operation. The benefits for the Chinese economy are obvious: improved processing yields, additional value-added in China, increased foreign currency earnings from a natural resource, and better quality products for local consumption.

Avoiding the risks of diversification

Given that the financial numbers looked attractive for the project as a whole, the issue for Nisshin was how to gain the benefits of a competitive source and additional local profits, without losing focus on its core, oil processing activities. In the absence of any well-developed market through which the various by-products of its activities could be sold locally, there was a danger of getting dragged into potentially distracting activities, like retail marketing and distribution of oils in China, which were incidental to the Nisshin's primary objective – securing competitive supply. This risk of becoming bogged down in a network of ancillary businesses as part of the *quid pro quo* for raw material access, is a constant problem in frontier markets. Failure to avoid this trap can dramatically increase the capital commitment required as well as dissipating scarce managerial resources in a quagmire of problems tangential to the main business.

For Nisshin the solution lay in its choice of Chinese partners. At first sight, a venture involving four separate Chinese partners in addition to four Japanese companies including Nisshin might look like a decision-making nightmare. But each partner has a clear role and one which, if properly performed, should reduce the potential complexity of the operation for Nisshin. The role of Dalian Oil & Grease Industrial General Mills is as manufacturing partner. It provided a skeleton staff of skilled employees to run the new plant and train new operators recruited through open advertisement. It also continues to assist the joint venture in meeting the various needs of its manufacturing operations where local know-how and relationships are invaluable. The Jilin Provincial Grain & Oil Trade Corporation handles the sourcing of raw soya beans for the venture as part of its much larger local grain trading operations. Harbin City Longliang Grain and Oil Sales Department acts as distributor for the oil products in the Chinese local market. The Dalian Export and Trade Development Corporation, meanwhile, provided land in exchange for an equity share, and associated infrastructure services – essential in a frontier market where shortages of water, electricity, or fuel, and inadequate transport and maritime loading facilities can cause frequent disruption and impair productivity. Among the Japanese partners, Mitsubishi trading is responsible for international sales of products that are not utilised directly in Nisshin's Japanese operations. Of course bargaining between these partners over transfer prices is robust. But the basic goals of consistent supply, volume expansion and high productivity are largely compatible. The individual roles of each partner tend to be discrete. Both are essential prerequisites for the effective operation of a venture where such a large cast of different parties is involved.

In the service sector, input pre-emption generally focuses on sites. It is no accident, for example, that the Moscow McDonald's occupies a high profile position on the corner of Gorky Street. McDonald's Russian partner, Mosopshrepied, owned the prime property and agreed to demolish a smaller restaurant to make way for the flagship store because it is no less than the food service branch of the Moscow city government. Sites for a string of future restaurants across the capital have already been found, examined and agreed; a task that continues to be one of Mosopshrepied's major responsibilities in contributing to the venture.

Levering off traditional skill bases

The availability of a local skill pool is often an even more important locational consideration on the global frontier than in a developed economy. Unskilled labour for simple processing and assembly operations is one thing, but individuals with a depth of specific skills and experience are often in short supply. In-house training is an important part of the solution, as we will see in Chapter 7. But the turnover of trained staff in regions where the base of industrial skills historically is weak, can prove crippling. Many investors have also found that training for specialist skills is easier if the individuals start with a basic experience in mechanics, engineering or even machine operation. Turning farm workers who have only recently left the land into engineering operatives can prove a long and difficult task.

Some locations offer the possibilities of levering off traditional skill bases that have grown up in the area. Thus, cities or towns with a long history in textiles, mechanical engineering, or heavy industry may offer investors advantages when they go to build their workforce in a related business. This consideration needs to be weighed against the initial impressions of overcrowding, or perhaps industrial decay, that may initially greet the visitor. In manufacturing especially, some frontier investors have found to their cost that the 'clean slate' attractiveness of provinces or cities without an industrial heritage needs to be weighed against an important downside: the possibility of an ongoing vacuum of skills.

Locations with a heritage in similar, or related industries are also likely to offer more opportunities for developing a network of local subcontractors and suppliers. In a number of today's frontier markets the former defence industries have left behind organisations and pools of individuals with well-developed, technical skills which a number of investors have successfully accessed.

The Minri Electrical Tools Company, a Sino-Japanese joint venture in Fujian Province 50 per cent owned by the Hitachi Group, is a case in point. The company makes some ten lines of electrical tools which enjoy a reputation for high quality and reliability. It comes as a surprise to many that, in addition to the 35 per cent of its parts requirements made in-house in the Chinese operation, a further 50 per cent of its components are supplied by over 40 local subcontractors. In contrast, many investors elsewhere in China have struggled to meet targets for local content, even where their requirements have been for fewer, and often simpler, components than those demanded by Minri. The secret lies in the fact that most of Minri's subcontractors and suppliers share a common heritage: they are specialised defence contractors. As a result, their staff offer a well-developed array of engineering skills. They also benefit from the substantial public investment in technology and equipment that was often denied to civilian industries. With the increasing importance of open market transactions they are eager to use these capabilities to increase their cash flows by selling to a joint venture.

Nor do potentially accessible pockets of industrial expertise always occur in the obvious places on the global frontier. The distorting impact of past central planning is an important reason why skill bases show up in some unlikely places while they are almost completely lacking elsewhere. In Eastern Europe in particular, planners were fond of designating one place the centre of (say) machine tools and another place the capital of (say) shoes. Such specialisation had the advantage of ensuring that no population group might be tempted into thinking they could be self-sufficient and thus could do without the paternal hand of the centre. Since politics generally had more influence on this allocation than economics, the logic behind the geographic spread of activity is often obtuse.

Careful research can pay dividends. Romania, for example, is probably not the first place most investors would look to lever off local aircraft engineering skills. But, in fact, the Romanian aircraft industry is the most advanced in Eastern Europe outside the Soviet Union. The country has seven aviation factory groups which employ some 341,000 people. Romania and Poland are the only two ex-Warsaw pact countries to produce helicopters. And during the sixties and seventies when Romania enjoyed 'most favoured nation' status in international trade, its aircraft manufacturers had strong links with the West, including licence agreements with Aerospatiale and British Aerospace. Having suffered a run-down during latter years of the Ceaucescu regime, industry insiders estimate that it is now at least 10 years behind the demanding standards of the modern aviation sector. However a strong base of skills and know-how remains – much of it relevant to a range of engineering industries well beyond aerospace.

Benefiting from proximity to customers

For other businesses, proximity to customers acts as the most powerful locational magnet. In some cases this is a direct reflection of transport costs. When Ready Mix Concrete acquired the Rüdersdorf plant mentioned above, a cash injection of some DM160 million was required along with a major rationalisation and reorganisation of existing operations. Yet by netting a plant 30 kilometres from Berlin, with 50 years material reserves, the company was able to lock in a long-term transport cost advantage in serving one of Europe's major, ongoing markets for infrastructure projects.

Increasingly, however, the argument for proximity to customers turns on access to information. As we noted in Chapter 2, a constant, timely and reliable flow of information about customers' needs and preferences is essential in frontier markets. Buying patterns and consumer preferences often change rapidly as the market develops. At the same time, the process of getting an unfamiliar product established demands a high level of customer communication and feedback. This was an important consideration, for example, when Tambrands Inc. began to explore joint venture opportunities to produce and market Tampax tampons in the former Soviet bloc. Representatives from smaller, more entrepreneurial states including the Baltic republics and Soviet Georgia were particularly enthusiastic about collaborating with Tambrands. However, the company was reluctant to establish its major market entry in any republic with a small population base.[5] On the other hand, Tambrands had doubts about pinning their strategy on forming a close alliance with the Moscow bureaucracy in a period of decentralisation and possible shift of power in favour of regions with direct access to resources. Ultimately the company settled on the Ukranian Republic as the location for launching a Tambrands Soviet joint venture. It offered direct access to a population of over 50 million, combined with an extensive industrial base and a strong agricultural sector.

In machinery, equipment, and industrial and commercial supplies businesses, information flows can be even more critical. Proximity to the customer makes it easier for a supplier to provide an adequate level of technical and maintenance advice in frontier environments where communications infrastructure is either lacking or routinely overloaded. ICL Computer's joint venture contract with Morflot, the Russian Ministry of Merchant Marine, to design, test and install a version of ICL's personal computer for use on ships at sea, for example, drew it to Morflot's base in St Petersburg. The partnership developed so that the joint venture is now involved in manufacturing, assembly, sale and distribution of personal computers to a variety of customers from the St Petersburg site. The fact that Morflot has branches in many of the major Russian ports gives ICL close to a nationwide distribution network capable of providing local service to the company's customers.

Accessing ancillary industries and infrastructure

A final, although often especially powerful locational magnet in frontier markets is the availability of ancillary services and access to infrastructure. Supply of these services can present a chronic problem for a poorly located business and prove a major management distraction. For most frontier businesses this issue has three facets:

- back-up services to keep imported equipment running
- the supply of utilities such as electricity, fuel and water
- the efficiency of local administration from planning permission through to customs clearance.

The availability of back-up services for imported equipment often adds to the pull of major cities. As the local manager of McDonald's in Moscow puts it: 'It helps in that other Western companies such as Olivetti, who supply and service the cash registers, and Panasonic, who make the computers used in the restaurant, also have offices in the area.'[6]

The importance of taking steps to ensure continuity of utilities in any location is not to be underestimated. Almost without exception, the supply of infrastructure in developing markets fails to keep up with growth in demand, special investment zones included. Non-price rationing is the most common result. Well-intentioned assurances or even written guarantees fall by the wayside when the local authorities are forced to prioritise increasingly scarce resources. China Otuska Pharmaceutical in Tianjin, for example, obtained local guarantees of water, gas, electricity and petrol supplies. But it is still faced with rationing when local capacity simply runs out. For some commodities, such as petrol, purchases on the free market (albeit at high prices) provide a safety-valve. For other utilities such as electricity, however, the price mechanism doesn't come into play. Loss of effective capacity, increased wastage rates and lower productivity are the inevitable consequences when supply is abruptly cut off. For these reasons an increasing number of ventures maintain their own back-up, power generation plants. Some, like the international textile company Coats-Viyella Plc whose yarn spinning operations are a major power user, have reportedly subscribed to debentures in a local power company as part of a deal to ensure supply continuity in China. Clearly the prospective supply/demand balance for supply of basic utilities and the scope for preferential access need to be important elements in any location decision on the global frontier.

Equally, the efficiency of the local government administration needs to be assessed. In some locations, government bureaucracy can prove an ongoing scourge, rather than a one-off hurdle. It is a common fallacy to view the efficiency of the local authorities as an issue only in the setup phase. The 'all will be well once we get up any running' attitude is a dangerous piece of wishful thinking. It is precisely because of the ongoing impacts of relationships with local authorities on downtime, productivity and pressure on scarce management time that they need to figure prominently in the location decision. Nor should any investor be beguiled by assurances from senior officials in a central administration that the path through local bureaucracy will be smooth by dictate from above. The reality of most frontier markets is that local administrators determine the practicalities of a business's operating environment. And they are driven by local networks of established relationships, incentives, past debts and old scores. In this environment, officials from the central government are usually unwanted outsiders whose interference must be tolerated but, if possible, shrugged off.

In fact, being well away from the central government can have decided advantages. When assessing different locations for its Chinese venture, for example, the Japanese leader in its market, Dainippon Ink and Chemicals was conscious that Shanghai and Tianjin both had large, established ink producers. But in choosing the Shenzhen Economic Zone they were also conscious of the enormous distance from Beijing, both geographic and psychological, and its influence on administrative flexibility; as well as the efficiency of customs clearance and transportation, given the heavy dependence of the region on trade through Hong Kong. Being part of a local network can have decided advantages.

Compromise or decouple?

The locational forces we have described: avoiding 'walled cities', pre-empting input supplies and sites, levering off traditional skills bases, benefiting from customer proximity, and accessing ancillary industries and infrastructure, almost inevitably end up pulling a frontier business in opposing directions. One solution is to choose a, single compromise location. But this approach can impose substantial costs on a business as well as forcing it to forego potential opportunities. Sooner or later many businesses need to consider the option of decoupling their various activities so that, for example, the sales and service functions can be located in one part of a frontier market and manufacturing in another. The peculiar geographic dispersion of activity on the global frontier, often the result of the heritage of politicised central planning we mentioned above, adds to the basic pressures to decouple that we observe in markets elsewhere. But dispersion of activities seldom comes easily to managers who fear a loss of control. To make decoupling work, a deep-seated prejudice in favour of the traditional headquarters (or even an enclave) may need to be shaken off. Again, a systematic approach to the problem can help.

Thinking through the activity chain

In many companies decisions about location tend to be discussed as if a new subsidiary were a single, indivisible entity. In reality, we know that any subsidiary comprises a bundle of individual activities which form a value-added chain of the type we illustrated in Chapter 2, Fig. 2.1. The chain comprises a number of primary activities from inbound logistics through to after sales service. Overlaid on these are a series of support activities such as procurement, technology development and human resource management which are required to allow the primary activity to function. In some cases these support functions are shared between primary activities. Alternatively, they may be independently supplied so that, for example, the maintenance and service function undertakes its own procurement or marketing and sales are responsible for their own human resource management.

Within any chain of this type each activity has various requirements for success. Production may require a competitively priced supply of skilled labour. Design and marketing may require rapid access to market information as well as skills. The availability of excellent infrastructure may be critical to distribution activities. R&D may be more effective if sited so as to make easy links with major universities or where it has good access to users of the product or service.

The traditional location tradeoff

It is highly unlikely that a single location will offer the best mix of requirements for every activity in the chain. The location offering maximum comparative advantage will differ for each activity. This means that there are strong forces driving the business to fragment its location across multiple sites. Each site could then specialise in a particular activity, allowing that activity to choose the most advantageous location to meet its special needs.

Such a company would undoubtedly gain considerable competitive advantage from simultaneously exploiting the benefits of all the best locations. The other key part of the chain, the links between the activities, however, would become much more costly and difficult to manage. Support services which are required by more than one activity may be uneconomic to provide for each activity alone. Economies of scale and scope in co-ordination and support services would be lost. While decentralisation has attractions, it is easier and often more economic to manage everything under one roof.

The result of these opposing forces is an uneasy compromise between fragmentation and concentration. The best overall location for a complete subsidiary will be sub-optimal for any of its activities viewed in isolation.

To take a simple example, suppose there are two locations, one remote from the main market and one in the centre of the main concentration of customers. In the first location, R, labour is cheap but market information is expensive. At the second site, M, the reverse is true: up-to-date, reliable information is abundant and cheap, but labour is expensive.

Labour and information are substitutes for each of the firm's activities. In marketing and design, for example, better information means substantially higher labour productivity. In manufacturing and maintenance, market information can improve labour productivity, but the gains are less dramatic than in other activities. As illustrated in Fig. 4.1, the venture's manufacturing and maintenance activities are best sited at location R to take advantage of low-cost labour. The design and marketing activities are best sited at location M to exploit lower cost information and better market access.

If the constraint that both must be sited together is imposed, one of these groups of activities will be forced to operate with an inferior mix of information and labour: either too far way from the customers or divorced from the

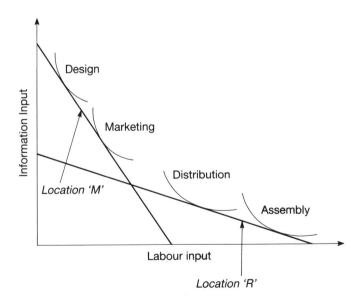

Figure 4.1   Location decisions: tradeoff and compromise

cheapest labour. Total productivity will therefore be impaired even if the subsidiary chooses its preferred location as an integrated unit. The potential benefits of greater geographic specialisation will be forgone.

In highly developed markets, two recent trends have been operating to open up new opportunities for decoupling of activities which had traditionally been forced together in a single location by the economics of co-ordination and provision of support services. The first is improvement in communications technology. The second is the increased availability of support services from third party suppliers. Dramatic advances in communications technology have made it possible for the different activities of a business to be precisely co-ordinated despite considerable intervening distances.

But even after the communications issues had been overcome, companies were still left with the problem of the economics of providing support services. Many of these support services, spanning activities from machine maintenance to printing services, are subject to economies of scale and scope. Unit costs could be reduced substantially by sharing these support functions across various primary activities of the business. While the sharing of support functions had to occur within the firm, activities had to stay under one roof, and decoupling was impossible.

Viable activity decoupling

Once these support functions are taken outside the firm, it is possible to achieve efficiencies by sharing the costs of support functions with other firms rather than across activities within the firm. A subcontractor or shared facility can enjoy the benefits of scale and scope, some of the benefit of which will be passed on to the user firm. Thus, through external economies it becomes viable to cost-effectively provide the necessary support function to enable an individual activity to be decoupled from other activities of its firm. Stand-alone design, marketing, or manufacturing units become viable so long as reliable and competitive third party suppliers of support services are available. Indeed, by using specialist third party suppliers of services to primary activities, they can often achieve higher quality services more responsive to their needs than was possible from a single support function inside the firm attempting to serve a range of primary activities with different needs.

In developed markets then, each *activity*, rather than a firm or an industry, is increasingly able to migrate to the location which maximizes its competitive advantage, as illustrated in Fig. 4.2. Production, for example, shifts from the 'compromise' location towards a 'labour rich' region, either in terms of skill availability or low costs. Meanwhile, the marketing function migrates to the best source of market information: a region with the most sophisticated customers or the city which sets the trend for the rest.

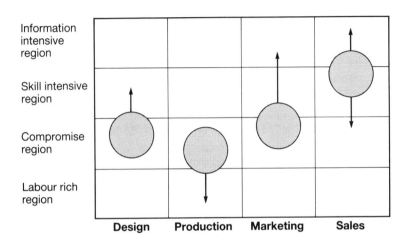

Figure 4.2   Activity decoupling

This concept of decoupling has three fundamental implications for business location strategy:

1 Individual activities are increasingly the appropriate unit of analysis for location decisions, hence the specialist needs of particular activities are increasingly important rather than the best compromise for the firm.
2 Communications infrastructure to permit individual activities to be linked carries increasing weight in the location decision.
3 Availability of high quality and cost competitive support services and functions in the form of subcontractors or networks of shared facilities, staff and information is now a critical element in the location decision.

Beijing. One office, but 'only scratched the surface' of the market. Need to open additional offices to cover enormous area and overcome service problems created by traffic congestions.

Midwest. (Key city: Xi'an). Land area of more than half size of USA, covered by a few 'obscure' agents. Sales push in Xi'an had already won share. Possible production base to supply other regions.

South and Southwest. (Key cities: Guangzhou, Chengdu, Changsha, Guiyang, Nanning, Kunming). Future potential 'beyond words'. One local office, selling older Tianjin products. Previous rationing by sales quotas.

Northeast. (Key cities: Dalian, Harbin, Changchun). One office, one agent. Considered to have great potential. Need to open additional offices and expand support for operations.

Shanghai. Successful operation with plans to open two additional offices. An important base for developing the market in areas surrounding the city considered to have great potential.

Coastal. (Key cities: Shenzhen, Macau, Quindao, Fuzhou, Zuihai, Ningbo). Three offices in region which included most of the fast growing SEZ's. Three additional offices at planning stage. Important to expand service network.

Figure 4.3   The Chinese elevator market and Otis activities by region in 1988

Source: Otis Elevator Company (B–1): China Joint Venture, Harvard Business School, Case No. 9-393-006

Pressures and obstacles to decoupling on the global frontier

The large geographic size of the markets on today's global frontier, along with trends towards political fragmentation and the resurgence of racial and cultural divides, are combining to increase the pressure on businesses to decouple their activities as a way of responding to local needs and peculiarities. The experience of Otis Elevator in China provides a good example of these pressures. During its initial years of operation from its base in Tianjin, Otis management was encouraged by the size and growth of the Chinese market. As its business developed, however, it also became increasingly aware of this market's complexity and the diversity of regional needs and buying behaviour. Local competition in the elevator business was also being complicated by conflicts between the central government's planning and co-ordination organisation and the priorities of regional authorities. In several areas, local elevator companies were directed and controlled by regional governments. The company concluded it would need to establish a network of local capacity for sales, support services and installation. By 1988 it had established eight registered branches across China. Yet, as outlined in Fig. 4.3, Otis believed it still needed to expand its infrastructure substantially, including the possibility of establishing a new production base in China's 'mid-west', around Xi'an as well as additional sales, support and installation capabilities in a long list of cities.[7]

Today's frontier markets are generating pressures to decouple activities across a geographically widespread network that are often even greater than those being felt in developed markets. But the communications infrastructure and third party support to facilitate the efficient operation of such a structure is frequently lacking. Once a production, installation, sales or service unit has been cut free from the cosy home base of its parent, the support functions and supply linkages that it needs to survive must be re-created. This problem can be solved in any of three ways:

- by establishing links with the parent location;
- by establishing links with a remote third party;
- by becoming part of a local network of firms with common interests.

The first option amounts to an attempt to use technology to run a dispersed network of units as a single, tightly co-ordinated entity despite geographic distance. An example would be for the new site, specialised in say design or marketing, to maintain its personnel and accounting records by using a computer link to the parent system. On the global frontier, however, inadequate communications infrastructure often renders this approach impractical.

The second approach means abandoning internal economies of scale and scope and building a self-sufficient site, be it for production, sales, distribution or service. Fixed costs and a minimum efficient scale often make this uneconomic – a fact some frontier businesses only discover when the bottom line turns to red. By duplicating various functions in several locations, this approach also multiplies the demand for trained staff – a scarce resource that many companies find constrains expansion even with a single-site operation. As an Otis executive commented: 'If we were to start from scratch in these other areas, it could take us 20 years to build capacity to support our business there, especially a capacity for support services and installation'.[8]

The third option involves replacing internal scale with external economies: reducing costs by sharing support and supply with other firms in close proximity. To do this, the new, decoupled unit must develop close links to a geographic cluster of firms with common interests. Finding ways to access the technical capabilities of local suppliers and service firms, or tap into pools of local market intelligence in a cluster are examples of this approach to levering off others nearby in a way which substitutes for (and often improves upon) the range of in-house services that might be available at the company's main site.

Cluster leverage

In many firms there is a prejudice in favour of an attempt to drive costs down by expanding their own throughput rather than by using a supplier or service provider who reaps economies of scale by serving a number of users. One venture we interviewed, for example, makes its own packaging materials. It is never likely to have the scale to be efficient. The argument given is that no suitable, local supplies are available in this frontier market. The real reason is probably that the managers often feel internalisation gives them greater control and that since the benefits are more proprietary, they offer more potential for competitive advantage.

This sentiment in favour of self-sufficiency is especially strong on the global frontier where third party suppliers and service providers often lack the capability to deliver. But in the cash and resource constrained environment that so often characterises frontier markets, self-sufficiency is a luxury few businesses can afford over the long term. The fixed costs are too high. Peripheral activities add to the pressures on a stretched management team and risk distracting attention from the core. Equally important, with the exception of pure exporters, the fact that sales are usually in local currency means that few businesses can go on importing all of their equipment, materials, consumables and services from abroad and ever hope to make a profit. To be successful, frontier businesses need to continually find new ways to lever off their local environment.

A strategy for gaining cluster leverage comprises three basic elements:

1 choosing a location where customers, local workers, suppliers, ancillary industries and possibly even competitors, are all learning rapidly and improving their capabilities;
2 developing an organisational culture and structure which encourages the business to learn from these other local market participants and to look for ways to benefit from the new opportunities created as these local players become more sophisticated;
3 a conscious policy of developing the quality and proportion of local content by seeking out and working with local suppliers of raw materials, industrial consumables and ancillary services.

Growth theory has long recognised that it pays to be located within a virtuous cycle where increasing customer sophistication interacts with improving quality among suppliers to drive economic development forward. More recently, Michael Porter has focused attention on these virtuous dynamics operating at the level of local, geographic clusters.[9] Adapting these ideas to frontier markets, the process may be characterised in terms of the 'pearl oyster' shown in Fig. 4.4.

The long-term advantage of being part of a suitable cluster comes from the chance to participate in the joint learning taking place within it. Increasing demand expectations, active competition on innovation, and advancement of suppliers and providers of support services all act as a spur to improvement. Frequent product improvement and innovation helps educate customers and increase their expectations. The cycle then continues: in the course of meeting increased customer demands the pool of knowledge shared among workers, suppliers and support services expands, providing a base for further innovation.

In choosing a location or network of locations then, it pays to put a subsidiary in a situation where it will be forced to keep pace with the rising demands of the most sophisticated customers in a frontier market rather than a site which breeds complacency through serving the least demanding laggards in a developing market. It also makes sense to arrange a network of operations that is situated so as to enable it to replace expensive offshore supplies and ancillary services as the capabilities of local supply and ancillary support improves. Likewise, it pays to be located in that part of a frontier

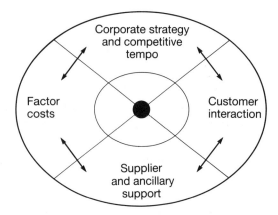

Figure 4.4   Sources of cluster leverage

market where factor costs are falling; either because new sources of land, labour or materials are opening up or because quality is improving due to a rapid upgrading of infrastructure, improvement in local training and educational institutions, or introduction of new technology into the extraction of raw materials. Finally, subject to the important caveat of avoiding competitors 'walled cities', it may be preferable to locate a subsidiary where the competitive tempo is high. This may seem paradoxical. But it is sometimes the case that being among tough competitors increases the performance of a business; with a visible benchmark and the energy of battle, staff strive for, and achieve more stretching targets. As we will see in Chapter 6, a failure to take the competition seriously until it's too late is one of the traps of operating on what seems like the open plains of a frontier market, especially for foreign firms.

DEVELOPING LOCAL CONTENT

Locating units or branches in the right kind of clusters of customers, suppliers and competitors, therefore, can provide powerful opportunities to lever off others for improved performance. However, any business that is no more than a passive bystander in a such a cluster is likely to gain little from this potentially fertile environment. Another important requirement, as we emphasised in Chapter 2, is an organisational structure that is able and eager to watch, learn and adapt as its local environment develops at a rapid pace.

For many businesses a major plank of that process of adaption is the ability to develop effective and efficient links with local suppliers and service providers. In short: successively increasing the local content in their overall activities.

The case of McDonald's in Moscow

When McDonald's opened its first restaurant in Moscow in January 1990 it covered any problems likely to arise as a result of relying on local support by a simple strategy: it imported everything that the operation could possibly need, from equipment to plastic cups. But as elsewhere in the world, it was the company's philosophy to supply its restaurants primarily from the economy in which it does business through a continuous and systematic programme to develop local content.

The strategy involved a two-pronged set of initiatives. The first of these was the construction of a processing plant at Solntsevo, some 40 miles south of Moscow, for the food supplies. This was the only time McDonald's had built – or felt that had to build – their own food processing facility to convert raw produce into a form ready for use by the restaurant. A large part of the company's total investment of $50 million is accounted for by this processing plant, which has the capacity to support an estimated 20 outlets. It took more than bricks, mortar and equipment to get this plant up an running including intensive, on-site training for local workers and management led by specialists ranging from English apple pie-makers and German meat processors to Swedish bread bun-bakers.

The second prong of the strategy centred on purchasing and supplier development. Purchasing staff worked in Russia for some two years before the restaurant opened its doors to serve 30,000 customers on its first day, settling at 50,000 per day by the end of the first year. They went out to farms and other potential suppliers and selected the most suitable candidates. Then began the process of training and investment to assure quality and a consistent flow of product. In the case of potatoes, McDonald's found that the tubers were being damaged during harvesting and transport. At first they imported specialised trucks to solve the problem. They have now found a Russian supplier of trucks that can help.

This kind of supplier development is continuous and ongoing. The company's area supervisor in Moscow described the process this way:

> 'At the beginning we had to import a lot of our paper products, and we still have to import one cup and one Big Mac box, but we have found Russian suppliers for sandwich wrap and Russian suppliers for the bags. It seems every month that our

purchasing agents have come up with something locally – we didn't have that at first. So as you do business more and develop more contacts, and find out who can supply you with what, you'll be able to increase the number of items. The trays are Russian trays; at first we had an imported tray – which happened to be too small and not sturdy enough – so we found a local tray, and that was the first stage. We now have another one that's even better, which we'll be introducing soon. Sundae spoons – we've found them locally now. That's just an ongoing progression of the company. All the time they're following different leads and finding different suppliers. We found a company that could make a paper bag for us that we could use as a takeout bag, but they didn't have the paper we needed, so our purchasing people found the paper and got it shipped to that supplier so they could make the bags. That's one thing that makes it a little more difficult, because a lot of times we're finding suppliers to help other suppliers.'[10]

The advantages for the Russian economy are obvious. But the driving force is not simple generosity. McDonald's sells it product in roubles. To make a profit it needs to have a high proportion of its expenses in roubles as well. This type of currency balance is an important factor behind the drive for local content across many of today's frontier markets. In order to capture this benefit, however, the investment of time, expertise and money in developing local supply is not to be underestimated.

The thrust to extend local content

Sagas of the trials of securing appropriate sources of supply on the global frontier are legion. Appropriate equipment for producing even relatively simple components is often lacking. When the local subsidiary of Japan Koei Machinery Company, which makes machine components for sale to other equipment manufacturers in Shenzhen, sought to locally source a plastic box in which to pack their product they found only one plant in the region with suitable equipment. After analysing the blueprint, this supplier confirmed they could handle the job and agreed to forward a sample. Several months later no response had been forthcoming. When the sample and the quotation was finally received, the price was higher than the going rate in Japan, largely due to the cost of overmanning on the production line. In other cases, suppliers have the equipment, but lack access to the necessary quality of raw materials. China Otsuka Pharmaceutical, for example, found that although the locally sourced bottles they tested had been moulded to the appropriate tolerances, they had been made of material which proved unstable. In Poland, Orient Atlantic's plans to export canned mushrooms were set back when it was found the cans themselves used soldered seams which are subject to concerns about lead contamination in the western market-place.

Shortages and delivery delays are also a frequent problem in many sectors. Some try to overcome these problems by maintaining a diversity of suppliers. As a manager at the Marriott hotel in Warsaw put it: 'Local sourcing is a test of adaptability', adding 'If you can't buy something from source A you've got to find source B and probably sources C and D and E, because you are going to need them at some stage as well.' Others rely on close, personal relationships developed with a single supplier to make sure they are at the head of any rationing queue – a particularly important consideration in China where few mechanisms exist for enforcing supply agreements and little hope of obtaining any redress for failure of suppliers to perform.

Some companies, particularly Japanese investors have taken close supplier relationships a stage further by involving key suppliers as equity partners in a joint venture. Of the four Chinese partners in the Tianjin Wanle Wool Garment Company with Ishii of Japan, for example, three of these are Tianjin-based organisations. The other equity partner, the Huzhou Worsted Mill, is located almost one thousand miles away in Zhejiang province. The reason is straightforward: Huzhou is a wool producing region and the mill controls a substantial local wool supply.

Other frontier investors, like Beijing Matsushita Colour CRT Company, have cemented their local supply links through technical assistance, investment and persistence – gradually expanding the proportion of local content over a period of five or ten years.

ALTERNATIVE SUPPLY STRATEGIES

There are, of course, alternatives to embarking on this arduous process of developing local content. The essential choices revolve around two sets of decisions: 'make versus buy' and 'import versus locally source' as illustrated in Fig. 4.5.

McDonald's in Moscow represents a hybrid case between identification and development of local suppliers (the bottom right hand quadrant of Fig. 4.5) and the strategy of local investment in in-house production (the top right quadrant). The Toyo Suisan Hainan Company has adopted the latter approach to supply its seafood processing business: it leases 700 acres from local communities on a three year rolling contract which it has turned into high-technology prawn farms. Others, such as wool garment producer

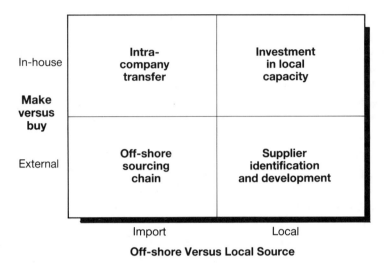

Figure 4.5   Alternative supply strategies

Shanghai Yin Feng, rely entirely on imported materials. This strategy is most common among ventures which export 50 per cent or more of their output forming what is known in China as a 'two ends outside' operation. Alternatively, exporters such as the Sanyo Electronics operation in China which assembles electronic control modules, draws its supplies primarily from sister companies, in their case both onshore and offshore.

A heavy reliance on imported supplies into frontier markets, however, is apt to face continued inefficiencies in the customs clearance formalities and paperwork that increases the length of the total pipeline and extends total lead times. Heavy investment in bringing activities in-house, meanwhile, is likely to put a downward pressure on returns and involve a business in a range of activities where it may lack expertise or home-country experience. Moreover, as a number of our case examples have illustrated, suitable local sources increasingly emerge as frontier markets develop and an investor's own local knowledge improves with experience. In the longrun, successful development of local suppliers is likely to play an important role in gaining locational advantage from an expansion into the global frontier. But it is a time-consuming process; this is precisely the reason it needs to commence at an early stage.

Just as in any market, the location decision on the global frontier presents two basic problems: no single location is ever ideal and once a firm puts down roots, 'lock-in' often makes it difficult to move. But in frontier markets, these difficulties are often more extreme. First, because a heritage of politically-driven, central planning has often distorted the distribution of existing capacity, potential suppliers, well-honed skills and even customer demand. Second, because the global frontier often lacks the efficient markets, transport and communications infrastructure that are necessary for supplies to move smoothly from place to place, and the disadvantages of a poor location are harder to overcome.

These peculiarities mean that choosing a single, compromise location on the global frontier can significantly handicap a business. So successful frontier strategy often means that activities within the organisation need to be decoupled: allowing manufacturing to migrate to a location that suits it, while the centre of sales and service is elsewhere, and logistics is run out of a major transport node.

The right network of locations, then, is especially important in order to compete in frontier markets. But strategies for locational leverage go far beyond identifying a favourable place to set up: they are also about *creating* new sources advantage within each location you choose. That means working closely with local customers to test new product ideas, building a network of support among local government officials and institutions, and developing cost-competitive local sources by searching out, and often investing time (and sometimes money) in promising local suppliers. *Frontier markets are not without potential for locational leverage, but compared with the more developed regions, advantages more often have to be built from the raw material available, rather than coming in a ready-made form.*

References

1 See Krugman, P., *Geography and Trade*, The MIT Press, Cambridge, Massachusetts, 1991.
2 See M.E. Porter, *The Competitive Advantage of Nations*, Macmillan, London, 1990.
3 Harvard Business School, Otis Elevator Company (A): China Joint Venture, Case No. 9-391-062, Publishing Division, Harvard Business School, Boston, Massachusetts.
4 Marco Polo, *The Travels*, Penguin, London, 1958.
5 Tambrands, Inc: The Femtech Soviet Joint Venture (A), Harvard Business School, Case No. 9-390-159, Boston, Massachusetts.
6 Moscow-McDonald's, 'Fast food at a cracking pace', *East Europe Business Focus*, Issue 5, November 1990.
7 Otis Elevator Company (B-1): China Joint Venture, Harvard Business School, Case No. 9-393-006, Publishing Division, Harvard Business School, Boston,

Massachusetts, 02163, USA.

8 Otis Elevator Company (B–1): China Joint Venture, Harvard Business School, Case No. 9-393-006, Publishing Division, Harvard Business School, Boston, Massachusetts, 02163, USA.

9 Michael E. Porter, *The Competitive Advantage of Nations*, Macmillian, London, 1990.

10 Interview with Glen Steeves, Area Supervisor, McDonald's Moscow, November 1990, originally published in *East Europe Business Focus*, Issue 5.

5

WINNING WITH FIRST MOVER BRANDS AND INNOVATIVE CHANNEL STRATEGIES

The idea of a marketing blitz aimed at frontier regions plagued with chronic shortages might sound like a nonsense. Faced with frontier markets starved of product, the logic of 'sell first, market later' often beguiles new entrants. Why waste money on marketing and advertising, they reason, when buyers will 'bite your hand off' for quality goods? Why 'over-specify' the product – something just a little better than the local offering will surely do? At best, this kind of thinking leads to lost opportunities. At worst, it is an express lane to disaster. In practice, frontier markets often develop a taste for 'up-market' quality in both consumer and industrial products with surprising speed. Those who have entered with a cheap and nasty offering can find it very difficult to shake off their 'down-market' image. Their early neglect of marketing and distribution can continue to plague them for decades.

Many of the most successful firms on the global frontier have claimed the high ground with top quality products early on. They invested heavily in marketing and advertising from the start, because they understood that they would never again get a clear run in an uncluttered marketing environment to establish their brand in customers' minds as number one. Some flooded emerging markets with heavy promotion even when they had little or no product available to sell – simply to secure a first mover advantage in establishing their brand. Likewise, early execution of strategies to pre-empt key distribution channels and strengthen the existing structure through direct contact with customers can pay dividends later on. In this chapter we examine the nature of these first mover advantages in marketing and distribution and how they can be won.

The paradox of up-market consumerism on the global frontier

'Young Mr. Yang had no qualms about spending $50 on a pair of imported jeans, a month's salary for the average Chinese worker. Shopping this week at Beijing's smart, new Yoahan department store with its Gucci corner was, he declared, chic. Mr. Yang, who described himself as an entrepreneur – a new class of cash-rich Chinese – was doing what millions of well-heeled young consumers do the world over.'[1]

That was how the *Financial Times* described the 'consuming passion of Chinese shoppers' in 1993. Meanwhile on Sundays in Moscow, a queue of 1,500 people wait for two hours to pay the equivalent of £2.00 for a single scoop of Baskin-Robbins ice-cream or £4.50 for a large one. IKEA is selling furniture in Hungary at prices equivalent to those in Western Europe.

There are a number of reasons why, time and time again, up-market consumerism comes to frontier markets much faster than most of us might expect. First, income statistics often give a misleading impression of the real spending power of consumers. Items like housing, health and transport that absorb a significant part of consumers' real incomes in most countries are heavily subsidised or even provided free in many of the emerging markets on today's global frontier. World Bank statistics show that in China, for example, only 5 per cent of household income is absorbed by housing, health, education and transport combined. In neighbouring Hong Kong more than 30 per cent of disposable income has to be allocated to these basic needs. This figure is almost 40 per cent in Korea. Since Chinese consumers spend so little on these 'public service' items, they have 95 per cent of their **disposable income** to allocate to goods like clothing, tobacco, and consumer durables.

The second reason behind the paradox of up-market consumerism is the high rate of saving on the global frontier. The Chinese save almost 38 per cent of their disposable income. Savings rates are also high throughout much of Eastern Europe. Because of these high **savings rates** consumers are able to purchase goods which might look unaffordable when measured against monthly incomes. High savings rates mean it is possible to buy goods like Mr Yang's imported jeans at prices equal to a worker's monthly salary. More dramatically, accumulated savings have underpinned buoyant markets in consumer goods, like the television sets discussed below, which cost 20 months salary when introduced. This also reflects the fact that two of the biggest outlets for consumer savings in developed markets: houses and automobiles, are generally not freely tradeable on the global frontier. Most valuable real estate is owned by the state, while the supply of imported vehicles is often restricted by currency regulations.

A third, related reason, is the role of **status symbols**. Seeing a product in short supply on the global frontier, one might be tempted to pursue a strategy of maximising sales volume. But shortages can transform otherwise mundane goods into status symbols. The more the product is in shortage, therefore, the more buyers clamber to secure the most up-market version available. If the product is a status symbol, then one wants the brand that others will immediately recognise as the best. Rather than initial adopters wanting low-end products, up-market consumerism appears early in the cycle. Smart companies establish their brand as a coveted jewel first and then broaden out to lower-end versions as the status value of scarcity disappears.

Finally, there is the **black economy** of the global frontier. Rapid growth, shortages, and a dearth of effective regulation offer enormous opportunities for fleet-footed entrepreneurs to move from rags to riches. They are helped along by the lack of frictional drag from taxes. They do not have to be millionaires. A small-time trader whose income reaches four or five times that of the average worker has very considerable purchasing power for consumer goods. Even if this group only represents 5 per cent of the population, they comprise a sub-market numbering tens of millions in regions like China, India or Eastern Europe.

Taking the high ground

Exploiting the paradox of up-market consumerism is one reason for capturing the high ground of a new market early on. But there are also other, long-term advantages to be gained by establishing an immediate reputation for premium quality and becoming a brand which both consumer and industrial buyers aspire to, even if this means initially restricting the target market. One of these best illustrations of the potential advantages of an initial focus on the high ground is to be found in the evolution of the huge Chinese market for television sets.

In the early 1980s Philips of Eindhoven, with the support of the Chinese government, sent a team of experts to investigate the potential market for colour TV sets in China. After visiting several major cities and provinces, this group reached the conclusion that the product would long remain out of reach of the mass market consumer. At the time, the cost of even a modest colour TV set was equivalent to more than one year's total earnings for an average Chinese worker. As a result, they forwent an opportunity to establish Philips as the brand to aspire to and were unable to take advantage of the up-market consumerism which was to subsequently emerge.

Sanyo of Japan took a different view. They reasoned that even if income was low, expenditure was also low. There were few outlets for consumer spending and many Chinese had a tradition of thrift. There was also a deep-seated tradition of family-based leisure life and a shortage of suitable leisure activities. Sanyo's local managers reported that people would postpone their marriage until they could afford to equip a new home with a colour TV set and that people would travel across China to the southern provinces to buy sets smuggled in from Taiwan or Hong Kong.

Sanyo had been a pioneer in China, entering with a representative office, followed by a number of small ventures in the early 1970's. In the late 1970's Sanyo's audio division had established a subsidiary to market and later to assemble radios and simple tape recorders in China. In the early 1980s Sanyo established a colour TV assembly line in China, exporting used equipment from Japan into a wholly-owned subsidiary in China. It was based entirely on kits supplied from Japan. After 1985 when Sanyo established Sanyo Semiconductor Shekou Co. Ltd, a limited proportion of parts, specifically transistors, were supplied from this sister plant located next door. The vast bulk of components, however, continued to come from Japan. Demand for the finished TV sets was strong and the company saw little need for heavy expenditure on advertising and brand promotion.

Between 1984 and 1986 the Chinese market for colour TV sets entered a period of explosive growth. Finished sets imported from Japan flooded in. Towards the end of this period as competition intensified and the government restricted imports, alarmed at the drain on foreign exchange, more and more local plants for assembling colour TV sets were established. By 1990 there were over 100 colour TV assembly plants in China. Sanyo continues to sell significant volumes, but its brand lacks strength. As competition has intensified, Sanyo have increasingly been forced to compete on price with other importers, and more particularly, with improved locally-produced sets.

One brand which many Chinese consumers distinguish as superior in this increasingly crowded market is Hitachi. Price realisation and sales reflect this esteem. This advantage comes *not* from the cache of a fully imported product – their sets are produced locally (although largely from imported components) by Fujian Hitachi Television Company – but the quality of their brand. When Hitachi entered the market in the early 1980s it did not need to spend heavily on marketing and advertising to sell its product in the short term. None the less, Hitachi believed it should invest in marketing to position its product at the top of the market from the beginning. It saw a unique, never-to-be-repeated opportunity to establish its brand by heavy advertising and promotion at a time when it could obtain a very high 'share of voice' in a market starved of appealing, professionally presented marketing messages. As competition has intensified this foresight has paid off.

The high-end strategy also seems to be serving Baskin-Robbins well in Moscow. Existing local suppliers make what Baskin-Robbins admit is a good ice-cream. But the Baskin-Robbins product sells at something in the region of three times the price of state-produced ice-cream. What Baskin-Robbins have added is variety (state brands are available only in vanilla and chocolate), branding and the right kind of retail presentation. They see their venture as a strategic investment – a unique chance to establish a brand and a presence. Money is also going into market research. They don't expect to earn immediate returns. At minimum, however, early high-end sales are paying for the cost of this brand-building investment. They offer a potential first mover advantage that it will cost latecomers much more to match as the market matures and communication channels are crowded with competing messages.

But success is obviously more than just a matter of throwing expensive, branded products at an emerging market. The right positioning requires careful tradeoffs between value, price and costs. These, in turn, have important implications for the right choice of manufacturing technology. In choosing the right balance the concept of the 'value line', described below, provides a proven tool.

UNDERSTANDING THE VALUE LINE

Viewing the global frontier as the natural home for obsolete products and technologies has all the dangers of myopia. Just as in the case of television sets above, competition in frontier markets often develops quickly. Entry decisions therefore need to look beyond initial scarcity towards sustainable, longer term positions. The choice of a quality level at which to compete is an important element of strategy for the global frontier. Two basic relationships dominate this decision: how the sustainable price premium varies with quality, and how costs differ between quality levels.

The 'Value Line' is the theoretical relationship between price and quality which appears to exist in the market. In Fig. 5.1, Brand U represents the unbranded, local product – in this case paper towels. On the global frontier this is often the product of a state company or a small local manufacturer.

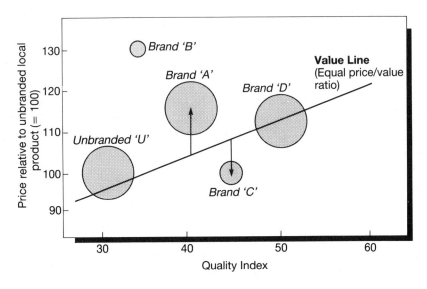

Figure 5.1   Using the value line to position your prouct
Note: Circle size is proportional to market share

Brands A, B, C and D represent four branded goods in the market.

Both the Brand D and the standard product U have roughly the same market shares (indicated by their equivalent circle size). Yet Brand D achieves its high market share despite its high price. The implication: customers feel the price premium for Brand D is justified by its higher quality. It is properly positioned in the market. Brand B on the other hand, is pitched at a price far above that consistent with its quality. As a result it has a very small market share, comprising those buyers who are fooled about its real quality. As those buyers gain more information, we might expect Brand B to lose even more share. On the global frontier, highly priced, fully-imported products are often caught in the Brand B trap. Rather than being priced so as to win a substantial segment of the higher end of the market, like Brand D, they are simply priced out of reach. Even when pursuing a strategy of 'taking the high ground', pricing must take into account the floor set by the standard local offering.

Working from that pricing floor, companies entering frontier markets need to answer three questions:

1   What is the objective difference in quality between the product I can offer and the standard, low-end product in the market?

2 What kind of price premium will buyers be willing to pay for this objectively high quality (the slope of the value line)?

3 How much extra price realisation can I get, over and above the basic price premium consumers will pay for objectively high quality, by investing in marketing and promotion?

The first step, then, in understanding the value line, is an objective assessment of quality differentials. For some products this is a job for the testing laboratory. In others, where after sales service plays a big role, for example, more subjective elements will also need to be considered. In essence, this task is no different from that required in developed markets. But all too often it's dismissed as unnecessary in frontier markets. In fact this first step is just as important as elsewhere.

A further potential pitfall also awaits the careless or ill-prepared: don't assume the definition of 'quality' in a frontier market is necessarily identical to the developed market norm. In developing markets, products are often pressed into a broader range of applications than elsewhere. Few manufacturers of rotary hoes and motorised tillers, for example, designed their products for towing trailer loads of crops, but in many developing markets their performance in this role is an important aspect of their quality. The grades of consumables and ancillary products available may also mean quality of durables needs to be redefined: the ability of a washing machine that can perform well with hard water and primitive detergents, for example, may be the acid test of quality, while an ultra-quiet purr is likely to be less important than elsewhere. (Indeed, silence may be interpreted as a lack of power!)

Setting the price

Answering our second question is often more an art than a science. Plotting the prices, quality levels and market shares of existing brands in the market, as in Fig. 5.1, can provide vital clues. Market research can also have an important role to play. Established infrastructure for market research is, of course, often lacking in developing markets. At the same time, the very fact that these markets are often emerging rather than mature makes it all the more necessary to collect data on consumer behaviour. Questionnaires may meet with a certain amount of initial bemusement or concerns about the long arm of authority. Ingenuity is required. As discussed below, for example, **demonstration stalls** can provide both a means of educating potential customers about new products and of collecting market research data to help determine the slope of the value line.

The third step in applying the value line methodology is to assess the potential for improving price realisation and market share through investment in brand marketing and promotion. As we have already mentioned, brand promotion can be especially effective in the early stages of the life cycle of a frontier market – building aspirations and providing the first movers with the chance to communicate with customers before promotional channels become overloaded with conflicting messages.

The aim is to secure a position like that of Brand A which commands a moderate price premium above that warranted by its quality without surrendering share. This reflects the successful use of advertising to establish an image among buyers which makes it more popular than its price or objective quality would lead us to expect.

The alternative strategy is illustrated by Brand C. It is actually underpriced compared with its true quality, presumably with the aim of rapidly growing the brand from its present small market share. This may be successful in establishing the base volume to support a local operation and become recognised in the market. But it also risks surrendering the high ground to competitors. If local consumers aspire to trade up as their wealth increases it may be left behind. The final decision obviously must be made on a case-by-case basis. What the value line framework offers is a way of laying out the different competitive options for quality positioning, pricing, and market share.

This kind of value line analysis is vital in frontier markets because, far from being well established, the rules of the competitive game are still being set. Yet an initial positioning, once it takes root, is difficult to throw off. A product's history has a habit of coming back to haunt it. One thing is for certain: you only get one chance to enter the frontier market afresh. Getting the positioning right from from the outset can help a brand for decades. Getting it wrong can leave managers struggling with the difficult task of repositioning a product and bogged down in a campaign aimed at trying to change all-important, first impressions in consumers minds.

Setting quality targets

The value line methodology can also aid in the choice of which technology to deploy. Figure 5.2 reproduces the same value line relationship between price and quality illustrated in Fig. 5.1. The costs of two different manufacturing technologies X and Y have then been plotted as an aid to deciding where to compete given the cost structure of existing technology.

The unit production cost using technology X rises quickly as quality

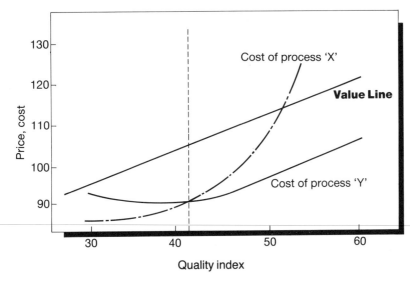

Figure 5.2   Using the value line to select the right technology

increases. This process is efficient for low quality, but causes a high cost for top quality where it produces a significant proportion of rejects. Technology Y on the other hand is unnecessarily sophisticated for the production of low quality grades. At the bottom end of the market it isn't cost competitive with technology X. But process Y can handle the production of higher quality with ease. Its reject rates remain low and its efficiency remains high even when required to produce quality of the highest grade.

The value line illustrated in Fig. 5.2, has two important implications for technology choice. First, it is clear that for a firm which intends to stay at the low end of the market, technology X will be the most efficient. For a firm which is aiming to take the high ground, technology Y will be a more cost efficient choice.

Second, by following through the logic of the value line, the possible costs and benefits of choosing a more *flexible technology* become clear. Technology X is more efficient for low grade production, but if required to produce above a quality index of 48 in our example, it becomes loss making. Conversely, while technology Y is less cost competitive at low grades, it offers much greater flexibility to profitably move up-market to higher quality levels if required. Profits can be maintained using technology Y even if the quality required exceeds an index of 60 relative to the existing, unbranded standard of 32.

The flexibility of technology to efficiently produce a range of different quality levels is a particular asset on the global frontier. With rapid rates of economic growth and an increasingly free flow of information, the quality standards required to serve the global frontier can rapidly catch up with those in developed markets. Manufacturers with inflexible technologies can easily find themselves stranded – unable to adjust cost effectively to rising quality norms.

We return to these technology issues in Chapter 6. In what follows, we take a closer look at the marketing, advertising and distribution side of the value line equation.

HARNESSING THE POWER OF ADVERTISING

On a March day in 1991 a marketing manger at Rank Xerox is involved in a scramble for press advertising space with his major Japanese rivals. A mailshot campaign to potential clients is under way. Rank Xerox has also taken slots on television to promote its wares.

The scene could be an office in New York or Paris. In fact, it's happening at Kiev in the Ukraine. Rank Xerox believe that an aggressive marketing campaign is an important ingredient for success on the global frontier. Establishing a firm base of brand awareness and becoming customers' preferred supplier are key elements of their strategy.[2]

Rank Xerox are not alone in using advertising early on in a campaign to access frontier markets. Advertising expenditure in the Czech Republic, Hungary and Poland has been growing by 26 per cent per year in the early 1990s. Across the globe in China, roadside billboards originally set up to display quotations of Chairman Mao and revolutionary slogans were being replaced with advertisements as early as 1979. Electronics companies like Matsushita Electric, Toshiba and Hitachi pioneered this roadside advertising. Today Japanese firms account for some 60 per cent of the total foreign advertising spend in China. Newspapers are their number one medium for this advertising followed by television, magazines and radio.

At first advertising on the global frontier has tended to meet some resistance. A new breed of managers in Eastern Europe found that conservative finance directors put a red line through the advertising budget on the basis that it was unproductive and unnecessary spending. Research in the area of household electronics found that consumers in Hungary were initially irritated by flashy Western-style advertisements appearing at a time that high inflation and a rapidly devaluing currency seemed to be taking these goods further and further out of reach. In China the new billboards were the focus of protest groups claiming that national interest was being betrayed; that advertising luxury goods that the people could not yet afford would lead to social unrest and rising crime.

Today, however, advertising has become part of the business culture of progressive firms in both China and Eastern Europe. Publications like *Advertising Age* and *Media International* are appearing on local managers' desks. Agencies like McCann-Erikson have opened up. Both local companies and multinationals are buyers. In Hungary, for example, one of the largest advertisers is now Hungaria Insurance. Advertisements for the products of joint venture companies like Pharmavit (which markets vitamin tablets) sit alongside those promoting Coca Cola and Nestlé products. In China the government is itself heavily involved in selling advertising services to foreign companies. Although still 'co-ordinated' by the China National Advertising Association, a part of the Ministry of Foreign Economic Relations and Trade, there are now numerous advertising agencies throughout the country. State organisations like the Beijing Advertising Corporation, the Shanghai Advertising Corporation or Gaungdong Advertising Corporation still control media buying for a 10–15 per cent commission. They compete for business. Beijing Advertising Corporation has staff trained in the USA, Australia, Hong Kong or Japan. With the rapid growth in advertising business, there are also many private companies who create advertisements and book the space through this network. Largest is the Japanese communications giant Dentsu, which has offices in Beijing, Shanghai and Guangzhou. Likewise, major US firms are represented.

Product or corporate image advertising?

The fact that when we interviewed a group of preschool children in China they were able to recall the names of more than a dozen major Japanese corporations is an interesting indicator of future potential and long-term strategic position. It is no accident.

Prior to 1985, along with most other organisations in China, companies like Matsushita, Hitachi and Toshiba were advertising particular products. The aim was to stimulate sales of imports of specific goods. Economic growth and deregulation combined with marketing led to a flood of consumer goods imports, like television sets and video cassette recorders into the country during 1985–6. National foreign exchange reserves drained away at an alarming rate. In response the authorities imposed tight import controls, reducing this flood to a relative trickle, even after allowing for the operations of smugglers. Similar problems have arisen in other frontier markets. Regulations in Hungary, for example, now require that before any product can be advertised, it must be available in sufficient quantities in the market. Television or radio advertising of alcohol, tobacco and pharmaceutical products is prohibited.

Companies have responded to these constraints in different ways. Some have simply canned their advertisements until an adequate supply chain can be sorted out. Others have sought out loopholes. To circumvent the Hungarian regulations, for example, advertising for alcohol, tobacco and pharmaceuticals utilises Radio Bridge (a channel of Voice of America) and the German/Hungarian speaking radio, Danubius, where advertisements for these products are permitted as long as they are in German or English.

The response of leading Japanese companies in China is perhaps the most interesting. When import restriction sharply reduced the flow of their imported goods after 1986, their advertising spend continued to grow. But it's objective changed. The advertisements were now directed at building corporate image, rather than the direct promotion of products. The emphasis shifted to developing the association between a corporate brand and strength, quality and leading-edge technology.

Only time can prove the worth of this strategy. Its attraction lies in the opportunity to lay down a base of consumer acceptance in a developing market at a time when competition for 'share of voice' is lower; at a time before consumers begin to be bombarded with a plethora of advertising messages; at a time when media rates are relatively cheap. It reduces the risk of creating resentment by advertising specific products when these are either unavailable in sufficient quantities or beyond the reach of most viewers or listeners.

The hope is obviously when the products of the corporation do arrive, they will fall on already well-tilled market ground; that they will benefit directly from a positive, quality, high technology image. And that they will be seen as coming from a reliable company, one which has 'stayed the course' and stood the test of time. This is particularly important on the global frontier where consumers suffer from fly-by-night operators and are sceptical of foreign companies entering with a fanfare, only to pull out when short-term profits fail to appear. Spending on corporate image in frontier markets has the obvious risk of little or no ultimate return. If our pre-schoolers are any indication, however, the long-term pay-offs might be large.

First mover advantages in uncrowded communications channels

Becoming a first mover in advertising in a developing market offers three potentially significant advantages:

- the advertising rates are generally low when the media industry is young;
- there is less competition for an individual's attention while the total volume of marketing messages aimed at consumers is low;
- less of any advertising message is 'cancelled out' by competitors' advertising.

In the early 1990s, China must be one of the few places in the world where $5,000 will buy you a 30-second slot broadcast on nationwide television. The *People's Daily*, the largest circulation newspaper in the country, costs around $150 per column centimetre (eight columns per page). Of course service is not always smooth. Advertisements are often cancelled or postponed with very little or no prior notice. Important national news always has priority; at times your promotion is simply 'bumped'. Given restrictions on the amount of air time or page space that can be devoted to advertising, the media seldom market their own services. The customer for advertising space is hardly 'king'. A fortunate prizewinner who must pay a commission for his or her allocation on time or space would be a more apt description. Payment is often required in advance. Television and radio stations generally don't collect information on the size and socio-demographics of their audiences. Print media know their circulation figures, but not the profile or their readers. For all these problems, a relatively modest budget by world standards still buys a great deal of air time or column-centimetres.

Advertisements in developing markets, meanwhile, are likely to grab the attention of a higher percentage of the audience than elsewhere. As one interviewee put it: 'Much of Chinese television is boring, many leisure publications are dull. When we see creative designs, strong colour and modern styles in advertisements, we take notice. The advertisements are interesting and impressive.' Some of the most effective advertisements are those which play a role in brightening up daily life. To do so, however they need to be more than 'catchy'; they need to be tailored to culture and aspirations to which people can readily relate.

Adopting a first mover strategy for advertising on the global frontier reduces the cost of building a brand because less of any message is cancelled out by similar advertising by competitors – the fate of a great deal of advertising in the West. As advertising grows rapidly in developing markets, the time window to exploit this benefit is closing. Increasingly this is leading companies to begin their advertising campaign to build awareness ahead of potential competitors even before either supplier has mass volumes of products to sell.

Mars Inc: an example of first mover advantage in Russia

The experience of chocolate maker, Mars Inc. in Russia shows just how successful first mover advertising can be. When it entered the market in late 1991, Mars began with an advertising blitz even before its chocolate appeared in the stores. Full-colour billboards were designed to make Russians curious about 'the chocolate that melts in your mouth, not in your hands' – a reference to the dubious quality of much of the local product. Others read 'Delo ili Igra, Sneekerz' ('Work or play its a Snickers'). A barrage of distinctly Western television commercials showed a 'hip' young man biting into a Snickers bar – to the Rolling Stones song *Satisfaction*, of course. This was followed up by further exposure through the company's sponsorship of the 1992 Summer Olympics. Moscow wholesalers estimate that Mars spent around $100,000 on advertising during the first three months. As a result, *Sneekerz* is now a Russian word. And the strategy certainly seems to be paying off. One of Mars distributors in Moscow was claiming sales of $5 million a month by mid-1993. They estimate that Mars' total sales in Russia had reached a rate of between $10 and $20 million a month eighteen months after its products were launched there. As one commentator put it: 'They virtually own the chocolate market here'. A manager for competitors Cadbury International adds: 'I'm full of admiration for what Mars have done in Russia.'[3]

Choosing the right media mix

A peculiarity of television in Eastern Europe is that advertisements for specialised, heavy machinery sometimes appear along with those for consumer goods. Three reasons are given to explain this phenomenon. First, the fact that rates for television commercials are often relatively cheap – in many cases there is little premium over rates of advertising in the press. Second, few technical or professional publications carry advertising. Third, there is little point in choosing a focused medium since there is a lack of research as to who the audience actually is anyway. The first is false economy. The latter two are simply fallacy. Choosing the right mix of media is just as important on the global frontier as it is elsewhere, and it is far from impossible.

The unlikely case of marketing pesticides in rural China illustrates the point well. The per minute cost differential between local television and radio in the rural market is small. But only 10 per cent of rural households own television sets. Some 98 per cent, on the other hand, listen to news and weather forecasts on the radio. And broadcasts of local radio operas are popular. Meanwhile, broadcasts from agricultural schools also have a wide audience. An intensive campaign of radio advertisements in the slots between these programmes was therefore launched by leading Japanese pesticide manufacturers. Special lunar calendars prized by rural residents and replete with high quality photographs (a rarity in a market where local printing quality is generally poor) were also widely distributed. These campaigns were complemented with entries in agricultural journals which detailed the appropriate use and application of the different specialist products.

The results were dramatic. Certain brands of Japanese pesticides have a level of unaided recall among farmers and agricultural technicians in the target rural regions higher than anywhere else in the world. A groundswell of popular pressure to obtain these products led the Ministry of Agriculture to respond with the necessary allocations of scarce foreign currency to purchase supplies of these products from Japan. Import of pesticides by Chinese farmers is now a well established and significant part of Sino-Japanese trade.

In most markets there exists a range of media appropriate for different kinds of products and target consumers. The trap of using television simply because it appears to be inexpensive must be avoided. The appropriate mix of media also changes as frontier markets develop. Historically in markets like Poland, for example, the split of marketing spend was 65 per cent to fairs and exhibitions, 15 per cent in the press, 15 per cent in outdoor advertising, 2.5 per cent television and radio, and 2.5 per cent direct mail. Press, specialist magazine advertising and direct mail have been a rapidly growing part of the media, taking significant share from fairs and exhibitions as alternatives open up for communicating directly with the customer at their place of business or home and the domestic marketing infrastructure improves.

These shifts in media mix also partly reflect the growing stock of research about the impact of different media and the profiles of their audiences. Seeing the potential of advertising revenue, publications throughout the global frontier are doing more to research their readership. All of the large Chinese advertising agencies, meanwhile, now have research departments capable of tracking brand recognition and estimating sales impact across most of the major provinces. Advertisers are no longer consigned to scattergun marketing on the global frontier.

NAVIGATING THROUGH LABYRINTHINE DISTRIBUTION CHANNELS

While the importance of early corporate image building and brand development in frontier markets is often underestimated, they are obviously only part of the marketing jigsaw. Performance of the distribution channel is equally critical, not only for sales volume, but also for product image and market reputation.

Whether emerging from a central planning or developing from a subsistence economy, frontier markets inevitably share at least one characteristic: labyrinthine, multi-level distribution systems. Contrary to some popular perceptions in the West, distribution channels do exist. The geographic spread of these networks is often impressive and they are capable of handling large volumes of goods. But there are three, fundamental problems with existing channels.

1 Their capability to act as a conduit for passing marketing and technical information from manufacturer to customer is generally very weak. This problem is aggravated by the multiple stages in the chain.
2 Channel performance has often been measured by volume instead of speed and responsiveness. In planned economies the manufacturer's responsibilities generally ended at the factory gate. Producers worried little about the marketing and sales of their products, hence there was no real pressure from manufacturers for improvements in channel efficiency.
3 Existing channels often have poorly developed capabilities in the provision of spare parts, maintenance and after sales service, especially for relatively sophisticated products.

The role of distribution in the kinds of planned economies from which much of today's global frontier are emerging was quite different from what we are used to. It emphasised physical throughput; scale rather than responsiveness and information. And it remained remote from both customers and manufacturers; the interfaces were simple and the interactions few. Lorries or rail waggons simply came, were loaded and unloaded, and disappeared again into a fog. Outward appearances may be changing, but the mentality lives on.

The experience of Sony in Poland

These problems, and the challenges they present, are well illustrated by a company like Sony in the Polish market. Sony enjoys an outstanding brand image in Poland: in 1992 it was rated number one in its product category by local consumers. The market for its product was also buoyant, reflecting consumers' high levels of Zloty savings and a large amount of US$ circulating in the country, much of it from remittances of Poles overseas. At the same time competition had begun to intensify. Arch rival, Matsushita Electric, for example, had begun to promote its Panasonic brand strongly with a massive poster campaign on buses and trams.[4]

To maintain its competitive position, Sony believes it is essential to preserve its strong market share in Poland and, most importantly, to continue to justify its reputation as the top brand by assuring consistent product availability and sales support, along with reliable after sales service. Historically, its products were distributed through an Austrian company, Mitte, who on-sold to Photex, one of Poland's 86 state-owned foreign trade organisations (FTOs). Photex had 1,010 retail outlets in Poland. Customers seeking after sales service, however, had to go to Photex's one service centre in Warsaw. Alternatively, they could deposit items in need of repair at one of eight designated outlets in Poland. Once per week these items would be transferred to the Warsaw service centre. For many consumers, therefore, getting service was inconvenient and turn-around times were slow. For customers who hadn't purchased the product from Photex, no service was provided, leaving them to the uncertainties of the unauthorised service sector. All spare parts and technician training, meanwhile, was provided through Mitte in Vienna, adding to delays.

As the Polish market developed, it was increasingly clear that this historical sales, distribution and service system, might not be up to the task. Photex, which had been a specialist, up-market retailer, was adding thousands of new product lines including toys, clothes, pharmaceuticals and foodstuffs. It was not investing significantly in its after sales service network. At the same time, while local service personnel were competent in working with products like stereos, they were judged to be less well qualified in repairing the new, more sophisticated products like compact disc players and camcorders based on digital and optical technologies.

Photex were also unwilling to reduce prices to speed up market penetration, wishing to protect their margins. The multi-stage distribution chain, meanwhile, locked Sony into high distribution costs. Partly as a result, a grey market was developing in Sony equipment, smuggled in from Germany or shipped from Singapore by entrepreneurs. Unauthorised service workshops, with no training from Sony, nor general access to Sony parts, were also mushrooming.

These kinds of issues are far from unique to Sony. In fact, they are typical of the kind of distribution and service problems which often threaten to undermine companies brand reputations and sales effectiveness in rapidly changing, frontier markets. They underline the critical need for an effective and evolving channel strategy in developing markets.

Alternative channel strategies

There are three basic approaches to the problems of extending sales, distribution and service channels to new and unfamiliar customer bases on the global frontier. The first is simply to offer product to existing third party channels, maintaining an effectively arms length relationship with the ultimate customers in the new market. The choice here is largely about how many layers of intermediary it makes sense to have between you and the final customer. The second alternative involves partial forward integration. For example, setting up a local sales office to support the third party channels. This may have a variety of functions: training the distributors' local staff, possibly supplying marketing and technical information direct to the ultimate customer; advertising to generate a 'pull' of customer demand through local advertising campaigns; providing after sales service with the local channels acting as a collection or information point. Another option is full forward integration into sales, distribution and service in the new markets. In the Sony example, all three would ultimately be viable options, but obviously not without a complex process of phasing out historical relationships in some cases.

The advantages of third party distribution

Accessing existing third party channels offers the advantages of sharing the fixed costs of sales, distribution and service across multiple products and/or brands. This is especially attractive when the density of demand in any local market is low relative to the fixed costs of the necessary network. The size of the advantage, meanwhile, depends on what proportion of these costs are product and brand specific. The more unique handling equipment, dedicated specialist staff or systems are required, for example, the less cost advantage occurs in the use of existing channels.

A similar advantage lies in the access existing channels may offer to scarce local knowledge or established relationships. Since these intangibles are difficult to buy and sell in the open market, often because they are embodied in teams of personnel, use of existing distributors or agents may be the only realistic way for a new supplier to gain a share of the potential benefits of this accumulated experience. Clearly this access comes at a cost in the form of the margin shared with the channel. It may, however, represent good value for money compared with the cost a newcomer would face in building and maintaining the local goodwill necessary to succeed. Leaving the problems of sales, distribution and service to local distributors may also allow a manufacturer to focus resources and effort on excellence in fewer activities and minimise costs of complexity.

Even relying solely on third party channels, however, it may be possible to strip out unnecessary layers of the traditional, multi-stage distribution chain which has tended to characterise the global frontier. Sometimes multi-stage distribution has significant value-added. It can provide a valuable role in 'breaking bulk' into successively smaller stock units where it is necessary to serve a dispersed and highly fragmented customer base. But multi-stage distribution systems increase the total amount of inventory in the pipeline. Their responses to changes in market needs are also notoriously slow. The more levels in the distribution chain, meanwhile, the greater the probability that marketing or technical information will be lost or misinterpreted as it moves down the chain. This is especially a problem for products which can benefit from exchange of information between the seller and buyers (and from buyers back to the seller), including training in appropriate use and maintenance.

For these reasons, manufacturers on the global frontier often seek to bypass some of the stages in traditional distribution chains. In China, for example, manufacturers and larger retail organisations are increasingly dealing directly with each other. Some of the more labyrinthine channels associated with the historical system administered by the Ministry of Commerce and the All China Federation of Supply and Sales Co-operatives are being bypassed. Even when some of the stages are effectively removed, however, over-reliance on third party distributors can still present problems.

Dangers of over-reliance on distributors

Sole reliance on existing, third party channels has a litany of potential disadvantages. Economic theory tells us that third party sales and distribution channels will generally spend less time and money on promoting a particular product, service or brand than would its manufacturer. The disadvantage comes from the 'spillover effect': one third party distributor spends the promotion money on a particular brand, only to find the customer buys the brand from the distributor next door. The classic case nearer home is the customer who spends hours of a sales person's time at Harrods discussing the merits of different brands of furniture, only to drive off to the nearest discount house to place the order. This inability to capture the full benefit of **sales investment**, discourages third party channels from spending as much as the manufacturer would on his or her own behalf.

The second potential failure of third party channels lies in the so-called 'chain of monopolies' problem. A local distributor who is the only supplier in a local area may set high margins, knowing that most customers will settle for convenience rather than travel far afield in search of lower prices. While the local distributor makes a tidy profit, the manufacturer loses out: he has gained none of the extra margin, but lost potential customers who are dissuaded from buying at all by the higher prices.

A third problem lies in the fact that while an independent distributor or agent wants to maximise total sales across a product category, he is likely to maintain more bargaining power over manufacturers if no one brand begins to dominate. Sellers will wax lyrical about the benefits of a tape recorder, but they usually will not want to convince you that a Sony is far superior than alternative brands at similar prices. The reason is simple: if local customers begin to get the message that Sony is the only brand worth buying, then if Sony were to begin to increase manufacturer prices and squeeze distributor margins, the distributor would be in no position to resist. On the other hand, by minimising the **differentiation between brands** in the customers' mind, but pushing the product as a group, he can credibly threaten to destock Sony in favour of, say, Philips. Up to a point, therefore, the objectives of the manufacturer and the distribution channel suffer from a degree of inherent conflict.

The fourth issue concerns the leakage of **proprietary technical or marketing skills.** Suppose a machinery manufacturer invests in training and possibly equipment to enable the local distributor or agent to provide reliable after sales service and high quality technical advice to users. He risks having provided a free advantage to his competitors whose equipment is supported and serviced by the same distributor staff, surrendering a potentially important competitive edge. The obvious solution is to force the distributor's service operation to be exclusively dedicated to your machinery brand. The equally obvious question then becomes: why not set up a wholly owned, local service operation yourself? The former cost benefits of sharing have already been lost by making distributor's operation exclusive.

Fifth is the danger that the existing distribution channels may become overloaded with complexity as they take on more brands and products. Distributors serving frontier markets face a constant temptation to keep adding new lines as development continues apace and manufacturers seek to extend their networks. If they succumb, the benefits of cost sharing may be swamped by the additional **complexity costs**, rendering existing channels increasingly inefficient over time.

Finally, the use of third party channels may be associated with loss of control by the manufacturer of important product attributes and risk of quality failure either in sales advice, customer training or after sales service. Obviously, quality failure is not to the distributor's advantage either. The downside for a manufacturer, including legal liability, however, may be an order of magnitude greater. Strict adherence to the same tight **quality standards**, therefore, may not be economically justified for a third party channel, especially with the short-term, 'quick money' mentality which characterises many traders on the global frontier.

A middle way?

These advantages and disadvantages of relying on third party channels to provide the sales, distribution and service support necessary to access new markets are summarised in Table 5.1. The obvious conflicting pressures mean that many manufacturers will need to consider a middle way. Their strategy must be to allow third party channels to undertake those activities where the advantages of spreading fixed costs of maintaining a network are great. In those functions where the potential disadvantages of reliance on third party channels is large, such as 'pull marketing', technical advice, user training and after sales service, they need to consider the use of exclusive representatives or taking them in-house. More often than not this strategy will require a degree of forward integration in the form of establishing a subsidiary in the local market. The range of functions undertaken by those subsidiaries will obviously vary with the product or service in question. For each case, the balance of cost advantages and control and quality disadvantages of transferring the activity to existing, third party networks will need to be decided.

The successful distribution of medicines by China Otsuka Pharmaceutical Company provides a good example of the effectiveness of this 'middle way' based on partial forward integration. China Otsuka is a joint venture between Otsuka, one of Japan's leading pharmaceutical companies and the Pharmaceutical Industrial Corporation of China. Its market research discovered a large potential demand for its products. The barrier was lack of information throughout the medical professions and hospital system. Partial forward integration, in the form of a large, technically trained sales team

Table 5.1 Advantages and disadvantages of reliance on third party channels

Advantages	Disadvantages
Shared fixed costs of common distribution, especially where: ● customer density is low ● a high percentage of network costs are fixed	Under-investment in marketing effort due to a distributor's inability to appropriate the benefits (the 'Harrods problem')
Access to accumulated knowledge of the local market which may otherwise take years to amass independently	The 'chain of monopolies' effect – high distributor margins provide a cosy life while the manufacturer loses potential sales
Opens up the 'inside track' to local relationships, some of which probably go back centuries.	Limited incentive to differentiate individual brands due to loss of bargaining power for distributor
Allows the manufacturer to focus on fewer core activities and a less complex operation	Leakage of manufacturer's proprietary technical and marketing skills.
	Loss of control over the quality of technical advice, service and sales integrity

who called on hospitals throughout the country, provided the break-through. By promoting the products, the convenience with which they could be administered using the correct procedures, and ease of patient use through direct contact with medics, they were able to unlock the latent demand. However, Otsuka decided to leave the physical distribution to the existing state system.

This mixed strategy has its share of problems. Co-ordination of marketing and physical distribution is one of the biggest headaches. China Otsuka Pharmaceutical sometimes launches a strong campaign of marketing and technical training in one city, like Shanghai, only to find the state distribution systems allocates the product to far away Zhejiang. The interests of the company and its channels diverge. Despite these difficulties, using the established physical distribution system in a huge frontier market with many delivery points has a massive advantage in terms of cost. The funds required to set up an extensive parallel distribution system for day-to-day deliveries would starve the rest of the operation of investment and weigh the company down with massive fixed costs. Partial forward integration, with the efforts focused on marketing and training seems an optimal, middle way.

The advantages of a direct sales force in frontier markets are not confined to products requiring technically sophisticated sales. Female underwear manufacturer, Beijing Wacoal, found it equally effective for their product. In introducing their Japanese and Western designs into the Chinese market, they found that advertising failed to stimulate sales. Dedicated promotion counters in department stores, staffed with saleswomen employed by Wacoal to discuss the merits and care of the Wacoal products, saw sales rise 56 per cent within the first year.

Some of the functions which entrants to the global frontier should consider putting into a local wholly-owned subsidary or joint venture company are summarised in Table 5.2. At minimum, involvement might be restricted to local customer research, provision of marketing materials or oversight of advertising campaigns. It may be useful to extend this to include activities such as retailer training and after sales service. As a company moves towards the bottom of the table, to a position of full forward integration, its level of control increases. But so do it costs. Taking additional sales, distribution and service functions in-house therefore involves a tradeoff which will be different for every business.

Full forward integration into sales and service

In some cases, full forward integration, with manufacturers providing full sales, distribution and service support through their own subsidiaries will represent the best option. This may also arise where access to existing channels is effectively blocked by the need to oust a competitor's existing product range from a channel in order for the distributor or retailer to maintain economic stock turns. Taking on a new manufacturer's product, for example, may require allocation of additional shelf space, or investment in warehousing and working capital which is not justified by the anticipated net increase in sales. Third party channels may be unwilling to take the risk of replacing established national brands with a new and untried product from elsewhere in the world. In this case the establishment of a sustained local sales and marketing effort by the manufacturer to generate customer pull for the brand, or setting up a parallel sales channel, may be the only viable ways to enter the market.

Of course, forward integration into sales, distribution and service should not be regarded as a panacea. Take the example of Chun Si Li , a Sino-Japanese joint venture in cosmetics. The company noticed that it was no

Table 5.2 Potential functions of manufacturers' local distribution, sales and service subsidiaries

	Consumer products	*Industrial products*
	General market intelligence	General market intelligence
	Local market research	Local customer research
	Brand and marketing management	Provision of promotional and marketing materials
	Retailer training	Distributor training
Increasing forward integration	Point-of-sale marketing and display	Technical advice and marketing
	Retail order taking	Sales order processing
	After sales service	Maintenance services
	In-store sales force or direct marketing	Manufacturer sales force or direct marketing
	Local stockholding	Local stockholding
	Physical logistics	Physical logistics
	Consumables supply	Consumables supply
	Packaging	Packaging
	In-home connection	On-site installation
	Final assembly	Product customisation

longer enough to rely on the cachet of being 'fully imported' to sell the product in a market increasingly saturated with foreign brands. In response they decided to forward integrate into sales, with a team of salesmen calling directly on retailers. Their approach was systematic and well executed. The salesmen were intensively trained in modern sales techniques; their territories were carefully constructed; and daily call routines, including which stores to visit and whom to contact, were established. But Chinese centralised purchasing traditions proved hard to break. The results were disappointing. It has now switched to selling with a few, high level sales people to the purchasing officers of large retail organisations at national exhibitions and conferences. For the present at least it is this strategy, rather than heavy forward integration, that works.

Forward integration may be necessary for different reasons in industrial products. In areas like machinery, for example, it may underpin a supplier's reputation for high quality technical advice and reliable after sales service – critical factors within the purchase decision for many industrial products. The 36 centres for technical sales, installation and maintenance which a company like Shanghai Mitsubishi Elevator has established around China, for example, has been a key driver of its success in this large, but highly competitive market.

For other companies, forward integration into distribution offers opportunities to exploit a broader range of their competences, as well as adding to control. Baskin-Robbins, for example, has a strong skill base in retailing as well as the manufacture of ice-cream. It is also the world's 'doughnut king', with 2500 shops. By forward integrating into retailing of its products in Eastern Europe, Baskin-Robbins can extend its source of advantage over existing competitors and probably better protect its position against future entrants. These stores also double as powerful marketing symbols. As their manager responsible for the business in Russia put it: 'After all, the initial commitment of £50,000 to set up a store is less than the cost of taking part in a major exhibition – something which is gone and finished after two to three weeks'.[5]

WINNING WITH FIRST MOVER BRANDS AND INNOVATIVE DISTRIBUTION

In sum, intuition may tell you that marketing spend is a waste of money at a time when they can't supply sufficient product. This intuition is often wrong: there are important arguments for taking the high ground in a frontier market while it is available.

One important reason lies in what we called the paradox of up-market consumerism on the global frontier. Disposable income levels need to be judged against other outlets for spending: since governments still tend to play a large role in life on today's global frontier, the proportion of income spent on education, transport and health care tends to be low. There are often few opportunities to invest in real estate in contrast to many developed markets where bigger and more luxurious housing is a major 'sink' for personal cash. Items considered mundane in many developed markets are still status symbols on the global frontier. Many people on the global frontier also resent having to make do with the world's third class offering. All of these forces act to favour up-market brands of many types of goods. And things initially get better for these brands as frontier market consumers get richer: more people can satisfy their aspiration to buy the top ranking brands. It therefore pays to build volume from the base of an initial perception of quality – not the kind of low-end product people can't wait to abandon.

At the same time, the early years in the life of a frontier market are often the most cost efficient time to build a brand: customers are impressionable, you don't have to break down loyalty to existing brands; since there are often few competing advertisements, you can achieve a high 'share of voice'; and advertising rates are often lower than they will ever be again.

So while a cheap and cheerful strategy may seem like the way to maximise initial sales volumes it is often not the way to build the future potential of a frontier business. Once established, an initial positioning is slow and difficult to change. A brand's history often comes back to haunt it. And you only get one chance to start in a frontier market completely fresh. Use tools like the value line to make sure you don't start off with a strategy you'll later regret. This kind of analysis of where to position your product on the price-quality spectrum also helps to inform other fundamental decisions like what technology to deploy and how much capacity to install.

Innovative distribution can also complement a good marketing strategy. For most businesses the historical quality of distribution support is inadequate. So there are three basic choices: to invest in existing distribution channels with the aim of improving their capability to act as a conduit for marketing information, technical advice and service; to abandon existing channels and go direct; or some of each.

Partial forward integration

The last of these approaches which involves partial forward integration, usually into marketing and service, leaving physical distribution to existing channels, is often the most fruitful. It seeks to strike a balance between the major advantages of using an existing third party channel: avoiding an additional lump of fixed costs and levering off existing customer relationships; and the advantages of going direct: better control of the customer interface and improved flow of information to and from the market.

Timely action

First mover brand-building and innovative sales, distribution and service strategies can play an important role in expanding sales on the global frontier. But they also help a company build a strong base of advantages which can help it withstand the inevitable increase in competition as the market develops andnew entrants are drawn to a proven honey pot. The apparent lack of sophistication of markets on the global frontier, combined with early excess demand for products, can lead companies to postpone stepping up their marketing, sales and service efforts until it too late. In the process, potential first mover advantages are surrendered. Looking to future competition on the global frontier, not just the present market situation, is essential right from the beginning. This rule applies far beyond marketing and distribution. As we shall see in the next chapter, planning for more competition in the future should influence even more fundamental choices for any developing market like which parts of the business should we be in?

References

1 Consuming passion of Chinese shoppers, *Financial Times*, 24/25 April 1993.
2 Rank Xerox in Kiev, *East Europe Business Focus*, Issue 8, March 1991.
3 N. Banerjee, Russia Snickers After Mars Invades, *The Wall Street Journal*, Tuesday, 13 July 1993, p. B1.
4 This example is drawn from IMD International, 1992, *Sony in Poland*, Case No. 392-052-1, Cranfield UK: European Case Clearing House.
5 'Baskin-Robbins – tempting the Russian palate, *East Europe Business Focus*, Issue 2, July 1990.

6

SECURING COMPETITIVE ADVANTAGE FOR THE FUTURE

One of the major attractions of doing business on the global frontier is the opportunity to escape the saturation of existing, well-developed markets. The object is to break away from an environment where growth means stealing from competitors a larger piece of a static cake. Frontier markets offer a welcome change: they are often short of product; demand is growing rapidly. So when a company begins operations on the global frontier it often enjoys a 'sellers' market'.

Resist complacency

Having more customers than product something most managers at home can only dream about. So being in a sellers' market can create a false sense of security. It is easy to slip into the belief that frontier markets offer a permanent escape from trench warfare against world-class competitors. But this is folly. Serious rivalry will eventually emerge on the global frontier too, as sure as night follows day.

Going to a frontier market doesn't rid you of competition forever. What early entry into a frontier market can buy you is *time* – time to pre-empt the competition that will inevitably follow. Smart companies use this time window to build a wall of competitive advantages that will help protect their initial positions when rivalry heats up. Others simply fritter away their initial jump on the competition.

Strategies that quickly secure competitive advantage for tomorrow are just as important in frontier markets as anywhere else, if not more so. What is different about the global frontier is the fact that future competition seems remote. So preparing for it seldom receives enough attention until after it's too late, when the opportunities to pre-empt competitors have already been passed up. The reason is that, in most frontier markets, managers are initially taxed by a very different problem: the fact that their supply can't keep up with demand. Their main concern is how to get the supply chain to deliver enough.

Anticipate keen competition

By the time the operation is running smoothly and managers have time to look up, they are greeted by a nasty surprise: the benign competitive environment they entered into has often undergone a transformation. While they have been concentrating on making the plants run and sorting out the distribution and supplies, new competitors have also been busy: bringing their own capacity on stream. Local incumbents have been learning new skills and improving their products and service levels, driven on by that most powerful of motivations: survival. An initial blush of sales driven by the novelty of new products and exotic, imported brand names may have passed. Entrants have begun to come face-to-face with the difficult tasks of developing repeat purchases and broadening the customer base to less affluent consumers. Growth rates slacken and competitors increasingly find themselves treading on each other's toes. As promised profits spiral downward, the catchcry of recrimination, 'Why didn't we foresee this in our plans?' is all too often heard.

This chapter is about ensuring those recriminations aren't around the corner. This means doing something to secure long-term, competitive advantage while the time is still ripe; to use that initial time window frontier markets offer before the familiar head-to-head competition becomes entrenched. And however uncluttered a frontier market starts out, sooner or later the problems similar to those in competitive, developed markets will emerge. The heady, initial growth rates will slow. At the same time, once the market is proven, new players will be attracted like bees to a honey-pot.

To pre-empt the coming competition and secure advantage for the future we first need to understand the dynamics of frontier markets. In particular, we need to focus on the fact that opportunities to invest in frontier growth can become cash traps: growth cycles which eat cash in the process of rapid expansion, but fail to deliver real shareholder returns. We then lay out some of the solutions: strategy to win the capabilities race, to assist the new venture to go on learning, and to secure control of pivotal activities along the value chain from raw materials to final consumer.

CASH TRAPS ON THE GLOBAL FRONTIER

Virtually every new business requires an initial injection of cash. This is often followed by a period of operating losses until the business passes its break-even level of sales and irons the expensive bugs out of its new operation. The prize that justifies this initial cash drain takes the form of promised future profits and, ultimately, cash dividends. Once the business has established 'critical mass' in the new market it will hopefully continue to grow and invest. At some point, however, net cash flows should turn from negative to positive, repaying the total investment plus a real return.

But there are some businesses where positive cash flow always seems to be just over the next rise. Whenever you survey the horizon there seems to be profitable opportunity out there. They often grow rapidly, absorbing cash into product redesign, marketing and advertising to educate potential customers, new plant and equipment, and inventory. Yet the day when the investment slows down and the cash comes flowing back in, never comes. These businesses are known as 'cash traps'.

In developed markets, cash traps are often associated with businesses where technological change is rapid and the life of each new generation is short – too short to repay the investment in development and launch costs plus a reward. Very low rates of customer conversion from one generation to another, necessitating continued high selling costs, are another important potential contributor to cash traps in established markets. This problem is common in products which are purchased infrequently, so that customer loyalty is difficult to carry through time.

But cash traps are not only a disease of developed markets; they are endemic on the global frontier. In both cases they share the same siren lure: their future always looks rosy at any point in time, but they never deliver. But the reasons why businesses in frontier markets turn out to be cash traps are often very different from those which create the same problem at home. On the global frontier, cash traps have four primary causes.

1 The frontier business becomes caught in an **investment stalemate**: groups of competitors keep pouring cash in the quest for scale economies and critical mass; costs fall, but prices fall even faster.
2 Competition intensifies, competitors look to differentiate their products in an attempt to break out of a cycle of falling prices. This **differentiation** adds costs. But the costly extras which support a price premium at home turn out to be less important to frontier consumers. Misguided attempts at differentiation therefore squeeze margins and cash flow still further.

3 As the business grows it becomes more complex. As the frontier market moves into adolescence, earlier homogeneous demand starts to fragment into segments requiring different products, different marketing and different types of service. In an effort to maintain its volume and market share, the company extends its range, adding new variety. This adds additional **complexity** and new fixed costs. In order to spread these costs across by winning new sales volume, the range is extended still further, forming a viscous spiral of ever-increasing business complexity, costs and cash absorption.

4 Rather than continuing along its initial development path, the frontier market turns in a new direction as it evolves. The early success formulae are rendered obsolete and new requirements for competitive advantage emerge. The pioneers find themselves poorly positioned to exploit the newly emerging segments and face impediments to restructuring their operations. Past cash investments provide a weak base for competing with newly arriving players, so the business requires further cash injections to restore its competitive position. But this adjustment faces **barriers to mobility**.

The avoidance of these four types of cash trap is a fundamental pre-requisite for securing competitive advantage on the global frontier. In what follows we consider the challenges presented by each one in turn.

Investment stalemate

As a frontier market develops, competitors tend to deploy better and better technology. One reason is that latter entrants need to look for an edge over those who are already established. Better technology is one way of offering that edge: either by lowering costs or allowing improvements in product quality. As the gap between the technology embodied in the pioneers' plants and those being built by newcomers widens over time, incumbents are forced to reinvest if they are to avoid getting left behind. This is exactly the kind of environment where stalemate cycles flourish: more and more investment, lower and lower costs, falling prices and a squeeze on margins. Its a game where the cash keeps going onto the table, but no one wins.

Play goes something like this. Suppose a competitor builds a new plant with larger capacity and more cost-effective technology then any of its rivals. In the short term, while demand in the frontier market outstrips total capacity, this large scale competitor makes high margins under the umbrella of prices which competitors with less efficient capacity have to charge to cover their costs. This position is illustrated in Fig. 6.1.

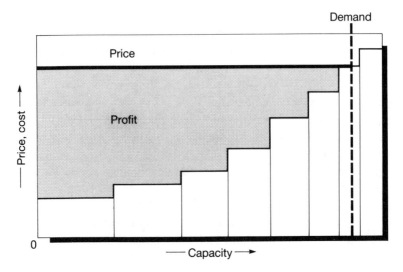

Figure 6.1   Early scale and cost advantages

The high profits reaped by this large scale operator are hardly likely to go unnoticed. By the time a new entrant comes to build a plant or an existing competitor decides to replace its plant, however, the technology has improved, possibly requiring an even larger scale plant. This is a frequent scenario in frontier markets where the early entrants have commonly deployed technology which has already been surpassed or second-hand equipment released by businesses in developed markets which are updating their plants (a point to which we return under the topic of 'technology strategy' below). The competitor therefore builds a plant which embodies the improved technology and seeks even greater economies of scale than his existing rival in an effort to lower costs in order to ensure his competitive advantage.

This large increase in capacity drives market prices downwards. Potential entrants or existing competitors then find they cannot make a profit on the basis of the prevailing scale and technology being used by existing firms. In the quest for competitive advantage they therefore build plants with yet better technology, lower costs and larger scale. But when these come on stream they drive prices down yet again. This scenario is illustrated in Figure 6.2.

Our original competitor's modern plant now looks sub-scale and high cost, yet it has often not fully returned its original investment and is far from the end of its productive life. If he writes it off and invests even more cash in

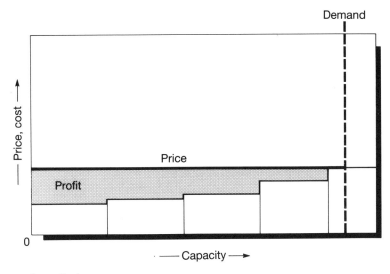

Figure 6.2   Stalemate

a yet larger state-of-the-art plant, total market capacity will be increased yet further. Prices will fall again as rivals initiate another round of discounting in an attempt to keep their plants full.

This is the stalemate cycle. Each competitor has to bet higher and higher cash stakes to play each round. Prices keep falling. The customers, rather than the investors, benefit from the cost reductions. While costs, and prices keep moving down together, no competitor can win. The industry becomes a cash trap.

A case history of stalemate

Take the example of Salgótarján Glass Wool, a Japanese-Hungarian joint venture manufacturing thermal and acoustic insulation materials for customers in construction, transport and heavy industries. In the 1980s Hungarian heat insulation standards had become increasingly strict, moving progressively closer to those common in Western Europe. This led to substantial demand growth for insulation products. Concurrently, the Hungarian business climate was improving. Market research in 1987 confirmed forecasts of strong future demand. A joint venture involving three Hungarian companies and a further three Japanese partners constructed a brand-new, large scale plant utilising world-class technology in order to serve the anticipated market.

Technology and staff training were successfully deployed, bringing the plant up to efficiency levels somewhere between six and eight times higher than those of a regular Hungarian company. Three years later, however, the performance of the venture began to be adversely impacted by what could become a long-term stalemate. The earlier high demand had attracted other new competitors; the original demand estimates proved to be over-optimistic; economic slowdown combined with increased competition, new techniques and reduced wastage in the construction industry led to falling demand. Producers of insulation are now facing a market in surplus. Because of the heavy investment in low cost capacity that the industry has attracted, even efficient producers like Salgótarján are suffering excess capacity and a squeeze on margins. Producers are now looking to exports as a way out of the impasse. But there is a risk that they will remain stuck between two worlds: product quality many of their East European neighbours can't readily afford and stiff retaliation from equally efficient Western producers determined to protect their turf.[1]

Avoiding investment statement

Stalemate cycles have been observed in many high volume, commodity-type businesses in frontier markets such as acrylic fibre, zinc smelting, paper, petroleum refining and steel making. Some strategists recommend avoidance of industries with these characteristics. Others suggest pre-emption to deter competitors from building capacity. However, pre-emption is often a high risk strategy. It involves continually expanding capacity ahead of demand growth. The theory is that by signalling to potential entrants that they would have to fight head-to-head for market share rather than just picking up excess demand if they came in, new competitors can be deterred. The problem is obvious: if this strategy fails, you risk ending up in the worst of all worlds – a market where both you and new competitors are struggling to fill excess capacity. Once established, plant capacity is often difficult to force out. The result is an aggravated stalemate where competitors slug it out in the quest for marginal volume at prices driven by variable costs.

There are three keys to avoiding the stalemate trap in frontier markets.

1 Recognise at the outset that cost advantages based on scale and plant technology are often temporary – they provide the venture with a head start. They buy time rather than delivering sustainable advantage.
2 Use this initial head start to invest in broadening the venture's sources of advantage: the aim is to reach a position where the business is 1 per cent

better than its competitors in 100 ways, rather than 100 per cent better in just one way; to build layer upon layer of competitive advantage.

3 Manage capacity expansion so as to avoid 'shocks' to the market which drive down prices when new capacity comes on-stream; price reductions which may be very difficult to roll back in the future. This means trying to bring capacity on-stream more incrementally, or smoothing the market impact of a new plant by initially diverting some of its capacity into export markets, gradually increasing the proportion going into the local market at a rate buyers can digest without heavy discounts.

Making sure that a frontier business quickly begins to broaden its sources of competitive advantage probably offers the best, long-run protection against the stalemate trap. One method is to begin building brands and strong distribution channels early, as discussed in Chapter 5. Another is to look for ways of segmenting the market into groups of customers with different needs, buying behaviours and price sensitivity and to adjust the product offering accordingly. Likewise the risks of stalemate can be reduced by developing the capabilities of the business to offer a package of product and service. Customer relationships based on providing a bundle of products, responsive logistics, technical advice and after sales service are often more difficult for competitors to break into than those where the customer gets little more than the product alone. Thinking in terms of a total **product-service bundle** is becoming commonplace in developed markets. But there is a risk that the long-term benefits of providing customers with more than the product *per se* are forgotten in the context of developing markets. Early opportunities for securing long-term advantage by broadening the bases are ignored at peril. In the quest to add value to a base product, however, it is necessary to navigate around another cash trap which awaits the unwary on the global frontier: ill-conceived attempts to differentiate the product.

Inefficient differentiation and the wrong kinds of service

Customers in a frontier market are seldom homogeneous. The geopolitics of today's global frontier, described in Chapter 4, mean there are important regional variations, widely different levels of development (like the gap between central China and her south east coast), and local needs. And inevitably, the standard product we sell at home doesn't quite fit. So there are demands for product adaption and and a range of models. And as the market becomes more crowded with competitors, the marketeers start segmenting – their favourite occupation – leading to calls for a further range of differentiated products.

But differentiating a standard product inevitably costs money. Likewise, adding new services to a product offering means extra costs. In some markets (usually those full of rich customers who are bored) differentiation has few risks. You can get away with adding irrelevant bells and whistles – like the video cassette recorder with a 64-button remote control – and charge a premium for difference (at least for a while). Unfortunately, frontier markets don't fall into this charmed group.

With lower real incomes and scarcity of industrial capital, frontier buyers tend to be less forgiving of product features that don't seem to be of much use. As we saw in Chapter 5, this does not rule out branded, high margin sales. Frontier customers will pay for differentiation. But, even more than in other markets, it has to be exactly the kind of differentiation they value.

Take the example of the Swedish furniture retailer, IKEA, in Hungary. Its joint venture partner, Bútorker, a spinoff from a state company, had 26 stores and supplies another 250 retailers throughout the country. In the joint venture store, opened in 1990, it sells IKEA goods in competition with its Hungarian-produced lines. Total sales are buoyant, despite the fact that the IKEA products sell at prices similar to those in Western Europe. The new products have proven complementary to traditional lines. The key lies in cost-effective differentiation. The IKEA lines offer functional, streamlined Scandinavian designs combined with a broader range of supplementary furnishings like cushions. These have proven popular with the well-to-do sector of Hungarian shoppers as well as many others with more modest budgets who buy individual pieces or supplementary furnishings alone. Another sector of the market prefers decorated furniture, replicas of antique furniture similar to old Italian or Dutch styles, which represents the majority of Hungarian production. IKEA's differentiation therefore meets the two basic tests: it provides uniqueness which customers value; and because it is based on designs suitable for high volume, automated production, it can be delivered at a competitive cost.

Satisfying these two criteria, however, is not always straightforward in developing markets. The strategy pursued by Beijing Tochiku Photographs and Pictures Limited (BTPP) illustrates some of the obstacles to successful differentiation. The BTPP partners observed the generally poor quality of photographic prints and reproduction on postcards, badges, corporate promotions materials, etc. in China. The joint venture therefore decided to differentiate its offering based on superior Japanese technology for printing from negatives. This involved the venture in some $4 million of investment in equipment and additional unit costs.

There was clearly potential value added for some customers. But for many more, the poor standard of their basic film negatives limited the extra sharpness an improved printing technology could deliver. The difference in the final product, therefore, was often minimal. Importing foreign negatives proved difficult and often failed to match users precise needs. Moreover, the quality of photographic reproduction, although often at the core of corporate communication in developed markets like Japan, was frequently a low priority issue for Chinese management strapped for cash.

No doubt the situation will change as the market develops. The success of differentiation on the global frontier critically depends on getting the timing right. Misjudging either the emergence of demand or the availability of inputs of sufficient quality can leave a business on the wrong side of the value/cost equation – adding too much cost compared with the ultimate customer benefit.

Similar considerations apply to design of a profitable product/service bundle. Adding service to a product can help secure established customer relationships and cement early sources of advantage as competition intensifies. Companies who establish an initial position on the global frontier through a strategy of 'expectations met and no more' (the lower right quadrant of Fig. 6.3) are exposed to market share erosion as new competitors enter. Supplying what customers currently want and no more

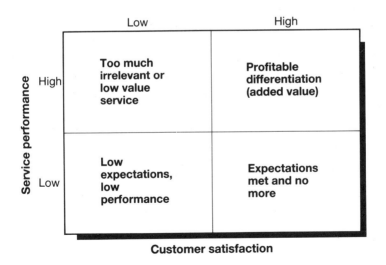

Figure 6.3   Adding the right kind of service

may be profitable for a time, but it does little to discourage customers from switching to another supplier who subsequently offers an equivalent product at a slightly lower price.

Companies with little experience in developing markets have also tended to slip into the lower left quadrant of Fig. 6.3: 'low performance, low satisfaction' by underestimating the service level demanded in frontier markets. Modern communications are quickly bringing expectations into line with international standards. While customers in developing markets may accept lack of service from traditional, local suppliers, they often expect a great deal more from a foreign entrant (regardless of the fact that such a standard may be difficult to deliver because of poor local infrastructure).

In some cases, success on the global frontier may require a more extensive package of services than that supplied in a developed market. Lack of familiarity with the product or correct operating procedures, for example, can necessitate more training and information than is the norm in developed markets. Forward integration into maintenance services and spare parts supply is more likely to be necessary on the global frontier where existing third party networks are apt to be inadequate.

Ready to thwart the quest to provide quality support and to secure existing customer relationships against future competition, however, lies another cash trap: the problem of 'too much irrelevant, or low value service' (the upper left quadrant of Fig. 6.3). The key danger here is that although developing markets require more of some types of service, other services which are critical in the context of developed markets may be of little value to customers on the frontier. The air courier and express cargo business is a good example. In developed markets, the emphasis has been on providing a standardised, streamlined service at maximum speed. For example, competitors vie for business on the basis of later pick up times for the same next day delivery. When the international courier company TNT joined with the Hungarian airline Malév to form TNT Malév Express, however, it quickly found a different definition of service excellence in Eastern Europe. The key purchase criteria was flexibility, rather than absolute speed. In a market where an express cargo service was relatively new, this meant working closely with customers to define how express cargo could help their business. If that meant finding a way to move live chickens or a jet engine rather than documents or computers, then so be it – good service in this frontier market was defined as 'not saying no'.

Profitable differentiation

There are two keys to avoiding the trap of inefficient differentiation in frontier markets:

- to invest in a very detailed understanding of what local customers really value, with particular care to avoid imposing inappropriate definitions of 'high quality' or 'good service' which suit a developed market environment;
- rigorous application of the basic test for profitable differentiation: that the extra customer value exceeds the extra costs involved.

Even with properly targeted differentiation, however, businesses on the global frontier are frequently asked to deliver a wide range of products and services from a single, and often small, unit. A spiral of ever-increasing complexity as new activities are added with the aim of meeting the wide range of demand in frontier markets (including trying to make up for the inadequacy of infrastructure or ancillary industries) represents the third, major cash trap.

THE COSTS-OF-COMPLEXITY SPIRAL

Most plans assume that as a business grows its overhead cost per unit of sales will fall. We suppose this will be the case because the fixed costs of the operation will be spread over successively larger volumes. Initial losses should therefore turn to profits as a new business expands.

The reality on the global frontier is often very different. Initially many ventures in developing markets enjoy the benefits of increased scale and cost spreading. But as they develop further, unit overhead loadings stop falling. In the quest for the growth that was their *raison d'être* in the first place, indirect *costs per unit* of sales actually start to rise as the business keeps on expanding.

More often than not, both local and headquarters management react with a mix of disbelief and bemusement: 'This is not supposed to happen, it defies the basic laws of commerce'. In the fact the cause is not to be found in a witch- doctor's curse. A more mundane, but no less powerful, set of forces are at work in the form of the 'costs of complexity spiral'. This particular cash-eating demon is illustrated in Figure 6.4.

In the quest for volume the business increases the variety of customers it serves and the the range of products and services it offers. The pressures to do so are particularly acute in frontier markets. Once a firm seeks to expand

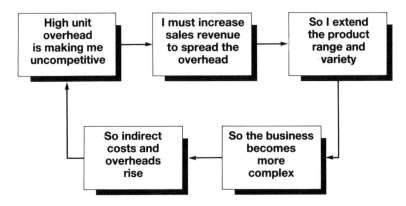

Figure 6.4   The costs-of-complexity spiral

its customer base beyond the few frontier market buyers familiar with the product (other multinationals for example), it is faced with the need to provide extra customer support: user training, maintenance backup or direct distribution to bypass the inadequacies of local infrastructure. The business comes under pressure to adapt its product to fit in with manufacturing configurations for which it wasn't originally designed, to adjust to the peculiarities of customers' locally-made equipment, or to compensate for the variable quality of local raw materials or inexperienced operators. These pressures are common for vendors of equipment and industrial supplies. Nor are those marketing consumer products immune: variations in everything from water quality to local customs call for adaption. This often results in extra variety and additional complexity.

The expansion path of a 50–50 joint venture between a Chinese computer factory and large Japanese electronics manufacturer, illustrates the process. The business began in 1987 as a relatively straightforward assembly operation for computer peripherals, drawing on components shipped in from Japan. By early 1988 there was pressure to launch a new printer, better adapted for the local market, and with it to source an increasing proportion of products locally. Two years later its capacity of 1 million units per annum was divided between numerous different models of calculators, computers, video cameras and players, video cassettes and office machines. Some 60 per cent of the inputs by value, and 82 per cent of the total number of components were sourced locally. Managing this complexity had become a major logistical operation. The ability to secure the right components and jigs on time and to achieve a smooth production flow was hampered by problems of co-ordination and information flow. With this additional complexity, the telecommunications infrastructure became an increasingly important obstacle to the company's progress. Credit control was aggravated by a growing and increasingly diverse customer base. Despite rising indirect costs, lack of personnel with the experience to manage a high variety environment added to difficulties.

From a perfectly valid desire or necessity to respond to the needs of local customers, the costs of complexity spiral can swing into gear. As volume rises, new variety and adaption increased complexity. With the increased complexity comes extra costs of management, co-ordination, planning, supervision, changeover and disruption. Unit overheads rise while market performance slumps.

Much of today's global frontier is emerging from a system which emphasised a culture of standardisation and routine. The system ground on to meet quotas, oblivious of fluctuations in market demand and deaf to changing customer preferences. As a result local managers and workers are often inexperienced in handling complexity. The costs-of-complexity spiral is therefore prone to pick up speed rapidly in these markets. Once the spiral establishes each new, albeit well-intentioned, step it further undermines performance. The operation risks becoming a continuous sequence of fire-fighting as employees and management are overwhelmed by a plethora of one-off tasks and temporary fixes.[2]

Part of the solution to the complexity trap lies in rigorously maintaining focus on core products and key strengths. In the world of opportunity represented by the global frontier it is easy to get diverted into side alleys; to fragment the customer base and proliferate products. At the same time, the need to adapt products and services to meet the non-standard, often diverse needs of frontier markets is a fact of life. The key to managing this situation ultimately lies in learning to control complexity, rather than simply trying to avoid it.

Controlling complexity

Three basic rules show the way forward in avoiding the complexity trap.

1 **Analyse** the operation to pinpoint exactly where variety adds extra costs. It's often not where you think, and where you think, it's not. Once these pressure points have been identified, relatively small investments in extra capacity or tracking systems can often solve much of the problem.
2 **Design** the product and the process to add variety at the latest possible

stage. Techniques like modularisation and standardisation of base components help contain the complexity problem to a manageable part of the activity chain;

3 **Invest** in careful design of processes and systems, not just the product and equipment. As we will discuss in Chapter 7, it is often the 'soft' side of the business infrastructure that creates most problems in developing markets; this is the area where staff are generally least experienced, yet they must face the inadequacies of external support and logistics systems that impose above-average demands. Many costs of complexity arise because systems were designed on the assumption of predictability and standardisation. The complexity of doing business in developing markets need not generate excessive costs if processes have been deigned to handle this challenge as the norm.

Designing products and processes to accommodate increased complexity is one example of the need to plan ahead for changes in the business as the frontier market evolves. Developing markets inevitably metamorphose as they grow. The final type of cash trap arises when a pioneer business finds itself boxed into a corner, unable to respond to these shifting sands.

BARRIERS TO MOBILITY: BECOMING BOXED INTO A CORNER

The problem of barriers to mobility is summed up by the old lament: 'Now it's clear I want to go there, I certainly shouldn't have started from here'. First movers often have advantages when they open up a lead in frontier markets. They can also be left marooned when the market changes course. Pioneers can be left locked into technology which rapidly becomes obsolete or product specifications that consumers quickly come to spurn in an environment of rapidly rising expectations. Existing distribution strength can turn to handicap if traditional channels are bypassed by new patterns of trade. Joint venture commitments, meanwhile, can prove the most problematic barrier to mobility of all. Those partners who seem best positioned early on may prove to be the laggards when the game gets into full swing. The capabilities required for success can change rapidly in frontier markets. Backing the winners of the past is no guarantee of future success. Becoming deeply entwined with a partner who proves slow to adapt to the new order may severely hamper a business in moving to the market position it desires in the future.

The easy answer is to find an accurate crystal ball. But heavy reliance on forecasts is dangerous even in mature markets. It is especially hazardous in the fluid environment of the global frontier. So it is critical to identify the sources of inflexibility a frontier business faces which will constrain its future market positioning (its barriers to mobility). The management can then take the necessary actions to guard against becoming boxed into a corner by investing in ways that increase flexibility and open up its options for the future.

Identifying and dealing with barriers

Barriers to mobility can be both internal and external to the business. External barriers to mobility can include channel relationships or brand image: once established, they are often very difficult and expensive to change. Any aspects of positioning which can only be changed with the acquiescence of parties like customers or distributors outside the direct control of the firm can act as barriers to mobility. Internal mobility barriers can act as equally potent constraints on the ability of a business to reposition itself when this is what a changing frontier environment demands. These include the established company culture: unquestioned assumptions, informal norms, short cuts and rules of thumb; systems and controls; and personnel practices as well as technology.

Three of the strategic weapons that are useful in fighting the build-up of barriers to mobility include:

1 Choosing the right sequence of market penetration: either the top down approach starting with a small, up-market segment and subsequently broadening the customer base; or the bottom-up sequence starting with a standard, low cost offering and incrementally adding additional value (bearing in mind the lessons of taking the high ground discussed in Chapter 5).

2 Investing in flexibility. Often the lowest cost manufacturing facilities or distribution systems are also the least flexible. They are optimised for a particular environment. But they can become dinosaurs when the climate changes. Sometimes it pays to choose technology, channels or systems that offer more flexibility, even if some short-term efficiency has to be sacrificed.

3 Continually opening up new options for the business by developing its capabilities to do new things.

Take the problem of choosing a sequence of expansion. The top-down approach has the advantage of associating the brand with high quality. As we mentioned in Chapter 5, this strategy helps to create aspirational demand for the product in a developing market. From such a launch pad, the customer base should expand as individuals and organisations increase their spending power over time.

However, there are risks in attempting to penetrate developing markets from the beachhead of an up-market niche. Competitors may be able to capture the mass market with a lower cost product. By deploying a bottom-up, volume strategy their costs may fall rapidly as they reap economies of scale and learning. Once large number of customers experience competitors products, they may be difficult to dislodge. Customers may wish to stick with the brands they know, even as they trade up with higher wealth.

On the other hand, the bottom-up approach carries its own risks. Suppliers who held market share with a low-end product in the early days of a poor frontier market may be spurned as consumers become more sophisticated and aspire to better quality. Competitors who deploy this strategy may find it hard to shake off a cheap and nasty image. Strong market penetration early in the game may leave them boxed into a corner by this barrier to mobility later on.

The most effective strategy, then, depends on likely patterns of consumer behaviour, the potential for repositioning brands and retaining existing customers, along with the size of potential advantages from economies of scale and rapid accumulation of experience through high volume sales. These considerations need to be weighed up on a case-by-case basis for each product. The general point is this: once a business embarks on a particular sequence, it is often difficult to change course. Choosing the wrong sequence can leave a business hemmed in by high barriers to mobility. Too many companies let the sequence they follow on the global frontier emerge either by default or as a result of short-term pressure for initial sales. The sequence of market penetration, instead, must be a centrepiece of any strategy for developing markets.

There is also a premium on investing in flexibility on the global frontier. An operation perfectly attuned to the market conditions which existed when it was planned can prove a disaster if things have changed by the time it comes on-stream. In developing markets there is a high risk of gaps opening up during the interval between planning and implementation. Building in sufficient flexibility to cope requires adaptable equipment and plant design. In some cases this means the most advanced equipment. In other instances it will argue for a more labour intensive, sometimes lower technology option capable of handling a range of different products and specifications.

Increased flexibility can also come from early importation of components which require highly specialised equipment and skills. Through an initial focus on more adaptable activities, like final assembly, a business can help avoid making irreversible commitments prematurely. Likewise, early emphasis on activities like service and maintenance can provide a route to learning before committing to manufacture of particular products and locations with technology which will be difficult to change.

Recognising the pace of change

Finally, we must never forget that a rapid pace of learning is one of the hallmarks of frontier markets. Customers, suppliers and competitors are accumulating knowledge and experience at a rapid rate; they are often on the steepest part of the classic learning curve. The implication is clear: any business that is not continually expanding its capabilities will rapidly be left behind. Few businesses on the global frontier can be established and left to churn out profits simply by repeating their original formula. Yet it is a common illusion that simply transferring modern technology and investing bags of cash will be enough to guarantee success in such 'backward' corners of the globe. The comfortable pace of technological and product diffusion which characterised the 1960s and 1970s will not be repeated as we move to the next millennium, even in frontier markets. Many managers have been surprised just how fast the gaps between frontier markets and their developed cousins are disappearing. A key strength, therefore, is the ability to continually generate new ways for the frontier business to compete. Opening up an initial lead is not enough, maintaining and increasing that lead is the challenge. So frontier businesses often find themselves in the capabilities race.

THE CAPABILITIES RACE

No matter what their faults, established businesses on the global frontier, be they former state enterprises, family firms or joint ventures whose roots go back into history, have one big advantage over newcomers: local knowledge. In the course of doing business over the years these 'incumbents' accumulate a large array of capabilities and assets. They know how to get their materials sourced and how to run a local manufacturing facility. They have established relationships with customers and a local workforce as well as suppliers and ancillary industries. They have the capabilities and infrastructure required to manage distribution and service networks to support their product.

Long-established frontier companies v. new entrants

These incumbents also have a problem: their knowledge, capabilities, relationships and systems often produce a final result which falls well short of what customers demand. This gap between what the existing players are supplying and what customers want continues to widen as the local market develops. Customers become more sophisticated and more wealthy. As a result they demand ever higher quality, service and flexibility. The challenge for existing businesses is how to learn new skills fast enough to keep pace with these rising demands.

Firms newly entering a frontier market also have one big advantage: they bring with them new bags of tricks. The ability to bring innovations in product, service, technology, processes and systems compared with existing standards in the market is their ace card. Their Achilles heel is lack of local knowledge and capabilities in frontier markets that are, and probably will remain, distinctive. To assume that entry means a clean sheet of paper is folly. The challenge facing the newcomer is to accumulate local knowledge and capabilities fast enough to allow it to successfully deliver the potential innovations they bring to the market. Few entrants fail because they have nothing new to offer a frontier market. They fail because they don't know how to deliver it in the local context: they can't get the supplies they need; they can't run manufacturing lines smoothly; the product gets stuck in the distribution channel; the sales force is ineffective; poor after sales service, lack of training or maintenance lets the customer down.

Entering a frontier market then, means running in a capabilities race: new entrants are racing to build up their local knowledge; established businesses are racing to learn how to match the newcomers' innovations. Entrants come with an endowment from their parent organisation: capital, equipment, technology, systems, skills. In the terms of Fig. 6.5 they must fill the 'localisation gap'. Incumbents are awash with local assets, relationships and knowledge; their problem is how fill the 'innovation gap'.

The innovation gap that incumbents face is the gulf between what their existing assets and capabilities can deliver and what a changed market is beginning to demand – a gap being filled, albeit imperfectly, by new entrants. To close this innovation gap involves incumbents in a potentially costly and slow process of internal change. New entrants, meanwhile, must close the gap between what their initial endowments can deliver and other

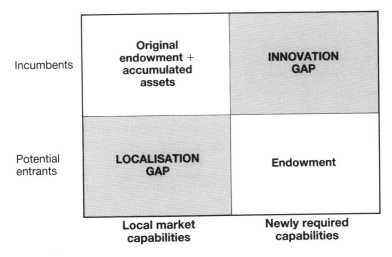

Figure 6.5   The capabilities race

product features, information and service support that incumbents have been able to offer based on their local experience, established brands, and distribution and service infrastructure – assets they have built up in the course of their history of supplying the market. Not all of these historic capabilities will be relevant to changed market conditions, but many will underpin attributes which are still demanded by consumers. The product may be new, for example, but many of the same supporting activities such as distribution or local maintenance may still be required. To close this gap entrants will generally need to replicate some of the capabilities enjoyed by established firms. The more distinctive the frontier market is destined to remain, (as we might well expect for China, for example) the wider the localisation gap to be filled.

The relative handicaps in the race to fill these gaps will depend on two sets of factors. First, the size of the gaps being opened up by changes in the market. Is the market undergoing revolution or evolution? Specifically, how much of the historic assets and capabilities continue to be relevant (determining the size of the localisation gap) and how significant are the innovations introduced by entrants (determining the size of the innovation gap).

The second important set of factors is the difficulty of replicating the assets required to close these respective gaps. For incumbents the magnitude of the problem will generally depend on the amount of change required and the degree to which change is unfamiliar to incumbents rather than routine. For entrants the difficulty of the task depends on the process by which local capabilities must be replicated.

In some frontier markets, therefore, local capabilities will be both important and slow and costly for entrants to accumulate. In this case, more of the new entrants are likely to lose the race against incumbents. By the time they overcome the constraints and costs of replicating the necessary local knowledge and capabilities, incumbents will have already closed the innovation gap and undermined the differentiation entrants initially enjoyed. Such markets have high barriers to survival.

Thinking through barriers to entry and survival: a case history

Take the example of Shanghai-Mitsubishi Elevator Company. When the partners, Shanghai Machinery and Electric Corporation, China National Machinery Import and Export and Mitsubishi Electric of Japan began to examine the market in the mid 1980s, the huge market potential was obvious. Both the Chinese partners and Mitsubishi enjoyed a choice of numerous routes to enter the market and were each courted by multiple joint venture suitors. Barriers to entry, then, were not a problem. Finding a strategy which would ensure profitable survival over the longer term, however, was a different matter.

Driven by the growing pace of the late 1980s building and civil engineering boom, Chinese machinery enterprises began to introduce new elevator products, upgrade their capabilities and licence foreign technology as they sought to close the innovation gap. Foreign companies like Schindler of Switzerland and Otis of the USA expanded their Chinese operations, closing the localisation gap in alliance with local partners. The capabilities race was on. Over 300 manufacturers were involved. Many have since succumbed to barriers to profitable survival in this capabilities race.

Shanghai-Mitsubishi Elevator adopted a three-pronged strategy designed to win this emerging capabilities race.

1 They entered using world-class technology: computer controlled, AC voltage, frequency regulating elevator systems, known as VVVF. These offered the advantages of improved reliability, greater speed and quieter, smoother operation. In doing so, they opened up a wide, initial innovation gap over their competitors.

2 The company introduced waves of improvements in the form of nine new series of products over the next four years. Each new series took advantage of increased capabilities of the Chinese joint venture in quality manufacturing, installation and maintenance, as local staff became more

experienced and better trained, to extend the company's innovation gap over competitors.

3 The company placed heavy emphasis on developing the 'soft' side of the organisation: its skills, systems, culture and management style. This involved setting and monitoring detailed standards as well as continuous training in the Mitsubishi 'power = responsibility' management and co-ordination systems at all levels of the company. The details of these initiatives are described in Chapter 7. The important point here is that, by investing in these systems, the company was able to harness the power of local knowledge and use it to support the delivery of innovative technology to the market. A technological edge was matched by improved capabilities in the other areas necessary to support it. Even if a competitor were able to close the company's technical lead, it would still have to go through the difficult process of replicating a myriad of other capabilities before it could offer the customer an equivalent package of equipment, quality and service. The fact that Shanghai-Mitsubishi Elevator's innovation gap was broadly based and fed from deep within their organisation, made it all the more difficult for competitors to close the gap they had opened up.

The Shanghai-Mitsubishi Elevator strategy is a good example of the need to extend the focus of planning for the global frontier beyond simple 'entry' and onto the problem of profitable survival when the capabilities race gets under way. As our arguments in Chapters 2 and 3 also implied, structuring the business so that it can go on learning rapidly, both from its parent and the local market, is essential for success, and often survival, on the global frontier.

Securing control of the value system

Running faster than competitors is one thing, but it also helps if you can pre-empt the inside track. It is even better still if you can find a way of controlling how fast the competitors can run. By securing control over the supply of key components or activities on this global frontier, it is possible to do just that.

Vertical integration: security or liability?

Behind every product or service there lies a chain of activities running from the preparation of basic inputs through to directly servicing the final customer. In the past, certain companies sought to control new competition by vertically integrating right along the chain. It could be argued, for example, that virtually complete vertical integration from exploration to final pump is one of the reasons why the major oil companies have been able to see off successive challenges to their dominance throughout the world. New competitors who lacked this vertical integration not only had to compete with the majors, that had to buy from them as well. And it's hard to compete when your rival effectively controls the cost of your major input.

But as a strategy for securing advantage on today's global frontier, this kind of vertical integration has four hitches.

1 On today's global frontier governments are seldom eager to see this kind of vertical 'closed shop' emerge. After all in Eastern Europe, for example, a great deal of public policy is focused precisely on breaking these vertical monoliths up.
2 It means trying to be good at a long list of different things. There are usually enough problems to solve in frontier markets without trying to fight on a string of fronts at once. For most businesses, focusing on a few key activities, leaving the rest of the chain to others, increases their probability of success.
3 Vertical integration can drastically increase the financial and managerial resource requirements necessary to get the business off the ground. Some of the stages along the chain may absorb large amounts of capital or eat up the time of personnel with scarce skills for relatively low return.
4 Vertical integration often reduces strategic flexibility. Owning upstream component or materials manufacture may increase the difficulty of switching to substitutes if they become more attractive on price or improved technology. Firms who were integrated back into packaging materials, for example, have often been reluctant to change even in the face of lost sales. Owning a distribution channel may be an impediment if new, more competitive channels emerge.

Recognising these problems of complete vertical integration, however, doesn't mean it's necessary to abandon the whole idea of controlling your competitors' costs or product quality. The question simply becomes: 'In order to get into the driver's seat *which* activities within the frontier industry is it strategically important to control?'

Understanding the value system

In order to answer this question it is essential to understand the value system of which the business forms part. In Chapter 2 we illustrated the value chain of activities for an individual business comprising the chain of activities from inbound logistics through operations, outbound logistics, sales and service. Each supplier to that business will have its own chain of activities. Likewise, intermediate buyers (such as an equipment manufacturer who uses a component) or distributors and retailers will have their own value chains. Any business is therefore embedded in a sequence of these activity chains (known as a 'value system') as illustrated in Fig. 6.6.[3]

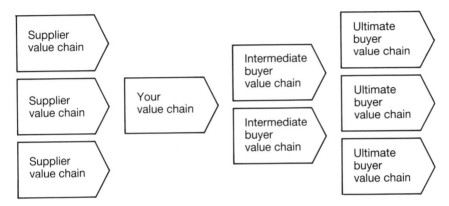

Figure 6.6   The value system

As frontier markets develop the structure of this value system tends to undergo significant change. Power and profit shifts throughout the system depending on where bottlenecks in capacity or scarcity of skills arise. If new manufacturers expand production capacity dramatically while retail sales channels grow more slowly, for example, the shortage of retail space will place distributors in a powerful bargaining position. If a large number of final assembly operations are set up in a developing market, suppliers of scarce, technically sophisticated components will become increasingly powerful. Their profits will rise as assemblers bid for a share of their output.

Just like the toll collector on a mountain pass, it pays to operate in bottlenecks of the value system: those activities where demand is increasing but it is difficult for competitors to supply because they lack the particular technology, skills, systems or other capabilities required. Heavy commitment of resources to parts of the value system where entry both by local and foreign firms is easy, in contrast, is likely to leave the business struggling with excess capacity in an overcrowded market. Firms who focus on the wrong parts of the value system also risk becoming hostage to those who control the bottlenecks, be they suppliers or intermediate customers. The choice of where to operate along the chain, therefore, is critical to securing advantage over the long term.

There are few general rules as to which activities within the value system are strategically critical. They will differ industry by industry and market by market. In some cases, having direct control of the customer relationship may be key. This may enable a business to better differentiate its product through direct experience of customers needs or the ability to support the sales effort with specialised technical staff from other parts of the organisation. It may also be a way to sidestep strong buyer or supplier power which would squeeze profits. It may raise entry barriers by keeping the markets for the intermediate products thin. It is argued, for example, that one of the main difficulties in entering aluminium smelting is that the dominant firms control such a high percentage of the downstream distribution and fabrication that there is virtually no reliable free market for the output of an independent of any size. In other industries the control of scarce raw materials or sites may be a source of advantage. In some businesses it is sufficient to control design, final assembly and marketing in order to exert control over the chain and win most of the profit, using subcontractors, licensees or franchisees to fill in the other activities required to complete the picture.

One of the most powerful strategies manufacturers have used to secure advantage within the chain is to become a major supplier of a core component or sub-assembly used by other manufacturers in a developing market.

CONTROLLING CORE COMPONENTS

Inserted in almost every modern calculator, digital watch, camera, telephone, facsimile machine, pager, piece of audio equipment, microwave oven – the list goes on – there are now LCDs (or Liquid Crystal Displays). Inside everything from cameras to printers there are small electric motors which require high precision. In many of the same products, along with virtually every piece of machinery and equipment there are ball-bearings. Even in developed markets, the specialist skills and technology needed to design and produce these components in volume and high quality make them profitable businesses. Similar examples exist in almost every type of business and value system. On the global frontier such components often have to be imported or are in short supply compared with the rapid growth in demand. Yet they involve an **innovation gap** that few firms on the global frontier are able to fill. Focus on becoming the major supplier of a core component to other frontier firms can therefore play an important role in securing long term advantage and pivotal, strategic position in the chain as the market develops.

The BMCC case history: securing control

One of the best examples of this strategy is the Beijing Matsushita Color CRT Company (BMCC). As Japan's largest consumer electronics company, Matsushita had watched the explosive growth in the Chinese market for TV sets between 1984 and 1986. Finished sets imported from Japan flooded in. Then came government restriction on imports as the authorities watched the drain on foreign exchange reserves with alarm. As a result, more and more local assembly plants for colour TV sets were opened by competitors, both local and Japanese.

Watching the rapid and large scale entry of new players into TV assembly, Matsushita doubted the profit potential of this part of the chain. Looking at the market in 1986–7 they were already too late to gain a first mover advantage in branding. In fact their fears were justified. By 1990 there were over 100 colour TV assembly plants in China. Intense competition was squeezing margins. Yet hopeful new entrants continued to queue up, the flood only stemmed by government refusal of many of the applications for new capacity.

Matsushita decided to take a different approach in the quest to secure a long-term advantage within the colour TV value system. In 1987 through a 50 per cent stake in a joint venture with four Chinese partners: Beijing Electronics Tube Factory; China National Electronics Import & Export Corporation, The Industrial & Commercial Bank of China, and Beijing CRT Factory, Matsushita established BMCC with total equity of $95 million. The product was not colour TV sets, but colour picture tubes to be sold to the TV assemblers throughout China.

The joint venture began production with one line on 1 July 1989 after 22 months of construction work. This first line produces 21-inch flat-square (FS) picture tubes for colour TV sets. A second production line was brought into operation in May 1990 producing 14-inch tubes and 19-inch FS tubes. The total capacity had reached 1.8 million units per annum by the end of 1990, with a staff of 1,450.

BMCC was the first to manufacture FS (flat-square) CRTs in China. They were sold at the same prices as ordinary CRTs of similar quality. Since assemblers can sell their TV sets at higher prices if they are equipped with FS CRTs, this policy rapidly established BMCC in the market. By 1990 demand exceeded BMCC's capacity with sales revenue of $124 million. The company showed profit in the first year of production, reaching profits of $36 million by 1990, placing it in China's top 500 ranking of enterprises for sales and profits. In the following year sales reached $200 million.

These results were based on production lines embodying mid 1980s vintage technology. Matsushita has now decided to introduce the next generation of technology for a 29-inch FS CRT which will take its production to four lines. This additional investment will take the total funds invested in BMCC to $360 million but this will be financed from profit reserves of BMCC. Each new line will add a further $100 million of sales.

BMCC now occupies a pivotal role in the industry. Excess demand for its components are such that BMCC currently restricts its sales to 40 of the more than 100 colour TV assemblers. It controls the 'mountain pass' of the value system. Its customers rely on BMCC not only for product but also for technical support. BMCC technicians are constantly on the road with customers to solve problems and collect information on product performance. As competitors slug it out in assembly and production of simpler components, BMCC has economies of scale and a capabilities lead which help to secure its advantageous position. Key to its strategy is the virtual control of the Chinese market for a core component – the picture tube – that all local TV assemblers need.

It's not just a matter of investment in hardware

In this chapter we have looked at a number of ways companies can cement an initial advantage over competitors, avoiding having to compete boxed in a corner, and navigating around terrain littered with cash traps. All of these strategies start from the same fundamental realisation: the global frontier may start out as a sellers' market, but it won't remain so for long. Frontier markets provide a window of time when growing demand and lack of entrenched, world-class competition mean head-to-head competition is much less intense. The issue is whether companies use that window well to secure advantages that will sustain their profitability when competition heats up.

In fashioning the right strategy to secure future advantage, an understanding of the potentially destructive dynamics of frontier markets is essential. Frontier markets suffer from stalemate cycles as newcomers are successively introducing new technology and driving down local costs.

Frontier customers are frequently unforgiving about irrelevant product features, so that ill-conceived differentiation will quickly drive a company towards the rocks. In the quest for growth – the *raison d'être* of a global frontier involvement – costs of complexity must be controlled. It's easy to find the product range ballooning faster than total sales, leaving local management with an impossibly complex task. It's also easy to let the range of activities get out of hand as you try to fill in for the lack of quality suppliers, suitable distribution and service support.

At the same time as avoiding these pitfalls, focused pre-emption of competitors is the name of the game. This involves:

- tying up prime sources of supply and channels of distribution (as we saw in Chapters 4 and 5);
- becoming the major local supplier of certain core components or intermediate products (so the competition is dependent on buying from you);
- finding ways to build your local capabilities faster than both the existing competition and future entrants can – ensuring you stay a winner in the capabilities race.

The prizes for success in this game, as BMCC illustrates, are substantial. But pulling it off is a tall order. And as the stalemate cycle cruelly demonstrates, investment in hardware alone is not enough.

References

1 Salgótarján Glass Wool, *East Europe Business Focus*, Issue 3, August/September, 1990.
2 See Hay, M. and P. J. Williamson, *The Strategy Handbook*, Oxford: Basil Blackwell, 1991.
3 Porter, M. E. *Competitive Advantage*, New York: Free Press, 1985.

7

BUILDING A FRONTIER ORGANISATION: 'SOFTWARE' BEFORE HARDWARE

Some of the resources that any new business needs travel well. Cash, for example, can be moved around the modern world quickly with little friction and cost. Much the same is true for most kinds of plant and equipment. There may be a few adjustments required and teething troubles associated with different climatic conditions, but by and large a team of engineers can generally get equipment to hum in a relatively short time-frame. The hardware of business is relatively easy to move around. Today there are thriving businesses that will provide a turnkey service to dismantle a plant in one location and transport, reassemble, and test it in a new home halfway around the world.

It is infinitely more difficult to transfer the organisational software of a business, everything from its systems and procedures to its know-how, culture and informal rules of thumb. These things are fragile travellers; difficult to identify as well as pack. They are also delicate flowers, acutely sensitive to their local environment. Richard Giordano, former Chairman and Chief Executive of the BOC Group summed it up this way: 'Hardware is not the problem – the molecules we process in our gases business behave pretty much the same way the world over; its moving people, culture, vision and values that is the real challenge of internationalisation.'[1] Yet these are precisely the things that give a multinational its advantage on the global frontier. Of course, investors bring cash and specialised equipment. But their real, long-run advantage often lies in the 'soft' technical, managerial and systems skills they are able to transfer because these are the very things local competitors and other entrants find it most difficult to copy or learn.

Not only is it more difficult to move the software of a business th[an] hardware, it also takes longer. If you try to transplant both ele[ment] together, the software is sure to lag behind. Being slower to take root, it will place a drag on the effective operation of even the best hardware investment. The implication is simple; so simple, in fact, that it is often ignored. The transfer of software must get under way before making a massive investment in hardware. Impossible? The kind of investments we discussed in Chapters 2 and 3 show the way. In this Chapter we explore the problem of building an effective frontier organisation in more detail. We begin by presenting a way to analyse exactly what organisational software needs to be transferred. Using actual experience, we then examine how it's done. Two themes recur time and time again: attention to detail and a mix of dogma and local adaption side by side.

ANALYSING THE 'SOFT' SIDE: THE 7–S FRAMEWORK

The first challenge in building a frontier organisation lies in determining exactly what software needs to be transferred and adapted. We know the business won't run without it. If left unmanaged a hotchpotch of bureaucracy and bad habits is likely to emerge in its place. But software is difficult to grip; more like a gooey mass than an engineering blueprint. The 7-S framework, originally developed by consultants McKinsey and Company, is a useful tool for thinking systematically about the kind of organisation a frontier business needs. It breaks the effectiveness of an organisation into seven interrelated elements – the seven S's:

- Staff – the human resources of the business;
- Superordinate goals – the fundamental values and aims that guide the organisation;
- Systems – all the formal and informal procedures that govern day-to-day activity;
- Skills – the distinctive capabilities or competences of an organisation;
- Style – how the management team spends its time and presents itself to staff;
- Structure – how the business is organised, reporting relationships, ownership links, etc;
- Strategy – the route chosen by the business to achieve success.

As Fig. 7.1 makes clear, all of the seven S's are interconnected and interrelated. A change in any one element has an effect on all the other variables. The diagram also illustrates the fact that it is difficult to make progress in one dimension (say, strategy) unless the others keep pace. If one or more lag behind, the 'diamond' will become warped and out of balance, exposing the the business to under performance. There is no hierarchy of importance. The critical element will change as the business develops. But the slowest cog will set the pace of all.

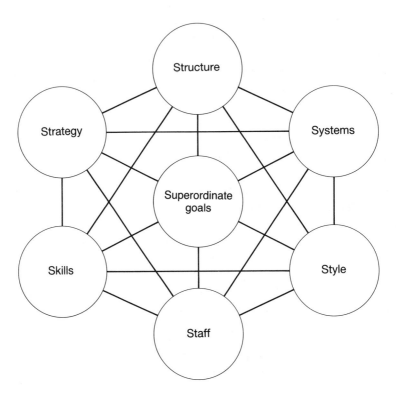

Figure 7.1   The 7–S framework

The harder S's – strategy and structure, are prone to running ahead of the pack. It is easy to redraw the organisation chart and tinker with the strategic plan. But real development only occurs when the softer, informal and less malleable S's keep up. This is true for any business. On the global frontier, however, the softer S's tend to require even more work – they frequently represent at best a void and at worst entrenchment, with counterproductive practices and norms. In what follows we focus on the lessons of experience on the global frontier with these, often neglected softer S's. The fit between strategy and structure is the subject of Chapter 8.

STAFF

Operating on the global frontier presents three sets of challenges in respect of staffing.

1 *Recruitment obstacles.* The problem of finding the right employees is often aggravated by poorly developed and inflexible labour markets. In many areas rural family employment has been dominant so the labour market remains undeveloped. In other cases the State dictate has historically constrained staff mobility.
2 *Inconsistent quality.* The range of skills and motivation among potential employees on the global frontier can be unusually wide. Often there are few familiar and reliable benchmarks against which to judge the qualities of an individual. There are also difficult tradeoffs to be made between experience, energy, bad habits and hangovers from a past regime.
3 *Motivation and retention.* The scarcity of specialist skills in frontier markets means that once trained, employees become a sought-after asset, wooed by competitors or entrepreneurial opportunities. At the other end of the spectrum, the continued existence of state protected sectors in many developing markets means the lure of an easy life, even at lower pay, is a constant temptation. Labour turnover is often high, with consequent loss of efficiency and skills. As we will see in the examples below, higher straight pay is often insufficient alone to motivate and retain a quality workforce.

While these problems are hardly unique to developing markets, they are often more severe than elsewhere. Some of the different solutions are outlined below.

Recruitment and screening

There is no single answer to the best source of recruits. The right approach varies with both industry and market. The important point, however, is to consider the full range of alternative sources rather than simply following the line of least resistance or, worse still, importing prejudices from home. Five main sources may be available:

- secondment or transfer from the existing operation of a joint venture partner;
- accessing surplus rural labour;
- recruiting school-leavers;
- government labour bureaux;
- open advertisement.

The secondment or transfer of staff from the operations of a joint venture partner has two potential advantages. First, it often provides access to skilled labour. With the right level of commitment and careful negotiation, some companies have gained access to some of the partner's most talented and motivated employees. The Shanghai Mitsubishi Elevator Company, for example, draws employees from one of its partners: the Shanghai Great Wall Elevator Factory with a complimentary product line. Since such transfers are viewed as a way to get exposure to higher technology and further training for the most ambitious, employees recruited via this route bring skills well above the norm available on the open market. In Hungary, meanwhile, Salgótarján Glass Wool draws many of its staff from Hungarian Glass Works which holds a 36 per cent interest in the venture. The selected employees are set much more demanding targets than their colleagues back at the parent. But with changed working methods, a different management style and better equipment, these experienced workers have quickly risen to the challenge. Salgótarján's productivity is seven times that of a regular Hungarian company.

Perhaps surprisingly, the second advantage often associated with secondment or transfer is flexibility. In practice, most agreements with frontier partners allow for those who don't make the grade or find the demands too great, to return to their old organisations. Beijing Sanyo Electrics illustrates the point. The joint venture agrees a recruitment plan with its part owner, Beijing No. 2 Computer Factory. Workers at this factory who are under 40 are invited to apply to join the joint venture should they be interested. Transfers are then approved by both partners. Of more than 100 staff recruited in this way not all have succeeded. But the joint venture company has avoided firing even a single individual. Those who found the production rates and working practices unpalatable simply returned to Beijing No. 2 Computer Factory under the agreement.

The downside of secondment, of course, is that workers often bring unwanted baggage: ingrained work habits and mindsets that may be difficult to change. Many companies prefer to start with an unskilled, but fresh, resourceful and malleable workforce. The rural hinterlands of cities and towns is a major potential source in most developing markets. The Beijing Oriental Friendship Furniture Company, a joint venture with a 40 per cent shareholding by Seibu Department Stores of Japan relies on a peasant workforce (often on temporary contracts) for one third of its total workforce producing commercial furniture on the northern outskirts of Beijing. In Hunan province red posters stuck to pillars advertise jobs in coastal textile factories. The floating army of workers the posters seek to attract first gathered pace around 1987. Today, around Chinese New Year in late January or February, when contracts are renewed, up to 90 million people move to industrial centres to take up temporary work as illustrated in Fig. 7.2. Reports of jobs in Shanghai's Pudong industrial zone saw 500,000 migrants move through in a matter of days during 1993.[2] Seafood processor, Toyo Susian Hainan Company, a joint venture in Hainan island also relies on temporary workers supported by a core staff of electricians, refrigeration specialists, boiler workers, security guards and cooks. Most of its workers are women under the age of 22. With a preponderance of low-skilled jobs, advantages for the company are flexibility, generally lower costs and avoidance of the complexity of welfare benefits generally provided to permanent employees.

Recruiting school-leavers

Other companies recruit the vast majority of their employees on longer-term contracts directly from secondary schools. The China Otsuka Pharmaceutical Company in Tianjin specifically targets high school leavers whose results in the university entrance examinations have fallen short of the cut-off for a university place by a small margin. Its advertisements, agreed with the local Medical and Pharmaceutical bureau, stipulate this requirement. The selection process that follows is rigorous, reflecting the importance of human resources in the company's strategy. First, it re-tests the candidates in mathematics, physics, chemistry and Chinese. Those who perform well in these written examinations are then interviewed by both Chinese and Japanese managers from the joint venture and systematically graded on an A-D scale. From this group, the best are selected to undergo a physical examination. For those who have survived this screening a personality test completes the selection process. Successful applicants are offered a three year contract with six months probation. Work begins with two months of structured, on-the-job training.

The cosmetics venture Chun Si Li Company in Hangzhou concentrates it recruitment on teenage women direct from schools. In an industry where

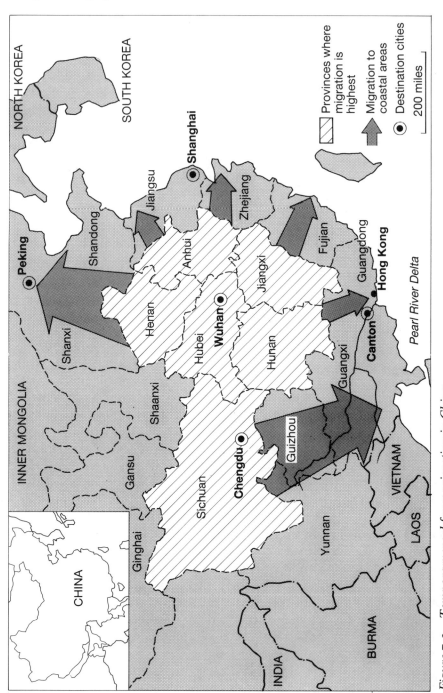

Figure 7.2   Temporary workforce migration in China

Source: T. Poole, 'Ninety million Chinese join the jobs march', The Independent, Wednesday, 3 March 1993, p. 12

work habits are more critical than specific skills, the company emphasises starting from a 'clean slate' rather than seconding the existing employees of its partner, the local cosmetics company Kongfengchun. The joint venture's marketing image and a 50 per cent wage premium over other factories in similar sectors make it attractive. But jobs are by no means open to all comers. With a view to lifetime employment, every candidate goes through three rounds of interviews; the Japanese management is directly involved at each stage. Successful candidates complete their training at the partner's plants in Japan.

The Sino-Japanese joint venture Shanghai Ace Travel Goods Company has taken its relationship with the secondary education system much further. It works with local secondary schools to help them develop a specific vocational course designed for their needs. In the classroom, students learn techniques for the manufacture of travel goods and the operating procedures and systems used in a modern factory. Practical sessions take place at Ace Travel Goods. At the end of the one year course most of these graduates are recruited by the company. With this highly specific training behind them and indoctrination in good housekeeping before bad habits have set in, high productivity levels are achieved quickly.

Other companies strive for a balanced mix of experienced workers and school-leavers. Shenzhen Hauri Automobile Enterprise, a Toyota affiliate in the booming Shenzhen Special Economic Zone, finds school-leavers are quick to learn but are less likely to stay in the organisation than older workers.

Recruitment through third parties

For some companies the established state infrastructure through local labour ministries has provided the recruitment solution. Beijing Tochiku Photography recruits from local residential districts by quota through the local labour bureau which administers written examinations and physical checks. While the final decisions are made by the joint venture's general managers, this route limits the company's direct control over the process. But those who do not reach the required standards on the job can be returned to the local district with one months notice. In fact, some 20 staff followed this exit route during the first two years. In addition, the local district takes care of housing and child care, allowing the company to focus on its core activities.

Yet there are tradeoffs involved in handing the recruitment problem to a local labour bureau. In China, for example, these bureaux typically limit the wage paid by a joint venture to a premium of between 20 per cent and 50 per cent over the state sector pay scale. This is often insufficient to motivate workers given the extra productivity demanded especially when some other joint venture companies pay premia of 100 per cent or more. The Sanyo Semiconductor Shekou Company recruiting through the local labour bureau was the first enterprise in Shekou to suffer a strike as workers demanded higher wages to compensate for workloads they regarded as heavy. Quality standards fell away sharply and the Japanese management decided to shut the plant for a week to conduct a quality check on all stock and work in process. With the introduction of new technology the workforce has since been cut by a third allowing a 'reselection' of employees.

Advertising and screening applicants

Recruiting hotel workers the Hangzhou Friendship Hotel, a joint venture with Murase of Japan located near Hangzhou's popular Paradise Lake, relies on open recruitment through advertisements followed up by an examination and interview. Looking for employees with specialist skills in Budapest, Citibank relies primarily on the local intelligence network. About three graduates per year are recruited straight from the Foreign Trade School and the University of Economics (where the deputy general manager is a member of the final examiners' committee). Apart from fresh graduates, the rest are found through local intelligence; the market for specialists is small and it quickly becomes known when someone of substance is about to leave another banking organisation. The lesson is clear: analyse your specific needs and consider the range of local options. But take the process seriously and get senior management involved in selection right down to operator level. Recruitment on the global frontier is a make or break decision.

Whatever the recruitment source, considerable variation in labour quality is often a feature of frontier markets. Screening systems are critical. They are a particular strength of Japanese investors who typically take enormous care in selecting the right staff, even at basic operator level. We have already described China Otsuka Pharmaceutical Company's rigorous, five stage process. Other leading Japanese investors, whether in high or low technology, deploy a demanding system of selection hurdles.

Reward and penalty

Having recruited the right cadre, the challenges of motivating and retaining these staff begin. Labour turnover is chronically high in the fast changing environment of developing markets. An unstable workforce is the enemy of productivity in many businesses. An innovative, sometimes complex mix of rewards and penalties is often required to successfully tackle these problems. On the Asian frontier, at least, Japanese investors have again led the way.

Alternative salary structures

Take the example of Beijing Matsushita Color CRT Company (BMCC). Each individual's basic wage is unique and confidential. It comprises three parts. The first component, of around 20 per cent of the total is determined by the employee's age. This rises rapidly between 25 and 36 years of age and levels out at age 50. The second component depends on the nature of the job with around 40 per cent of the total dependent on the rating for the post an individual occupies. The remaining 40 per cent of an individual's basic wage depends on his or her education and previous experience. Increases in this last component are based on 'contribution' to the company as determined by a half yearly performance evaluation. In addition, bonuses are awarded twice per year depending on the performance of the individual and the company as a whole over the previous period.

This system provides a series of different incentives designed to align company needs with those of the individual. The age component rewards loyalty and helps reduce employee turnover. The job rating encourages individuals to strive for promotion and to acquire more complex skills. Meanwhile, an individual can increase the contribution component by studying for an additional qualification after hours, as well as through meritorious performance on the job. Finally, the bonus system allows the company to reward its workforce for short-term results, while not committing the company to higher wage costs throughout the economic cycle.

The half yearly assessment procedure is clear and rigorous. Operators are rated on technical knowledge, skill and productivity; discipline, unity and sense of co-operation; and progress against previously agreed objectives. For managers the ranking is based on the quality of their planning; style and demonstrated leadership; co-ordination and co-operation; and contribution to educating subordinates. Rankings are fitted to a normal distribution (or 'bell curve') spreading employee's results across a range from AA (super-excellent), A (excellent), B (satisfactory), C (needs effort) and D (definitely needs more effort!).

Elsewhere the wage and bonus systems have been successfully augmented with recognition and rewards for contributions to operational improvement and innovation among employees. The monetary value is often modest. The world market leader in small electric motors, Mabuchi Motor Company of Japan, provides gifts like a handkerchief or toothpaste in recognition of suggestions for improvement from any employee. A monetary reward from £1 upwards follows if the suggestion is implemented. The philosophy: small rewards which are relatively easy to attain contribute most to motivation. Among the company's 4,500 employees at its Dalian plant in China, the approach seems to work.

Alongside reward, penalties for non-performance are also part of most systems in the Chinese context. Lateness, absenteeism, failure to adhere to procedures or safety regulations attract immediate reduction in pay or loss of bonus (which can represent up to 30 per cent of salary). Such structures were familiar to most Chinese workers from the days of 'big pot rice' – the concept of drawing an equal share from a single organisational pot. With few incentives for individual productivity, regulations and penalties played a dominant role. Although hardly loved, many Chinese associate regulations with order rather than repression. Rather than abandoning the penalty culture many Japanese- and Hong Kong-managed enterprises have used it as a building block to which they have added systems of reward. Carrot and stick together are much in evidence. At Toyota affiliate, Shenzhen Huari Automobile Enterprise, for example, employees are fined for every minute they come late to a roll-call of the workforce each morning. On the incentive side, welfare benefits attract worker attention in many frontier economies. They can be an effective way of motivating and retaining a workforce. But beware; they can prove a costly tangle of extra complexity, especially for a business starting out.

Welfare provision

Social welfare systems in many frontier markets are crumbling in the face of rapid change and ballooning public sector deficits. Others are becoming pitifully inadequate in the face of inflation. Many workers rightly fear falling through the cracks.

Some companies have chosen to allay these fears and attract the labour they want by constructing a virtual 'support city'. The electric motor manu-facturer, Mabuchi, put in place accommodation for their 4,500 workers in a complex comprising five residential buildings, a medical centre, bathing pools, shops, a hairdressing salon, a cinema, halls for everything from lectures to table tennis, and a sports ground. Large dining-rooms exist in both the residential complex and the nearby plant. Most of the company's workers are from the rural hinterland of Dalian; the average age is under 20 and 90 per cent are women. For this type of workforce in what is primarily a labour intensive assembly operation, the investment is more than compensated for by low labour costs. For other businesses, especially those requiring a smaller workforce of skilled or specialist employees, many with families, becoming embroiled in the residential property, entertainment and child minding business has proven a costly nuisance. Sorting out the problems with these unfamiliar activities in a new and changing environment has diverted scarce management time from the core operation. As one executive from a joint venture in the former USSR, put it, 'We had to wonder whether managing a music and dance school was really necessary for an engineering company. Doing business here was already complex enough without trying to run a self-sufficient city state.'

Others have chosen to share accommodation and welfare facilities run by their local partner as part of an existing, usually adjacent, plant. The benefit is clear: complexity is replaced with a simple sourcing contract. The disadvantage is more insidious. The continual mixing with employees from what is often a partner's old style operation and mentality can undermine progress in establishing the corporate culture and work ethic necessary to make the venture a success. In some cases attempts to get employees to identify clearly with the venture have been undermined by the fact that much of their social lives revolve around the partner organisation. In other instances, friction and jealousies arise from mixing a better paid, higher productivity joint venture workforce in the same residential and catering facilities as their cousins who have either chosen, or been forced, to remain with a traditional entity.

Those most experienced in operating on the global frontier have increasingly tried to home in on a handful of benefits that are really critical to their workforce. By focusing only on these benefits and allowing employees to use their wage premium to secure their other needs, the magnitude of welfare management has been contained. Throughout most of the global frontier, two types of benefits are becoming foremost in employees minds in the face of change: health insurance and pension provision.

As we move through the 1990s, companies like BMCC are putting the emphasis on medical and pension schemes. On this dimension there is a rapidly growing similarity between the benefits demanded in frontier markets and the priorities in economies like the United States. BMCC already has a sophisticated health insurance scheme in place. Despite a predominantly young workforce, a pension scheme will follow close behind.

SUPERORDINATE GOALS

A business whose staff are infused with the will to win is sure to out-compete a rival with even the most finely tuned pay and benefits system. There is no substitute for a sense of mission. The most successful businesses on the global frontier have at least one characteristic in common: their staff share a strong sense of purpose and pride in their company. They derive status and respect from being part of it, as well as monetary reward.

Speak to the shop-floor mechanics at Shanghai Mitsubishi Elevator Company (SMEC) today and within the first five minutes you will hear the same sentiments expressed time and time again. **Pride** – the company was ranked 18 among the 500 best mechanical engineering companies in China by the Association of Foreign Investment Enterprises; and that it was one of a handful of companies chosen for Gorbachev's visit in 1989. **Optimism** – that their company has a bright future despite an increasingly competitive market and the cyclical ups and downs of the Chinese economy which often aggravated shifts in the political wind. **Determination to excel** – surpassing competitors to become the best elevator company in China and have a place in the world industry within 5 years; overcoming the handicap of a late start compared with rivals like Tianjin Otis and China Schindler, to prove the Chinese proverb 'Youth are to be regarded with respect'.

Such an ethos among the SMEC staff is no accident. In other joint ventures, insecurity about the future and suspicion as to investors' motives are all too often the norm. People on today's global frontier are wary of being exploited for short-term gain. As one Hungarian manger put it in our interviews: 'There are so many people who think that this is the time of a new gold fever; 100 years ago they went to America to get rich quick; now the grandsons and granddaughters of these people come to Eastern Europe and promise everything. Everybody who has $5 in his pocket will promise $1 billion.' A Russian manager added: 'Whatever else, we are determined to avoid Western rape and pillage'.

Opportunities to build local self-respect are critical; especially in a world where comparisons with the economic miracles of Japan, the Asian tigers and even the postwar affluence of Western Europe are often portrayed as general failure of the frontier societies and their people, not just an economic malaise. Creating pride, optimism and the determination to excel requires communication of a strong vision and mission for the future along with policies to successfully build support for the company within the broader community.

Communicating vision and a mission for the future

Whether the business is in relatively low technology garment making or complicated electronics or sophisticated pharmaceuticals, a vision of future progress and stretching goals is essential. In any developing market, managers and workers know instinctively that things are changing rapidly; that there will be winners and losers; that standing still means decline. Energy and loyalty will only be forthcoming to an organisation that can demonstrate that it offers a way forward.

The appropriate channels for communicating a vision of future success and the goals which must be achieved to make it happen vary by company and national culture. Some of the goals that have proven most powerful in motivating workforces on the global frontier include:

- attainment of world-class benchmarks for quality and productivity;
- winning export orders in international markets;
- recognition from local governments, dignitaries and foreign visitors;
- successive upgrading of technology or product sophistication as the local business learns.

Every Monday and Thursday mornings at Shanghai Yin Feng Garments (SYFG), a joint venture involving Seiko Industrial of Japan, the day begins with a company-wide meeting. All staff sing the Yin Feng company song and recite the staff regulations. Managers discuss the production and quality targets and plans for the future. At one of those meetings employees celebrated winning approval from the International Wool Bureau to carry its distinctive 'Pure New Wool' symbol of quality on their products. The increasing fashion sophistication of products manufactured by the company also provided tangible evidence of the company's progress towards its stated goal of supplying high value-added, fashion products to the Japanese and world markets. Its target of exporting 90–95 per cent of its output having been met, it then set about upgrading its product mix. Having begun with sewing of simple trouser designs, the venture has progressed to dresses, coats and higher value items as the capabilities of the workforce have expanded with experience. Ultimately SYFG is aiming at the high fashion end of the international woollen garment business. The mission is clear and motivating. Progress towards it is obvious to all. So are the means of achieving it: first class products, first class procedures and first class credibility as a supplier.

At the Bútorker-IKEA furniture retailing partnership in Hungary the story of stretching goals is repeated: 'If we were to meet in 10 years time', say managers, 'Bútorker's image would be completely different. We aim to export product to foreign markets and one day to open retail stores in countries like Austria'. At Beijing Sanyo Electrics Company, the communicated goals included introduction of successively more complex products from calculators to computers, tape recorders to video machines. Ultimately the mission is to launch products developed locally. Internal communication channels include an in-house newsletter informing employees of the company's progress against targets and highlighting outstanding performance by particular departments.

China Otsuka Pharmaceuticals, meanwhile, set a clear requirement to match international product standards and export a significant proportion of its production. Today over 30 per cent of its output is sold in Japan and Hong Kong. Employees take pride in the nationwide reputation of the company and the fact that over 16,000 national and international visitors, including many powerful figures, have inspected the operation.

Throughout the world, of course, high-minded objectives and stretching goals can meet with employee cynicism. The global frontier is certainly no exception, especially when foreign partners are involved. Continual reminders to each individual of their contribution to these objectives are essential. Successful companies repeat this message with monotonous regularity. At the regular Monday morning meeting of Beijing Matsushita Color CRT Co.'s 1,500 staff in the main square around which the plant is constructed, the president's message was now familiar:

> 'BMCC is like a boat in the ocean. Never feel complacent because it is big and sailing well. It can sink at any time because of just a small hole. Small mistakes in day-to-day operations are like small holes.'

And yet, he knows this will not be the last time the parable will be told.

Building community support

Children whose birth was registered on the first of January 1987 in the city of Shanghai enjoy a special distinction: they are 'Mitsubishi babies'. Because they share their birthday with Shanghai Mitsubishi Elevator Company (SMEC), they receive a small gift from the company each year. They are also invited to a range of activities arranged by the company. In August 1990, the home of one of these 'Mitsubishi babies' caught fire. On the day of this personal disaster, SMEC sent two employees with food, drink, clothes and other articles for the baby's use to the family. The company plans a scholarship fund to encourage some of these children to study architecture and elevator technology in later years. This is just part of the company's determined campaign to win the support of the local community in their host city.

Responsiveness to local needs pervades the SMEC's image. The company's specially selected Shanghai telephone number, 430-3030, is another reflection of a careful approach to its external face. The pronunciation of '4' in Chinese sounds like 'Yes' and '30' sounds like Mitsubishi

On the third anniversary of the opening of Shenzhen Huari Automobile Enterprise the managing director and deputy managing director each received a cash award for their contributions to the local community. The impact on the company's cash flow was less than dramatic: the prizes were of 100 RMB (or about £10). But these awards represented the culmination of a determined policy of building community support through a mix of sensitivity to local needs and high standards of service. Given the frequent newspaper articles praising the venture, it may never need to advertise. Over 2,000 people inspected the company's operations during those first three years.

Across the other side of the globe, investment bankers Daiwa Europe are running a financial training course for Eastern European managers. Attendance is free. Initially promoted through central banks the word spread about the course. Delegates were drawn from Bulgaria, the Czech Republic, Hungary, Poland, Romania, Russia and the former Yugoslavian states – including countries where Daiwa formerly had no business contacts. After an intensive five weeks delegates returned home with heads full of information and suitcases full of business cards. Their message to Daiwa: 'Run many more such courses. You are unlikely to lose by staging them in terms of contacts in the first place and ultimately much more.'

Many investors in developing markets may see themselves as new Messiahs, or 'wise men' from the East or West. To them the value of what they have on offer should be self-evident. But the reality is very different. 'Barbarian raiders' might more aptly describe the initial perception of many locals. A detailed public relations plan for frontier markets can never start too soon. It plays an essential role, not only in winning co-operation from the local community, but equally in building the pride, loyalty and motivation of employees.

But in winning local community support, PR hype alone is not enough. It needs to be backed by deeds as well as words. At its most fundamental, this means achieving a basic alignment between the company's mission and superordinate goals with the needs of its host community. Ryan International, the first Western company to win a share of Poland's huge coal mining industry, illustrates the point.

The scale of Eastern Europe's environmental pollution problem is now well known. In parts of the former Czechoslovakia, the concentration of sulphur dioxide in the air exceeds 1,000 micrograms per cubic metre – the World Health Organisation recommends a maximum level of 60 micrograms. It is estimated that 95 per cent of Poland's surface water is undrinkable. Tap water in Krakow was identified as an industrial waste in a 'blind test' conducted in the United States. Just two petrochemical plants in the Urals churn out 200,000 tonnes of toxic waste into the atmosphere annually. And so the list could go on.[3] The problem throughout much of Eastern Europe is that governments can neither afford to close the offending factories down, nor to clean them up.

Like a number of other companies Ryan International, a subsidiary of Digger plc, could have attempted to enter the Polish coal industry as an open-cast miner. The experience of some of its rivals suggests the welcome might have been less than enthusiastic. Instead, recognising the growing environmental problem with waste material from the existing Polish mines, Ryan proposed a project based on the purification of discard tips and the export of the recovered coal. It proved an excellent opportunity to enter the market. Nobody had been able to tackle the problem before and no established interest groups would be threatened by a project recovering discarded coal and at the same time cleaning up the environment. Investor and local goals were well aligned.

Given the high wastage rate of existing Polish mining technology its first plant produced over 111,000 tonnes of coal a year. As tougher environmental regulations begin to bite, the company is on the right side of the trend with its environmentally friendly project. In the recovery process coal discard is washed and any impurities put back into the soil can support grass and plant life. A deal with local authorities is then made as to what to do with the purified discard heap. Ryan has since been approached by other Polish mines which would like their waste purified for profit.

In setting superordinate goals to build community support and motivate partners and employees, it clearly pays to find a way to swim with the tide of local needs. The keys to doing this are twofold:

1 Start by analysing the problems the host community faces, not with a ready-made package for 'progress' or a home-made problem of how to dump obsolete technology or slow moving stock.
2 Look for an alignment between your company's resources and solutions to these emerging problems so that future success and growth of the

venture will be of benefit to both sides.

As we explore in Chapter 9, the analogies for success on today's global frontier are those of 'win-win' alliances in the face of pressures for change rather than the colonisation, however paternalistic, of the past.

SYSTEMS

The right staffing policies and superordinate goals are, as the 7–S model reminds us, only part of the requirements for an effective organisation. Overcoming the problem of what the Chinese call *tong chuang yi meng*: same bed, different dreams, is one hurdle. But as Jim Mann put it in his book entitled *Beijing Jeep: The Short, Unhappy Romance of American Business in China*, frontier organisations often fail on a less philosophical plane: at the level of a dirty and unswept factory floor.[4] Embedding the right systems deep within the organisation is essential for success. Without them productivity and quality will progressively degenerate, even in the best designed and equipped facility.

When taking over an existing operation on the global frontier, or even when deploying a sprinkling of experienced local workers and managers to get a new operation up and running, the systems' challenge is twofold. First, existing systems and work habits may need to be cleared away. Then new procedures can be put in their place. Unless these systems' issues are tackled even a motivated and energetic workforce may achieve little. As the Siemens director of East German projects puts its: 'That the people on the shop-floor in former years didn't work in an efficient way, which we normally expect, is definitely not due to the people but to the system they were working in. I'm optimistic if we change the system and the people who are symbolising that system, then shop-floor people will work as efficiently as . . . in West Germany.'[5]

As we discuss below, Japanese companies have been among the most effective in transferring systems like Total Productive Maintenance and Total Quality Control onto the global frontier. But they have also found that to do this job properly takes determination and time. As a Japanese manager at Salgótaján Glass Wool in Hungary cautions: 'We can only go step by step in training [according to] the Japanese system. They know the basics now. The first step is simple working discipline. The next step will be group work: small separated teams, each working together . . . And the next one [is a] total quality control system. We have two-and-a-half years for that. Step by step.'

Total Productive Maintenance and five more S's

Across the global frontier the noticeboards in Japanese ventures extol the virtues of the five S's.

- *Seiri* (order) – procedures for each employ to manage the flow of materials through their area to avoid losses, incomplete batches, mislabelling, combining the wrong materials, applying incorrect production processes and excessive safety stocks.
- *Seiton* (tidiness) – determining the appropriate layout of materials, equipment and tools depending on their frequency of use and the sequence in which they must be accessed.
- *Seiso* (cleaning) – continually inspecting equipment and work areas to ensure they are free of dirt, waste and foreign matter that will cause accidents, defects or hide malfunctions, much in the way an infantry soldier is taught to oil and polish a gun ready for action.
- *Seiketsu* (personal cleanliness) – best illustrated by the increasing numbers of shop-floor workers today who wear light-coloured smocks. Significantly, they are favoured by many Japanese organisations because they show the dirt! This acts as a continual reminder to workers and managers alike that they should be striving for ways to eliminate everything from oil mist to dust and paint thinners, improving safety, reducing waste and making for a more efficient and pleasant workplace.
- *Shitsuke* (discipline) – in respecting cycle and break times, following correct operating procedures, using protective clothing, accurate recording of times, materials and costs.

The five S's may seem like innocuous terms; 'motherhood' statements. But it is the lack of these basic standards, systems and procedures that has caused many large investors in the global frontier to struggle with poor quality and low productivity from expensive plants. As illustrated in Fig. 7.3, the five S's can have a pervasive impact on costs, efficiency, quality, downtime, safety and even employee morale. It is because of the very simplicity of these relationships that they are often ignored or unseen.

The five S's are an example of the kind of systems that, in our observation, form the backbone of organisations combining Japanese efficiency with low labour costs and growth market opportunities on the global frontier.

Initially these systems were implemented to deal with what are often glaring inadequacies in the procedures that have historically pervaded many of today's developing markets. Once these basic ground rules are firmly embedded, the organisation can build on this base towards the ultimate

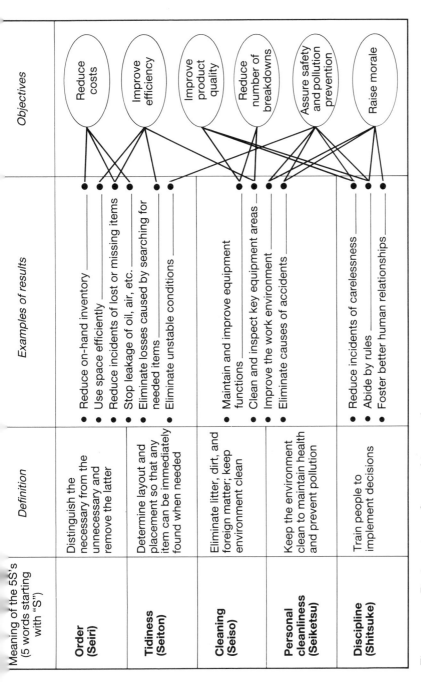

Figure 7.3   Basic systems, far-reaching results

Source: Y. Takahashi and T. Osada, Total Productive Maintenance, Asia Productivity Organisation, Tokyo 1990, p. 127

goals of Total Productive Maintenance (TPM), the successor to Total Quality Control.[6]

The immediate object of TPM is straightforward: to maximise the productive capacity of a given operation through total employee involvement in productive maintenance throughout the enterprise. The philosophy is that if every employee understands the equipment he or she uses and has primary responsibility for monitoring, managing and maintaining it, then potential problems will be arrested before they show up in breakdown or poor quality output. TPM involves systems for formalising the five S's; creating a smooth and continuous materials flow; analysing the relationships between equipment performance and output, quality, cost, delivery rate, safety, pollution and employee morale; maintenance planning; training of employees in self-initiated maintenance procedures; and re-design to reduce maintenance and improve efficiency of maintenance processes. The same philosophy is also applied to office-based activities. Here the systems seek to streamline unnecessary paperwork; eliminate duplicated files and databases; re-design forms to reduce the chance of error; and maximise the effective utilisation of office space and equipment.

Systems in practice

Some examples serve to illustrate these systems at work. On the trouser line at the Shanghai Yin Feng Garment Company (SYFGC) the production system is designed around 80 individual tasks. Sewing on a right-hand pocket takes 9 seconds. The maximum variance for this operation between pieces or workers is an incredible 0.5 seconds. Any higher variation and it would destabilise the co-ordinated flow of work along this line; each of the other 80 tasks is similarly timed to make sure the whole runs like the gear train of a well-oiled machine. Looking more closely, it is evident that every worker sewing pockets picks up the cloth between their index and middle fingers to feed it into the machine. Such is the level of detail to which the procedures have been worked out. After two years of constant instruction in this production system by Japanese supervisors and four waves to training in Japan, operating speed at SYFGC now averages 95 per cent of Japanese plants. At some procedures SYFGC's workers are already faster than their Japanese counterparts. But this system is about more than just speed. The task definitions and procedures are designed to embed quality into the manufacturing process. Posters around the plant continually remind staff that 'quality is number one' – a theme emphasised by the fact that quality levels are the primary driver of individuals' pay. Line management focus on a systematic cycle of continuous improvement following a series of P–D–C–A (Plan, Do [or trial], Check, Action) routines, backed by analysis of process control statistics on time and quality. This may be Shanghai, rather than Osaka, but the system is every bit as sophisticated and tightly run.

At Mabuchi Motor Dalian, every worker follows tight procedures which embody the five S's in what the company calls '50PPM management' – cleanliness, order and worker attention to detail that results in no more than fifty defects per million small electric motors produced by the factory. Associated with each regulation that operators must follow is a reminder that to be successful the company must meet the standards of the world's most demanding equipment makers, not just exceed the quality of others on the global frontier.

Despite an exclusive focus on local market needs, Toyota affiliate Shenzhen Huari Automobile Enterprise also base their standards on world-class performance. The gulf between TPM and the entrenched habits of a traditional Chinese auto-repair shop was daunting; exhortations were soon forgotten. Again, systems provided the way forward, despite the diverse nature of the maintenance work. The daily routine varied in line with the repairs necessary to a particular vehicle. But by providing detailed procedures which could be repeated over and over again, along with a way of monitoring the process, not just the final result, old habits were gradually replaced with new.

Cleanliness and order are major challenges in many frontier markets where standards inherent in daily life are frequently inconsistent with an efficient, modern plant. At Toyo Suisan Hainan Company, which processes and snap-freezes seafood, vegetables and oriental snacks such as Chinese dumplings, one worker described the quality requirement this way: 'I never thought it was possible that I would work in a plant that was cleaner than my own home'. Here, systems not only ensure cleanliness, but also efficiency; just as in SYFGC's trouser line, the process of trimming and cleaning a squid for refrigeration in Hainan was designed in detail by an engineer.

Tight operating procedures, TQC and TPM on frontier production lines are also mirrored in successful white-collar functions. Throughout much of today's global frontier, systems are required to help reorientate the focus from unit volume towards value. As one Hungarian managing director put it: 'It might sound strange, but earlier money was something very abstract here; it was provided for the project by the state. In this [joint venture] case, it needs to be clearly seen by everybody as the shareholders' money for which we are responsible. The new situation necessitates a major shift in accounting, costing and budgeting systems, and increased precision.'

Introducing new accounting and financial control systems is not necessarily a quick or easy task. Government regulations can also hamper the process. Ryan International in Poland, for example, had to begin by running two sets of books in parallel – one according to Polish and one according to Western accounting principles. Even when the government introduced international accounting standards, Western accounts continued to present problems for their Polish partner. In addition to securing the services of a Western accounting firm, Ryan found itself flying in a senior accountant from Britain each month to spend a week working with the Polish accounting staff. It was an expensive solution, but according to the company, its only real alternative. As one manager put it, 'You cannot take a nation which has accountants who have been brought up on a book of local regulations which is 2,300 pages thick and dictate that they, as of next week, next month, next year even, will adopt all the accounting conventions of the West.'[7] Weaning an organisation off former systems that both pervade its activities and provide accepted scorecards is as much the task as putting a new one in place. But it can be done. Beijing Sanyo Electrics, for example, now successfully operates a system calling for rolling monthly budgets, created through a bottom-up process at departmental level, consolidated by central accounting and approved by the General Manager. These procedures play a vital role in inter-departmental co-ordination and conflict resolution as well as allowing each department to track its individual progress.

The importance of getting systems right in a developing market is indisputable. The main lessons for how it's done may be summarised as follows:

- enormous attention to systems detail – no task is too small or insignificant to benefit from a well-planned routine;
- involvement of every employee and giving individual responsibility;
- formal mechanisms for co-ordination and conflict resolution (and conflicts in frontier markets abound) across the company as a whole;
- step-by-step improvement of systems from a firm base of the five S's;
- tight monitoring of compliance to systems and procedures.

SKILLS

Widespread training and skill development at all levels of the organisation is required before the kinds of systems we have described above can be implemented effectively. Such training is not only a necessity for operating efficiency; it is also an important source of staff motivation and community goodwill. Perhaps above all else, the global frontier looks to foreign investors to play a major role in developing the skills of local workers and managers.

There are three main planks to a successful training strategy for the global frontier:

- secondment of local staff to the parent or a sister subsidiary for training;
- training on the job;
- appropriate use of expatriate managers and technicians for training.

In many cases, each of these elements needs to complement the others, rather than being viewed as alternatives.

Secondment to the parent

The know-how, procedures and corporate culture that makes a home operation successful are notoriously difficult to codify. When written down in manuals, the rules, procedures and systems often seem trivial or unnecessary. These documents are more effective as a source of reference and clarification than as a means of communication. Formal instruction is often an equally inefficient means of training a frontier workforce. A recent study of classroom effectiveness, for example, found that at best 40 per cent of the material taught was received by the student. In most situations the loss of information was 75 per cent.

Many of the most successful frontier investors have tackled the problem of transferring know-how, systems and culture head-on. Over a three-year period, Shanghai Mitsubishi Elevator has sent over two hundred of its employees to Japan for training through secondment to local operating divisions. Prior to this experience, few believed that it would be possible to apply the daunting rule book which sets out the company's operating procedures in practice. By the time they returned some of these rules were simply second nature; others became targets they strove to match back in China. The Warsaw Marriott Hotel, aware of the reputation of East European restaurant staff for less than cordial service, sent a group of trainees to Marriott hotels in the USA for some four months. The aim: to immerse them in the 'Marriott way of doing business' alongside acquiring technical skills like the use of the company's worldwide computer systems. These people became the core of the local management, aided by a sprinkling of expatriates. Every year, China Orient Leasing seconds seven or eight of its Chinese staff to work in its operations abroad for between three and eight months. China Otsuka Pharmaceutical rotates all of its managers through a three-month assignment to its sister operations in Japan. After a programme of training, Seimens routinely seconds its East German staff to its established operations in the west of the country for between one and three months 'to observe the principles in practice'.

We could go on listing examples. But the point is this: although 'total immersion' of frontier staff (including linc operators) through overseas secondment is expensive, it has been found to more than repay the investment many times over through its effectiveness as a training mode. This is especially true in respect of training on the global frontier by virtue of the fact that so often basic assumptions and mindsets, not just bad work habits, need to be reformed. Overseas secondment takes employees away from the frontier environment where historic beliefs are in danger of being continually reinforced. It also places them in an environment where, if they do not embrace the company's values, systems and work practices they are in a tiny minority. When a secondee is surrounded by sometimes hundreds of people working within established systems, the pressure to conform is intense. Given time, unfamiliar 'regulations' enter the psyche to become 'normal routines'. There is also a positive demonstration effect: the systems are shown to produce results. As a result many Chinese workers seconded to Japan, for example, return to their homeland with a determination to get their colleagues to outperform equivalent teams in Japan at their own game.

On-the-job training

Of course, not every employee can be shipped off to sister subsidiaries for secondment. It may be necessary to transfer substantial numbers, sometimes hundreds of people, in order to gain a 'critical mass' of those with the desired skills and mindsets. But almost inevitably these people will need to train others.

A large part of the training that secondees can provide to their compatriots on return can come through practical demonstration; the way they, themselves, learned from colleagues overseas. This task will be made easier, however, if local employees are provided with more formal types of training designed to enhance their skills and knowledge. Supervisors and managers also need to be given clear responsibility for the training task. This means commitment from the top. It is no accident that the President of Beijing Matsushita Color CRT, recognised as one of China's most successful joint venture operations, requires his managers and supervisors to spend no less than 50 per cent of their time on staff development.

In training as elsewhere, the golden rule of frontier markets applies: take nothing for granted; don't assume. Basic training in systems and procedures needs to complement improved technical skills. China Otsuka Pharmaceutical is a good example of the kind of sustained, systematic approach to training that has underpinned success in an industry where quality failures can have catastrophic effects. The company trains its employees on a continuous rota, with 10 per cent of workers engaged in formal training at any time. Courses cover operations management, total quality control, production record keeping and reporting, and basic financial management and administration, in addition to special skills that differ by department. Performance in examinations for these courses feeds directly into the skills and education loading in each employees pay package. Not surprising, workers at Otsuka take training seriously. Equally important, by training all employees in a common set of systems and terminology the company stands a good chance of embedding its culture deep within its frontier affiliate.

Utilising expatriates

Sometimes flooding the frontier operations with expatriates may seem like the fastest solution to the need to an extensive programme of training. But in practice, parachuting large numbers of ill-prepared expatriates onto today's global frontier is likely to be a recipe for disaster. They are unlikely to know when to adapt a foreign system and when to be unbending. They often find it hard to distinguish the reasons why new techniques are not put into practice: such as lack of complementary skills, group resistance to change or the need to remove the obstacles before a particular approach will work. Inadequate language skills or lack of cultural awareness can obviously hamper effectiveness, especially in certain roles.

Beyond choosing enthusiastic and culturally-sensitive individuals to do the job, perhaps the most important key to using expatriates lies in distinguishing their three potential roles:

- Visionaries
- Coaches
- Technical specialists

In many successful new ventures on the global frontier, a senior expatriate has played a central role in guiding the medium term development of the organisation and providing a sense of stability, a signal of the parent's commitment and a longer-term vision around which local staff can rally. Ideally this individual should be experienced in the local culture. But above all, expatriates who fulfill the **visionary role** need to be in a post for an extended period of time, something in the order of five years. Given this individual's role and the fact that many staff tend to identify the company and its mission closely with such a person, careful succession planning is critical. High turnover at this level is frequently disastrous.

Those playing a **coaching role** are generally managers with considerable functional or line experience whose task is to establish the major departments within the organisation and build a local team capable of taking over. The horizon here is commonly between two and four years, full time. The ability to devolve responsibility and develop others is obviously just as critical as knowledge of the way the multinational works. Cultural sensitivity and willingness to assess, learn and adapt where necessary are more important that past experience in this role.

Finally, there is often a place for **technical specialists** to bring local individuals up to speed with particular technologies or techniques over a relatively short period of time. Tight definition of the task and its scope is key here. In many cases it is most efficient for these individuals simply to present their knowledge to local personnel as free-standing tools or techniques relatively free of context and prescription. Local managers and expatriate coaches can then wrestle with their appropriate application and adaptation to meet the needs of the local operation. In this case a series of flying visits may be ideal.

The evolution of expatriate involvement in establishing Citibank's Budapest operation illustrates some of these import distinctions. On startup Citibank transferred seven, permanent expatriate staff to the Budapest operation. The four whose primary task was to build effective local teams to handle the bank's main business areas had completed their task and moved on within two years. Five years after establishing the operation, two senior expatriate staff remained: the general manager and the corporate banking group head. In addition the bank initially drew on the expertise of other expatriates on the basis of one-, two- or three-week stints to provide support in areas like credit control, credit analysis training, marketing and selling.

Through **two-way secondment**, from the frontier organisation back to the parent and then seconding expatriates into the local organisation, a multinational can instil its systems and skills into a frontier business. This is also part of the process by which the venture develops a distinctive management style. Like the other six S's, however, management style is subject to conscious policy which can alter the long-term effectiveness of the organisation which emerges.

STYLE

We began by defining 'style' as 'how the management team spends its time and presents itself to staff'. Among the seven S's, it is notorious as the one difficult concept to pin down. And different styles will be appropriate for different types of businesses depending on the industry and the venture strategy for long-term advantage. Achieving a fit between style and the other S's, including strategy, must be a primary objective.

Despite these differences, three general points stand out from our observations of businesses in frontier markets:

- the importance of layout in both factory and office;
- the power of role models and visible signals;
- the effectiveness of styles that would probably be considered unduly hierarchical in the context of more developed markets.

Walk into a large, open floor space where materials flow directly and sequentially from one station to the next and you cannot resist a sense of ordered movement. The subconscious messages abound: time is critical, bottlenecks or quality failures in one area impact on those downstream, the work groups are interdependent. Contrast this with a multi-level facility, floors piled with work in process, work groups obscured from one another by corners or physical dislocation. The workplace itself is therefore an important determinant of organisational style. Some of the most successful frontier ventures repeat the ordered pattern in their office layouts. At first the massive open areas with 'schoolroom' layout of desks comes as a surprise. But in a frontier market where co-ordination is constantly upset by erratic market conditions and poor infrastructure and where historic over-manning, especially among clerical workers makes 'free-riding' endemic, managers quickly point out the benefits. Such a layout is easier to supervise and monitor; it is more difficult for newspaper readers to go undetected; and communication and co-ordination between different departments is facilitated enabling more rapid responses to an unpredictable market environment.

At Mabuchi Motor Dalian, the scene is of open work spaces punctuated with a series of coloured caps. Junior workers with less than three months experience wear white caps. Those with more than three months experience and on-the-job training don grey caps. A green cap signals the production monitors and yellow their deputies. Highest in the pecking order are the pink caps worn by quality control investigators. The signals are many: experience and extra training is rewarded with a visibly higher status; the promotion path is clear; quality activities justify the highest rank on the floor, not a lowly afterthought.

Continuously signalling the importance of quality to local staff is one of the biggest problems faced by many frontier organisation. Tight systems are part of the answer but management style also has an important role to play. Quality control is a particularly difficult issue for Daiken affiliate, Japan Daiichi Kenchiku Service Company which provides office cleaning, building maintenance and property management services in Shenzhen. Their reputation for quality is made or broken at the customers' premises; away from the watchful eye of factory floor inspectors. In this environment the company's hands-on style of management plays an important role in reinforcing messages of quality and customer service: twice a month all of the managers and office workers participate with the front-line cleaning gangs.

Managing organisational style

More generally, the working habits and lifestyles of senior, especially expatriate, managers are an important contributor to the management style that develops throughout the organisation. We cannot expect senior management or expatriates to live the life of an ascetic. But ostentatious living or excessive 'distance' from the workforce caused by everything from physical isolation to language barriers send the wrong signals to others about the way they should manage. Given that there are inevitably cultural barriers associated with managing on the global frontier, informal signals can play a major role. In our interviews it was surprising how many of the staff at successful ventures derived motivation and energy from the observation that senior management worked hard, were concerned with operational detail, had a thorough knowledge of the business, and limited their pay and perks (even though most received only a nominal local salary and were compensated offshore!). Almost without exception among the least successful frontier businesses employees had a very different perception: the venture was 'exporting huge profits' (even though many of these firms were in fact making losses); that senior management were remote and out of touch with what was going on; and most damaging, that promotion meant the right to do less work, rather than more. We found exhortations or statistics proved unconvincing in the face of the reality employees could see in their daily work; among determinants of morale and productivity, management style proved to be key.

But the proactive management of style needs to go beyond informal signals. Frontier managers need to pay special attention to the impact on a company's style of the way decisions are taken, the system for approving different levels of expenditure, and the pattern of meetings. Decision-making at Shanghai Mitsubishi Elevator illustrates the point. It evolves around four main meetings. First is the weekly management meeting attended by the heads of each major department like manufacturing, sales or personnel, along with senior management. Chaired by the managing director, it reviews operating performance and plans for developing the business. The company's competitive position in the market often dominates the agenda. In some other frontier organisations, by contrast, we often found the pattern of decision making routinely ignored competition: the market was simply left out in the cold. Number two in the pecking order is the monthly quality meeting. Presided over by the chief engineer, its prominence in the structure is no accident. Third, a weekly production co-ordination meeting emphasises the importance of a smooth production flow and on-time delivery to customers. Finally, all middle managers, including the heads of sections or workshops within each department meet weekly to discuss changes in the external political and economic environment and how these will impact on the flow of orders and staff motivation and morale. In most developed markets it would probably be unusual to discuss these issues with such a wide audience, many several layers down from the top. But most frontier organisations are especially subject to the vagaries of a rapidly changing, often erratic environment; a fact that needs to be reflected in mechanisms which help the organisation to rapidly respond at every level.

The most successful frontier organisations we studied also tended to share unusually tight definitions of each individual's responsibility for particular results and their corresponding decision-making power. This might appear as excessive bureaucracy. However, whether in China or across the globe in Eastern Europe, managers continually expressed frustration with the problem of overcoming time-honoured behaviours of avoiding responsibility and looking to others, usually superiors, to make even trivial decisions. Clear devolution of responsibility and power proved an effective weapon in this battle. But this was not the wholesale decentralisation of decision-making power and overall, bottom-line responsibility that is becoming increasingly popular in the West. Instead, both responsibility and power were tightly circumscribed within a framework of procedures, rules and approval systems (often even for relatively small expenses, designed to promote a culture of 'every penny counts' cost consciousness).

In different ways each of these elements: layout, role models and hierarchical decision making in the most successful frontier organisations aim at a management style designed to promote a sense of order and tight control.

This is probably not surprising given the destabilising forces that abound in developing markets. Operations on the global frontier are often chaotic. In the face of rapid growth and often inadequate infrastructure, constant 'fire-fighting' becomes the norm. Destructive habits of the past reappear. In this environment the efficiency of the operation can suffer badly without a management style which promotes order and stability, continually acting as a force to bring business back on track.

'SOFT BEFORE HARD'

Beijing Matsushita Color CRT Company (BMCC) brought its first line into production on the 1 of July 1989. More than 250 Chinese staff had already spent six months training and studying in the company's plants in Japan. These operators and managers formed the backbone of the BMCC's workforce, now over 1,500 strong. A company slogan translates as follows:

> 'Every good quality CRT justifies the hard work of every member of our employee team. And we make high quality personnel before we make products.'

The motto might be summarised as 'soft before hard'. This philosophy emphasises the need to begin building the infrastructure of staff, skills, systems and style ahead of products and manufacturing lines. It recognises that the 'soft side' of a business often takes longer to put in place than the hardware.

Many frontier ventures start life in a very different way. A shiny new plant is greeted by a group of eager, but inexperienced staff. While employees learn, efficiencies remain low. Meanwhile the costs of servicing the capital tied up in capacity continue to mount. Starting from a low productivity base, managers continue to struggle to improve productivities and speed up work rates; norms established by an early gentle pace of activity prove difficult to dislodge.

Sceptics, of course, quickly point out that it's impossible to develop an organisational infrastructure before putting the expensive hardware in place. The strategies of some of the leading companies on the global frontier has proven them wrong. Starting out, large scale secondment, like that implemented by BMCC, can play a decisive role in building organisational capacity ahead of needs. But maintaining a continuous reserve of soft capabilities is an ongoing process. The strategy of sequential development from local representation, through trading, technical advice, and processing contracts, building to a full-service local operation, discussed in Chapter 3, opens the way to building an effective frontier organisation over a realistic time-scale. Many of the skills and systems necessary to take each successive step can be developed within the previous business base. To successfully move along such a path, however, organisational structure also needs to evolve. Maintaining this fit between strategy and structure is the topic of Chapter 8.

References

1 Author interview, 1991.
2 Ninety million Chinese join the jobs march, *The Independent*, Wednesday, 3 March 1993.
3 Rodenbeck, C., Counting the Cost of Environmental Change, *East Europe Business Focus*, July/August 1991.
4 Mann, J., *Beijing Jeep: The Short, Unhappy Romance of American Business in China*, Simon & Schuster, New York 1990.
5 Interview with Erich Gerard, director responsible for co-ordinating Siemens' East Germany projects, 1990.
6 See Takahasi, Y. and T. Osada, *Total Productive Maintenance*, Tokyo: Asian Productivity Council, 1990.
7 Ryan International: cleaning up the Polish coal industry, *East Europe Business Focus*, October 1990, pp. 17–20.

8

FITTING STRUCTURE TO STRATEGY

'We know where we want to go and what we need to do. Somehow the structure of our organisation seems to drag us off in other directions. You feel it fighting against you, not with you. Of course we try to cut through the "boxes" to get things done. But with a young business in a chaotic market like this, its important to have procedures and routines. Formality is important; people need to know where they stand. That's a problem because the design of the "boot" is basically wrong.'

This is the way one manager described the frustrations of his frontier organisation; at the heart of his problem is a lack of 'fit' between the strategy and the organisational structure of the business.

This chapter is about achieving the four main dimensions of that strategy/ structure fit:

- choosing the right, basic architecture: a processing agreement, a wholly-owned subsidiary or one of various forms of joint venture;
- putting in place the right set of channels through which to exchange products, people and information with one or more parent organisations;
- developing an effective internal structure, both formal and informal, that defines specific tasks and responsibilities, distributes authority, while also facilitating co-ordination across the business;
- aligning the structure with the local institutional and regulatory framework, as well as the policies of home country governments.

Before embarking on this task, two cautions are in order. The first is by now familiar: beware unquestioned assumptions. Any structure we choose is based on a set of implicit premises about the way organisations work. And these tend to be environmentally specific – especially if we have packed a 'cookie-cutter' structure from home. But as we have constantly found in previous chapters, frontier markets often demand that we turn these premises on their heads. The most important gaps between the presuppositions on which structures are built in developed markets and the common realities we observed on the global frontier are summarised in Table 8.1. Two key point stand out: don't build a structure that solves the same old problems you are familiar with – the frontier often presents a different set of conundrums; and beware of assuming that a known structure will produce a

Table 8.1 Dangerous presuppositions about organisational structure on the global frontier

Presuppositions	Common frontier realities
1 The structure is for an organisation located in one site	The organisation is decoupled across multiple sites (as was discussed in Chapter 4)
2 Our formal structure will drive the informal structure	The informal structure is often driven by cultural and socio-political forces external to the business
3 The structure needs to control the power of strong, functional departments – the functional barons	Functional capabilities are poorly developed and need to be nurtured rather than controlled
4 Middle management represent unnecessary overhead – flat structures work best	Middle management is the linchpin of the organisation in an environment where individuals often shy away from responsibility, and where the need for control and on-the-job training is exceptionally great
5 The structure needs to provide senior management with a clear set of levers through which to control the business	Before top management can control the business through a set of levers it needs a structure that will help it to build an organisation that has something at the end of those levers
6 Wholly-owned subsidiaries avoid most of the internal conflicts associated with joint ventures	Wholly-owned subsidiaries have about the same amount of internal conflict as joint ventures; the conflicts are just deeper in the organisation and take longer to surface

known result – the input/output equation in frontier markets is usually unique.

The second caution is that trying to fit structure to strategy on the global frontier can be frustrating, so never forget that the perfect organisational structure is an Eldorado. The real task is to fashion a workable compromise between conflicting demands. Strategy/structure fit is an imperfect science. And the demands of a strategy change as it develops; so any structure must balance the need to provide a solid anchor for the business, with room for it to manoeuvre.

PRINCIPLES OF STRATEGY/STRUCTURE FIT

Since Alfred D. Chandler's seminal work on the interaction between strategy and structure published in 1962, three prerequisites for maintaining the strategy/structure fit have been confirmed time and time again by research and experience:

1 the firm's strategy should be a primary determinant of the way it chooses to structure itself;
2 as strategy changes, organisational structure also needs to change at a similar pace;
3 restructuring must tackle the informal, as well as the formal structures that exist in any organisation; changing structure involves much more than just redrawing the organisation chart.[1]

Since most of these principles seem like common sense, it is perhaps surprising how often they are contradicted in practice, especially on the global frontier. On closer inspection, the reasons for this failure become understandable (as we will see below). From time to time it may be necessary to contradict the basic rules of the strategy/structure fit. But such decisions should be the result of careful thought, rather than lack of awareness or stumbling into unintended traps.

Structures that won't fit the strategy

Host government restrictions are one reason why the kind of structure a strategy demands sometimes can't be implemented. Requirements for minimum levels of equity participation, or even control, by a local partner for example, are common in developing markets. But throughout the global frontier, these kinds of restrictions have been progressively easing. Sometimes the joint venture form is accepted by default; other alternatives available today, including processing contracts, alliances, and wholly-owned subsidiaries are excluded from consideration. When choosing a basic architecture the first lesson is this: keep an open mind toward different organisational forms.

A second important reason why decisions on structure sometimes end up departing from what is best for the firm's strategy lies in the nature of the negotiation process. During the 'heat of battle' of a negotiation, the emotive issue of organisational structure often becomes an end in itself; the idea that it is a means of achieving a certain set of strategy goals gets lost. The structure that emerges at the end of this process is a careful compromise among considerations which are peripheral to the main strategic thrust, or worse, inimical to it. The important lesson here is to keep on reminding yourself that organisational structure is a means, not an end goal.

Even if a business starts life with a good fit between its strategy and its structure, time and changes in strategy often conspire to throw the balance off course. Despite the impression that strategy documents may seek to engender, changes in strategy are seldom entirely planned. A firm's strategy partly emerges in the course of day-to-day decisions and as it accumulates experience in a particular market. Henry Mintzberg drew attention to the power of this process of **emergent strategy** in developed markets, as we discussed in Chapter 3.[2]

Strategies that keep changing

On the global frontier, emergent strategy almost inevitably plays an important role because markets are in the process of *being created*. Rather than simply serving a well-defined market segment, the frontier business constantly faces new, often inexperienced customers joining the market. New suppliers are often entering at a rapid rate. The behaviour of these players is generally unknown; preferences, tastes, habits and competitive reactions are in the process of being formed. The application of products in a new, frontier environment is throwing up new challenges. The participants in a frontier market are generally on steep learning curves. All this change and uncertainty puts enormous pressure on a strategy to respond, not on the basis of foreign prejudice and standard routines, but by learning from local experience and adjusting accordingly.

These adjustments in response to new discoveries and local developments mean the strategy tends to change through a long succession of small increments. But without a discontinuity, a watershed, or a conscious, planned shift in direction, there is nothing to perpetrate the reorganisation in structure that might become necessary to maintain its original fit with the strategy. Formal structures, at least, tend not to change through a series of small increments. The fact that there are winners and losers in most reorganisations, and that pride and 'face' are at stake, create powerful forces that resist even minor change. This is added to the fact that many structures are made rigid by the ink of legal contracts and organisation charts. Change in organisation structure means a major upheaval and a possible new round of both internal and external negotiations.

What happens, therefore, is that structure tends to stand still. The accumulated changes in strategy open up a gulf between the needs of the business and a structure that is more or less set in stone. As a result of this gulf, the structure starts placing a drag on progress toward strategic goals. The initial 'fit' has come undone because structure tends to lag behind, producing the kind of frustrations expressed in the quotation at the opening of this chapter.

In the rapidly changing and uncertain environment of the global frontier, it is a constant problem to maintain the fit between strategy and structure as the organisation learns and new strategic directions emerge. At least one implication is clear: structure cannot be treated as entirely fixed. Instead, managers need to give special attention to changes that help their organisational structure keep pace with their emerging strategy. A restructuring (such as the decision to decouple activities within the organisation) may be the sign of good management, not a signal of defeat.

Recognising the informal structures

Finally, our third principle of maintaining strategy/structure fit was that informal, as well as the formal structure needs to change with the evolving strategy of a business. Organisational structure is similar to an iceberg, you can observe the formal structure at the tip above the waterline, but a mass of informal structure is hidden below. This informal structure comprises currently accepted practices and ways of doing things or getting things done, temporary alliances and networks; debts and obligations; tacit norms and expectations that govern behaviour.

Again, the informal part of organisational structure deserves particular attention in businesses on the global frontier. In an unfamiliar and culturally distinct environment, the mass of the iceberg is even more difficult to see and understand. Nor is it a simple matter of expatriates relying on the experience of locals. Much of the social environment within a joint venture of a foreign-owned subsidiary will be new to them as well. Old rules of thumb and remedies, may not apply. The fact that ventures on the global frontier are often creating new, and unknown organisational creatures argues that there is no substitute for *exceptional sensitivity to informal structure* and a hands-on approach to managing it through the soft S's discussed in Chapter 7. The aim is not to attempt to eliminate the informal structure (such an objective is doomed from the start), but rather to nudge and bully it into a fit with the venture's strategic goals.

CHOOSING THE BASIC ARCHITECTURE FOR A FRONTIER ORGANISATION

The basic architectures of a foreign presence in a developing market fall into four main categories:

- wholly-owned subsidiaries;
- equity joint ventures with one or more large and well-established local companies or institutions;
- equity joint ventures with small or medium-sized enterprises;
- processing agreements.

Which structure is ultimately most appropriate will obviously vary case by case, depending on the particular combination of resources, needs and aspirations associated with a specific project. But a useful point of departure in analysing the potential fit between structure and strategy is to focus on two major dimensions: the degree of technological sophistication required to successfully execute the strategy; and the degree to which the business needs to be integrated with the local, frontier market. The implications of these strategic needs for choices about basic architecture are illustrated in Figure 8.1.

Weighing-up the options based on Fig. 8.1

When the required level of technological sophistication is high, and with it the need for control by the foreign investor, and the venture can operate with a low level of integration with its local market (by using imported supplies and/or exporting its output, for example), then a wholly-owned subsidiary is likely to be attractive.

On the other hand, if the venture's strategy requires it to be highly integrated with the local market, necessitating local knowledge, access to

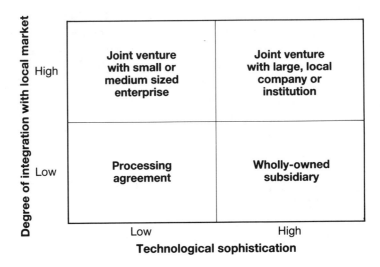

Figure 8.1   Choice of basic architecture

distribution, supply lines, and influence with various levels of government, then an equity joint venture (where a local partner has a substantial shareholding alongside that of the foreign investor) is likely to provide a better fit.

If the process is technically sophisticated, requiring the partner to have access to a substantial base of skills and a critical mass of distribution and supply capacity in order to contribute effectively, then a joint venture with a large, local company or organisation will be favoured.

Contrast this with a strategy that involves a relatively simple process and minimal resource commitment by the partner, but needs to be highly integrated with its local environment. In this case a joint venture with a small or medium-sized local partner may satisfy these objectives, while offering the foreign partner more flexibility and greater control.

Finally, if the level of technological sophistication and the extent of integration with the local market required by the venture are both low, as might be the case with a relatively simple assembly operation using imported components and exporting the finished product or assembled module, then a processing contract is more likely to be the best option.

Within this basic framework we now turn to examine each of these options for basic organisational architecture in some more detail. This involves a closer look at the fit with the strategic imperatives of different types of foreign investors. Because mutuality of interest is a key ingredient in any partnership, we must also assess the advantages and disadvantages of different architectures from the local partner's perspective.

Wholly-owned subsidiaries

Wholly-owned subsidiaries offer three main types of advantages to a foreign investor compared with other basic architectures: maximum control, greatest opportunities to capture learning, and reduced risk of technological leakage.

Mabuchi Motor Company decided on a wholly-owned subsidiary when its fact-finding studies concluded that 'strict production management' would be more difficult with a joint venture. Technological leakage was also a consideration. Management believed that the general trend of technological diffusion was inevitable, and that they must give local workers the training necessary to do their jobs properly. But it wasn't about to choose an organisational form that would speed up the process of 'technological dissipation'.[3]

The general manager of Shenzhen Koei Machinery Company, which assembles electronically-controlled valves, admits that setting up a wholly-owned subsidiary from scratch wasn't easy, but he believes what the company learned during the process is a lasting source of competitive advantage. Dealing with a plethora of government bureaux within local and regional government, each organised for vertical communication rather than horizontal communication proved a time-consuming and frustrating task. It took a full three years from initial investigation to gaining a site with what the Chinese call '*san tong yi ping*' or 'four connections and one levelling' (in other words, connections to the major services like electricity and water, and ground works) for a plant which took only six months to construct. This is perhaps not surprising, given that some 75 'chops' (or stamps of approval) by local authorities can be required. On the other hand, it is worth pointing out that a similar lead time is not uncommon for the complex negotiations required to set up a joint venture.

In choosing to set up one of the first foreign, wholly-owned subsidiaries in Poland in 1990, the British chemicals multinational ICI sought the advantages of tighter control over its product positioning and better access to information about the local market. ICI has a long tradition in Eastern Europe. It was first represented in the former USSR in 1926 through agents working for the company. In the mid-1970s ICI began building up its East European network, establishing at least one representative office in each country. In Poland, for example, it had representation in Warsaw, Lodz and

Wroclaw with a combined staff of 25. But ICI believes that registration as a Polish company will enable it to develop a necessary infrastructure for distributing and marketing its products in Poland and get closer to its customers in ways that representative offices cannot support.

A number of potential disadvantages need to be weighed against these attractions: lack of know-how about how to operate locally; gaining the right entrées into local administration may be problematic; access to distribution or scarce supplies may be more difficult. But such downsides should not simply be taken for granted. When Mabuchi Motor set up in Dalian in 1987, wholly-owned subsidiaries were still a rarity in China. One of the primary reasons was a fear that relations with Chinese authorities might suffer from the absence of a Chinese partner well-versed in the Chinese way of doing things. But being the first, wholly-owned foreign subsidiary in Dalian was apparently not without its redeeming merits. Mabuchi received special consideration not only from the Dalian Economic Development Commission, but also from other government agencies involved.

From the host nation's perspective, wholly-owned subsidiaries are in many ways the least attractive form of investment. None the less, there are substantial benefits to the local economy: new jobs, tax revenues, introduction of new technology and training of workers. Wholly-owned subsidiaries also help to form a local cluster, of the type discussed in Chapter 4, that can act as a magnet to other investors including major joint ventures

It remains a fact, however, that the most successful wholly-owned subsidiaries on the global frontier are still operations that demand only modest integration with the local market environment: they tend to assemble imported components for re-export, or market and distribute foreign-sourced products. When the set of interactions between a frontier venture and its local markets grows in complexity, involving local suppliers and service providers, labour with developed skills and experience, complex logistics and precise financial engineering to maintain the balance between local and hard currency, a joint venture structure can offer significant advantages and increased, long-run potential.

Joint ventures with large, local companies or institutions

Across much of today's global frontier, large local companies are often well-established state enterprises, usually major players in the existing domestic industry and with close links to national and local governments. The primary advantage of a joint venture with this type of institution is access to a substantial stock of potentially complementary skills, resources rand market elationships. Successful ventures of this type are not simply a stopgap solution to a foreign firm's unfamiliarity with a frontier market: they develop into true partnerships where each party continues to contribute to the venture's ongoing development.

Having a joint venture partner with access to formidable resources can substantially reduce the capital contribution a foreign investor needs to make. This fact comes as a surprise to many potential foreign investors who assume that the full burden capital backing is inevitably something the overseas partner must shoulder. Of the $100 million capital behind the Beijing Matsushita Color CRT Company (BMCC) in 1987, 50 per cent came from the Chinese partners. The majority of this cash was sourced from bank borrowings, but the debt remains on the books of the local partners: the funds were used to purchase equity in BMCC. Total investment is planned to rise to $400 by the mid-1990s with expansion of the operation, but the bulk of this will be financed from BMCC's retained earnings.

IKEA's retailing partner in Hungary, Bútorker originally planned to contribute 45 per cent of the costs of constructing their new, 12,600 square metre outlet in Budapest. The Hungarian Credit Bank was to finance a further 5 per cent on through an equity stake. Due to unforeseen cost overruns – including the need to widen an access road and move water supply lines and telephone cables that had been driven through the originally empty site by the local council, who then failed to come up with the money to fix the problem – Bútorker was unable to meet the full amount. It therefore decided to let IKEA take a further 13 per cent equity share. In the final event, the local partners contributed more than 35 per cent of the total funding.

More usually, the local partner's resource contribution comes in the form of land and buildings and equipment (especially ancillary plant like boilers and transformers). But the reduction to the foreign investor's financial exposure is no less real. In the case of the cosmetics joint venture Chun Si Li Company, the Chinese partners provided the joint venture with land, buildings and ancillary equipment valued at $440,000 plus a further $350,000 in cash. Again, a proportion of the cash contribution was borrowed from banks. Of the $4 million start-up capital for Beijing Stone Office Equipment Technology Company (SOTEC), the Chinese office equipment maker, Stone, contributed $1.2 million in the capitalised value of Chinese-character software, a figure agreed with the Japanese partner, Mitsui. Stone also provided land, buildings and equipment to the venture to make up the majority of its 50 per cent equity stake.

This joint venture deal also gave the new SOTEC access to Stone's highly skilled computer staff. As one of China's largest and most successful private corporations, Stone had attracted a pool of individuals who were not only some of the country's most technically qualified, but also ambitious and confident enough to forego the welfare system of state enterprises and the 'iron rice bowl'. SOTEC was able to quickly tap into a team with a strong sense of unity and hunger for achievement that, even after years, Mitsui alone might not have hoped to build. As we noted in Chapter 7, many other joint ventures with substantial, local organisations have enjoyed the benefits of access to secondees who provide a launching pad of critical skills. Without this access these new businesses would have faced a much more protracted process of building an effective staff.

The right local partner, with an extensive distribution network and sales force, can also provide an ongoing flow of market intelligence that it would be very difficult for a wholly-owned subsidiary to obtain. Stone's office equipment group, for example, provides SOTEC with a steady stream of new product ideas through its contacts with the market. Well-established customer relationships, built up through Stone's past service to customers, enable SOTEC to test new products and involve users in developing new ideas. As a newly arrived outsider this type of market access would probably be impossible. As we saw in Chapter 4, an established local partner can also provide access to scarce supplies and services. On today's global frontier, where free markets often exist only in the theoretical world of official pronouncements, this kind of access can be critical.

Some benefits of a joint venture

Importantly, significant benefits also accrue to a local organisation from continuing to make a substantial joint venture work. Advantages like access to new technology and skills; management, production and control systems; and cash injections, are all well known. But others are less widely appreciated. For some local partners, one of the major benefits is the freedom to operate part of their business without the constraints of State intervention. Perhaps surprisingly, joint ventures in today's frontier markets can do many things that local enterprises, caught in a web of formal or informal political interference, cannot. One manager in Eastern Europe put it this way: 'Forget who is supposed to own us. As a major [local] enterprise, every decision passes through the general directorate, the ministry, thousands of officials. And every bureaucrat has their own problem to add. Part of our business still has all of that. But in the joint venture part, there is a relative freedom over wages, financial control and foreign trade operations. So here we can go forward.'

For other local partners there are positive spillovers on the image of their own products that can help their sales outside the joint venture. This was one reason the Chinese partner in the cosmetics venture Chun Si Li, for example, was keen to distribute some of the joint venture's production. The discipline that can come from participating in a joint venture can also help to increase the international competitiveness of the partner's own core business. The Hungarian furniture retailer, Bútorker, underlines this point: 'From working with IKEA we learnt the importance of quality standards and fulfillment of deadlines in a very tangible way. This has had a positive effect on our management and workforce. They have begun to be more involved in the running of the business and have solicited much more co-operation from our manufacturers'.

Converting land, building and equipment into equity in a joint venture can also provide the local partner with a financial gain. Local relationships and market imperfections sometimes enable a partner to buy land or building well below their true market value. (Local communities, for example, often wish to keep major companies 'sweet'). Liquidating such an asset on the open market might be decried as profiteering. But transferring it to a joint venture in exchange for equity is likely to be more acceptable. Even if such an asset is transferred to the joint venture at a price lower than the foreign investor would otherwise have to pay, the local partner can still log a capital gain. Of course this is a 'paper gain' in the short term. But by helping the partner to justify a larger equity stake than it could afford if it had to subscribe cash, it promises to translate into higher cash dividends in the future. Not surprisingly, the use of such asset transfers is a popular way of securing an equity stake in a joint venture.

The management of many local partners are also fond of the publicity and national accolades that are often associated with concluding a substantial joint venture agreement. This can also be an advantage for the foreign investor: with this kind of publicity, there is enormous pressure to make the venture work. Failure will bring disgrace.

Possible disadvantages of joint ventures

Demonstrable success can propel the top management towards the status of national heros. But herein lies one of the potential disadvantages of forming a joint venture with a major local company or organisation: their definitions of success may not be the same as your own. The top management of established, local organisations have been known to judge success by the total number of workers, land area or the total value of plant and equipment under their control. This 'bigger must be better' mentality can lead to conflict with foreign investors who use profitability as the scorecard.

Moreover, the bigger and more visible your joint venture partner, the more probable that national objectives will become entwined with those of the venture itself. Speaking of their failed bid to form a joint venture with Beijing Elevator Company, then China's largest elevator organisation, an Otis Company official commented on such an experience: 'The Chinese government obviously wanted technology, but we were not willing to provide our newest technology to them. We believed their appetite was too big! They did not need the latest technology. We thought we were fair by giving them what was appropriate and what they could absorb without too much difficulty'.

One way to avoid these disadvantages may be to take the wholly-owned subsidiary route. As we have seen, however, spurning a local partner may mean forgoing a string of potential advantages which flow from a joint venture structure. Faced with these conflicting pressures, a joint venture with a small or medium-sized local enterprise sometimes provides the answer.

Joint ventures with small or medium-sized enterprises

A small or medium-sized partner obviously lacks the financial capacity of a large, local organisation. It is unlikely to have the same depth of staff skills or distribution power as its larger cousin. It will usually also lack the same clout with national government and civil service. This problem is aggravated if the product tends to rank low in national priorities. A company with medium-sized partners in the fashion and garment retailing business, like Beijing Wacoal which produces and markets lingerie, for example, has perhaps not surprisingly found it difficult to fight its way to the top of the list for regulatory approvals and import allocations. Despite the problems the company has faced using substandard local nylon, the Ministry of Foreign Economic Relations and Trade (MOFERT) has been unwilling to grant the company an import licence. It is also unable to obtain quotas to import additional motor vehicles for use in its operations.

However, choosing a small or medium-sized partner may offer compensating advantages to a foreign investor compared to a tie-up with a major local organisation or with a wholly-owned subsidiary. Specifically, this type of joint venture enables the foreign investor to exert greater control of the venture than would be possible with a larger, more equal partner, while enjoying some of the advantages of local market know-how and relationships at the same time.

This architecture seems to work particularly well when the two parties are able to achieve a division of responsibilities within the business that accords with their respective skills. Take the Hangzhou Friendship Hotel, a three star hotel venture jointly owned by The Hangzhou General Travel Bureau and a private Japanese company. The hotel is located near the West Lake, one of the region's major tourist attractions, with 40 per cent of the traffic accounted for by Japanese tourists and the bulk of the remainder being Chinese expatriates. This business comes mainly through distributors such as the China International Travel Agency, China National Travel Agency and China Youth Travel. Broadly, the Chinese partner handles logistics and external relations, including marketing – areas where local knowledge and connections are key strengths. The Japanese partner, represented by two expatriate managers, takes responsibility for service quality, internal systems and staff training and management. Here the Japanese experience has greatest value-added in a local environment not renowned for efficient and responsive service. The same is true at Industrial & Commercial International Leasing Company, a joint venture between the local branches of three Chinese organisations: a bank, a trust and investment company, and a trade financier; and Tokai Bank of Japan and Banque Indosuez of France. Business comes primarily through referrals by the Chinese partners of their existing customers. The foreign partners, meanwhile keep tight control over systems and vetting procedures, deploying a substantial number of expatriates.

This kind of division of responsibilities is repeated in the manufacturing sector. Dalian Nisshin Oil Mills, the soya bean processing operation described in Chapter 4, involves multiple, medium-sized partners, one dealing with the supply of raw soya beans, another with local sales of oil, a third with international trade and yet another with local infrastructure and supply of utilities. The primary roles of Nisshin is to provide technology, systems and quality management to the manufacturing operation and to act as purchasers of the soya bean meal. At Zhejiang Sanmei Tea, which makes branded green teas, there is a similar type of specialisation between the partners.

Typically then, in joint ventures with small or medium-sized local partners, the local organisations handle those activities requiring a high degree of interaction with the local markets and institutions, while the foreign partner focuses on technology and operations management.

Of course these arrangements are not without interdepartmental conflicts.

And these can be aggravated by formalising the divide between different cultures and possibly engendering divided loyalties. As we noted above, some investors look to a wholly-owned subsidiary structure in an attempt to avoid these problems. But simply choosing to establish a wholly-owned subsidiary is not panacea for potential frictions within the organisation, especially when the strains have their roots in different cultural norms. A manager of Mabuchi Motor, who operates a successful, wholly-owned subsidiary in Dalian, provides an interesting perspective:

> 'Actually, the conflicts in wholly-owned subsidiaries are just as great as in joint ventures. The difference is just that the conflicts in a joint venture are more obvious and come to the surface at an earlier stage. After the initial period, if a joint venture survives and management from both sides have settled the main conflicts, then the venture can function quite smoothly. Whereas in wholly-owned subsidiaries, the conflicts emerge later and are less obvious. A lot is going on beneath the surface. When the wholly-owned subsidiaries replace expatriate managers with local managers, the conflicts begin to appear. Industrial relations are another kind of conflict in wholly-owned subsidiaries. They are not as obvious as management conflicts, but more difficult to settle.

PROCESSING AGREEMENTS

Processing agreements, which we introduced in Chapter 3, generally share the following features:

- the foreign partner provides raw materials or components for processing or assembly, but retains the ownership of stocks, work in process and finished goods throughout;
- all finished output returns to the foreign partner;
- the local organisation undertakes the processing or assembly in exchange for a fee per piece or tonne completed to the required quality standard;
- if the wastage of materials and/or components (other than defects) exceeds an agreed standard, the costs are deducted from the processing fee;
- the foreign partner often provides a small number of staff to monitor quality, provide technical advice and liaise with its headquarters on supply and logistics (often on a six-monthly rotation);
- in many cases, the foreign partner ships specialised equipment to its local partner which, at the conclusion of the arrangement is repatriated overseas (in many frontier markets, the sale of this equipment locally is prohibited by tariff and import regulations);

- the foreign partner may also make a limited investment in upgrading the local organisation's facilities (such as building refurbishment) with the aim of assuring quality standards can be met;
- these types of processing contracts are typically for a two or three year duration, although they are often renewed if the results are positive.

Processing contracts offer a number of advantages to a foreign organisation wishing to begin doing business in a developing market. The required capital investment is generally very low. The foreign company pays only on results (although there are obviously some fixed, setup costs). The exit costs involved in concluding the arrangement are also minimal.

For these reasons, the processing contract is a particularly suitable architecture when the aim is basically to arbitrage differences in labour or material costs between a frontier market and other locations. If this arbitrage opportunity disappears as a particular market develops, an international firm can readily respond by moving elsewhere; it is not 'locked in'.

Case histories of processing lines 'on loan'

Recent developments in the Polish raw food industry illustrate this strategy/structure symbiosis at work. Poland is one of Europe's major producers of mushrooms with annual production exceeding 130,000 tonnes. The raw quality is generally high. But exports to Europe and the USA have been constrained by problem of maintaining that quality to acceptable Western standards, from picking right through to consumption. Nor can most of the small companies and co-operatives that comprise the Polish industry afford to finance the $500,000 or $600,000 required to install a complete mushroom-processing line.

Processing contracts have provided a way of breaking the impasse. European and American food companies have provided these processing lines 'on loan' for installation into the processing facilities of local organisations. The foreign firms then contract to buy raw mushrooms from various local producers. Their own quality control contractors or staff reject substandard shipments before they enter the plant. The blanched, processed mushrooms are then inspected again before authorisation of the agreed fee to the processor.

These arrangements have some obvious attractions to local businesses, especially those caught on the wrong side of the rapid structural adjustment that usually accompanies the emergence of frontier markets: jobs for idle workers; new volume to increase the utilisation of existing facilities and support plant; hard currency earnings; an infusion of new skills, especially in quality control and operations management; and experience with new technology.

Recall the case of the Japanese electronics firm, Omron, which we discussed in Chapter 3 which has electronic blood pressure and body temperature meters assembled by the state-owned Dalian Recorder Factory. Dalian Recorder lacked the capital, technology, parts supply and sales channels to support a fully-integrated joint venture. It did, however, have a trained workforce and support infrastructure that were under-utilised because of import competition against its core electronics products.

A number of foreign firms had proposed sourcing deals to the Dalian Municipal Government to access these idle pools of skilled labour. The stumbling block, however, was an unwillingness of the Chinese authorities to take the risk of purchasing specialised equipment to supply a processing service with an uncertain future. Omron overcame the problem by lending the equipment to Dalian Recorder at no cost, initially for a period of 2 years. Two Japanese technicians were also seconded to Dalian Recorder to handle the logistics of supply and shipping as well as quality control. $50,000 was invested by Omron to refurbish the buildings allocated to the project by the Chinese partner. In exchange, Omron was able to negotiate an attractive piece rate for the work. And Dalian Recorder selected some of its best, young operators to work on the line.

This processing contract proved successful for both sides. After 2 years the line was handling double the volume originally envisaged; from 3 initial product types, the operation had developed the capability to handle 10 different models. Omron gained cost efficient assembly capacity up and running quickly, with little commitment of capital and personnel. For the Chinese the processing contract brought in cash, absorbed idle labour, expanded the skill base of its workers, and introduced new manufacturing systems, procedures and disciplines.

Uncertainty and distrust with contracting

At the end of the day, however, the balance of power in most processing contracts remains very much in favour of the foreign firm. Even in friendly arrangements, the local organisation must work with an implicit threat constantly in the background; the threat that its partner will move the contract and the associated equipment to another local producer. Superficially, this power play may seem like an advantage. But it also has downsides in the medium to long term.

The uncertain life of processing contracts under the threat of switching acts as a deterrent to long-term investment in the venture by the local partner. Quality is limited either by the partner's current infrastructure or what the foreign firm provides. There is little motivation to innovate, especially where experimentation or disruption could risk immediate efficiency for an unknown and uncertain future benefit. The resulting frustration is common in processing agreements as they age: local partners can see scope for improvement and development of the venture, but they find themselves in a structure where the incentives are fundamentally opposed to acting on these ideas.

Perhaps most significant of all, the local partner has little incentive to help the foreign organisation learn about the local environment. Quite to the contrary, there is the risk that if the foreign partner learns too much it may abandon the processing agreement in favour of a wholly-owned subsidiary. Faced with an uncertain future, the local organisation is more likely to act as a sponge than a teacher, soaking up whatever technology and know-how it can gain from the foreign contractor while it has the opportunity.

Of course the foreign firm may use a processing contract as a vehicle for familiarising a core of its own staff with the frontier environment as a step toward a more complete and permanent presence. But any suspicion that this might be the case will further encourage the local organisation to be tight-lipped and learn as much as it can unless it can be convinced it will be part of any future development. As we discussed in Chapter 3, a processing contract may be a step on the staircase of developing a solid frontier business. If it is to play this role, however, it needs to be managed as a co-operative source of learning from the start; a true partnership from the outset.

BENEFITS AND PITFALLS OF VARIOUS FRONTIER STRUCTURES

Each basic architecture, then, has its pros and cons; there are 'horses for courses'. Some of the disadvantages of any particular choice of structure can be alleviated by sensitive management. With careful planning, one structure can sometimes be used as a stepping-stone to another. But a keen awareness of the inherent advantages and disadvantages of each organisation form is an essential starting point; these considerations are summarised in Table 8.2.

Table 8.2   Basic architectures – pro's and con's for the foreign investor

Architecture	Advantages	Disadvantages
Wholly-owned subsidiary	• maximum control • greatest opportunities to capture learning • reduced risk of technological leakage	• poor access to local know-how • weak links with local authorities • lack of access to distribution or scarce supplies
Joint venture with large, local company or institution	• access to local skills and resources consistent with scale • established market relationships • partner contribution can reduce cash investment • political clout	• large visible joint venture partners increase likelihood of economic decisions being hijacked by 'national goals' • local managers likely to be driven by size rather than profit • reduced control and flexibility
Joint venture with small or medium-sized enterprise	• greater control and flexibility than with large partner • may provide unique access to niche skills or specific sources of supply • potentially good relationships with local government	• difficulty in gaining regulatory approvals and quota allocations from national authorities • partner's lack of resources and weak skill base may constrain growth
Processing agreement or contract	• low capital requirement reduces financial exposure • payment only on results • low exit costs avoid 'lock-in' • incentive to minimise learning by foreign investor	• local partner's insecurity reduces its motivation to invest or innovate • possible technological leakage

STRUCTURING THE RELATIONSHIP WITH PARENT ORGANISATIONS

The type of relationship between the frontier venture and its parent organisations, or the other partners involved, is heavily influenced by choice of basic architecture as in Table 8.2. In a processing contract, the two-way flow of resources and information between the foreign and local organisations is limited and well defined. It takes the form of materials or components, completed products, specific equipment and limited technical advice.

In the case of a wholly-owned subsidiary on the global frontier, the basic challenge is to set up channels through which the parent's technology, know-how, systems and corporate culture can be transferred into an unfamiliar and unstable environment. As we saw in Chapter 7, the organisational structures to achieve this may include a framework for secondment of expatriates, programmes of training for local staff back at headquarters, formal allocation of responsibilities for providing support to the new venture and so on. Transfer from parent to subsidiary is, indeed, a critical task. Equally important, but often neglected are channels for the new subsidiary's ideas and discoveries to flow back to the parent. Structures are required, for example, for the experience of the frontier subsidiary with new types of customer needs to feed back into the process of product design and research and development; for competitor intelligence gained locally to be registered back at HQ; for potential new sources of supply for the corporate group unearthed by the local subsidiary to be followed up by purchasing personnel at the centre. Every company will have different ways of achieving these kinds of feedback. Often the annual strategic planning and budgeting process can play a pivotal role. *The point is that structures to facilitate feedback need to be put in place; learning on the global frontier is not a one-way flow: the parent organisation, as we noted in Chapter 2, must also have ways of learning too.*

All of these needs apply to joint ventures. They also present two additional issues:

1 What kinds of structure need to be put in place to control a joint venture's access to information within the parent organisation?

2 What are the appropriate mechanisms for measuring the parent's investment in a joint venture on an ongoing basis?

Without an appropriate structure for controlling a joint venture's access, the parent organisation can become a 'leaking bucket'; encouraging a kind of free-for-all, treasure hunt by joint venture staff as illustrated in Fig. 8.2.

Even in a spirit of partnership and co-operation, it is as well to remember that proprietary technology or information transferred to a joint venture earns a parent only a percentage of the profits it may produce. Especially where its equity interest is low, the parent may be giving away its know-how

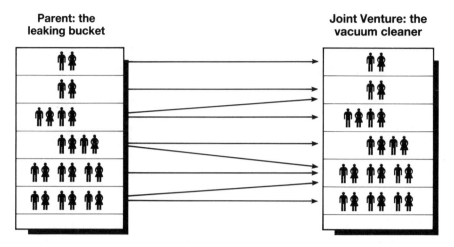

Figure 8.2   The 'leaking bucket' – a common result of lack of structure

too cheaply. Worse still, the top management of the kind of 'leaking bucket' illustrated in Fig. 8.2 doesn't have a total picture of exactly what information has been given out. These are particular problems when the joint venture partner has other co-operative relationships in the frontier market or other parts of the world; cousins (and sometimes potential competitors) who may benefit from formerly proprietary information.

Avoiding the 'leaking bucket' syndrome

One effective way to deal with these issues is to establish a 'gate-keeper structure'. As illustrated in Fig. 8.3, requests for information and assistance from the joint venture are directed to a single individual, or small team, who has the responsibility of assessing these requests and approaching the right person within the parent organisation. After a response has been prepared, the gate-keeper reviews, and possibly adapts, the information before passing it on.

Such an arrangement may appear excessively bureaucratic, slow and unresponsive. Sometimes the nature of information flow between parents and subsidiary means the gate-keeper structure is unworkable, even if routine communications are excepted. But some of the less obvious advantages of using gate-keepers to manage the parent/subsidiary interface need to be considered: these individuals can save the inquirer time because they know the structure of the parent and who to approach; as they gain

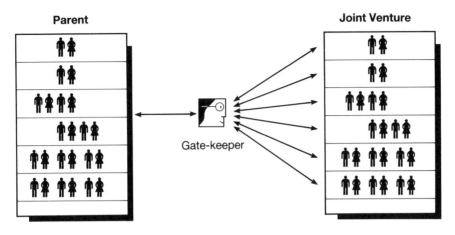

Parent   **Joint Venture**

Gate-keeper

Figure 8.3   The 'gate-keeper' structure

experience dealing with both organisations, they are able to translate and restructure requests and responses so as to make them more useful to both sides; and they can provide top management with an overview of the time and information it has invested in a joint venture to aid future decisions and help pinpoint weaknesses.

Quantifying the benefits of frontier operations

This leads us to the second issue we identified: how to measure the parent's investment in a joint venture on an ongoing basis. Ask any finance director how much his or her company invested in a piece of manufacturing equipment or an acquisition and, hopefully, you will receive a quick and precise answer. Ask about the total investment in a joint venture to date, and the same person is likely to scratch their head. This is because much of the total investment that goes into a joint venture is usually 'soft': technical advice, visits, know-how, systems, training – the kinds of investments where our accounting systems find it much more difficult to quantify the costs. What was the value of Matsushita's investment in on-the-job training of 250 Chinese staff in its Japanese plants in preparation for the startup of its 50 per cent joint venture Beijing Matsushita Color CRT Company? How much is the continuous flow of proprietary garment designs worth that Wacoal of Japan transfers free to its 44.1 per cent-owned producer in Beijing?

Without a way to monitor, and ideally quantify, these 'soft' investments in joint ventures, it is difficult to assess the overall profitability and returns from the frontier business. There is no easy solution. But an increasing number of companies are structuring the relationship between a parent and its joint ventures or subsidiaries such that, in so far as possible, time, know-how and other types of 'soft' investment are *sold to the frontier venture* rather than transferred gratis. Otsuka Pharmaceutical licenses each of its products and processes to its 50 per cent-owned venture in China for cash. In Hungary, the Salgótarján Glass Wool joint venture paid for nine months consulting time of technical specialists sent by one of its foreign parents to supervise preparations for the startup of a new production line.[4]

This kind of structure provides a way of tracking exactly what the parents are putting into any venture on an ongoing basis. Again, this information can act as an important aid to decision making. And such a structure has positive spinoffs: it makes the joint venture think more carefully about what it really needs from the parent; the joint venture becomes more demanding about the quality of support it is receiving (often spurring the providers to improve); and it can increase the impact of soft investments by the parents – as we all know, things you have paid for tend to be valued and used with care; that which is free is often squandered.

INTERNAL ORGANISATION

Clearly every organisation must develop a unique internal structure appropriate to the scope of its activities (self-standing sales or manufacturing units obviously require a different internal structure from fully-integrated businesses); its customers and products; its stage in the life cycle; and its choice of basic architecture. It is not our purpose here to list the many possible permutations. Rather our discussion in this section focuses on some of the problems of internal organisation, some successful solutions, which have recurred in our interviews and case studies of frontier businesses around the world.

Two basic problems most frequently emerge.

1 Difficulties in building an organisation with the full range of functional capabilities required to support a modern business; notably chronic weaknesses in the areas of logistics, quality control, and sales.
2 The challenge of developing an internal structure that allows top management to delegate responsibility and encourages middle managers to

accept that responsibility and to take decisions, while still maintaining tight control.

The first of these generic problems is perhaps not too surprising. It arises right along the spectrum from joint ventures with state enterprises through to new, wholly-owned subsidiaries. Its root cause lies in the various forms of central planning that have been common throughout most of today's global frontier: be it in China, eastern Europe or the Indian subcontinent. Most local managers and staff lack experience of certain critical functions either because they were virtually non-existent in their organisations (e.g. a sales function, as distinct from order-taking), or given a low priority by the prevailing performance criteria (e.g. quality control), or the responsibility of someone else – usually distant bureaucrats (e.g. logistics). Describing a system that limited his organisation's experience with different business functions and its historic isolation from the market, a Czech manager summed it up this way: 'Once a month a lorry came and loaded what the business had produced and took it away; another lorry came and delivered the wages.'

Structuring according to local need

Many successful frontier organisations we studied have taken a three-pronged approach to dealing with this problem:

- they have adopted a structure where the divisions between groups are primarily along functional lines (grouping similar activities from right across the business together in one department, such as a single sales function),
- they have given weak areas, like quality control or logistics, a high profile within this functional structure;
- they have skewed the allocation of their expatriate managers towards the weak functions with the aim of building these up quickly.

The first of these policies flatly contradicts the direction in which organisation structures are headed in the developed world. A functional structure may be defined as one in which common, or similar activities are grouped together to form functional areas, or departments, like finance, marketing, sales, production, design, logistics, personnel, and quality control. Responsibility for the performance of each function rests with a department head. At home, managers have become increasingly concerned that the functional departments have become too powerful and insular within their organisations. In an attempt to achieve better co-ordination and compromise between departments, responsibility is being shifted towards cross-functional teams and task forces. And hierarchical chains of functional command are being pared back as companies 'de-layer'. Middle management layers have become unfashionable. Seen as an unnecessary overhead, they are being unceremoniously chopped.

But such flat, cross-functional structures cannot work unless they can draw on a strong, and relatively balanced, set of functional capabilities and systems. On the global frontier, this prerequisite is seldom satisfied. At least initially, the internal organisational structure has to be designed to develop a basic strength in each functional area, to pin clear responsibility on particular people, and to give top management a well-defined set of levers they can use to control the business. And middle management layers are often essential to much of this. The flat, network organisation might be an ideal, but it is doubtful that most frontier businesses are ready for it.

Using middle management to the full

Look at the internal structure of Shanghai Mitsubishi Elevator Company (SMEC), detailed in Fig. 8.4. Visiting SMEC, one can see that this structure demonstrably works; a fact confirmed by the company's excellent results. But it would be enough to make a trendy organisation consultant from New York or London cringe. It is dominated by functional departments and sections: sales section, installation section, metal forming workshop, technology department, personnel department, local content section, and so on. And SMEC believes that middle management – the heads of each section or workshop – are the linchpins of line management. It expects them to take full responsibility for the performance of their function against its monthly targets. Each of these individuals also undertakes a continuous programme of training designed to 'build a team of hard working, technically sound, and managerially capable people.' The chain of command within this structure is very much vertical, along functional lines. There is a clear view that, at least on the Chinese frontier, people and organisations are not ready for the ambiguity of matrix management, despite its admirable goals. The emphasis must first be on building functional strength.

Note also that quality control and logistics, two functions that need special attention on the global frontier, report directly into the managing director's office. The same prominence of the quality control, cleaning and logistics functions is evident even in a venture with a more restricted span of activities, as illustrated by Fig. 8.5 which details the internal structure

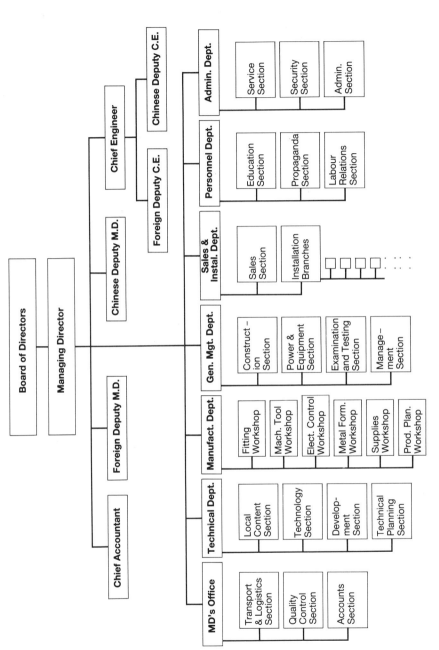

Figure 8.4   Organisational structure at Shanghai Mitsubishi Elevator Co.

adopted by Beijing Sanyo Electrics Company – a unit that assembles consumer electronics and office machines.

Functions that have been traditionally weak in the frontier markets also tend to have the largest presence of expatriates, at least in the early stages of a venture's development. China Otsuka Pharmaceutical is organised around eight functional departments: production, technology, finance and accounting, quality control, material and property management, sales, personnel, and logistics. A Japanese deputy general manager oversees the technology and logistics functions. Japanese middle managers head production, sales and finance. Expatriates have been replaced with local mangers to head other departments once a strong foundation has been laid down.

Management and delegation

The second major problem of internal organisation we identified on the global frontier was the challenge of delegation of responsibility and decision making, while at the same time maintaining tight, overall control. Again the heritage of central planning throughout much of today's global frontier is in a large part to blame for many local managers' reluctance to take decisions and accept responsibility with its associated risks. A system of 'collective neglect' was preferred as the safer option. Tight, functional structures have also helped here too. A functional structure has the merits of simple and direct lines of communication; clarity of job definition and accountability; and enables the chief executive to directly monitor the development of each functional capability (rather than dealing with, for example, managers who are responsible for all aspects of a particular group of products). These qualities are useful in frontier environments where it may otherwise be difficult to pin down responsibility.

Despite these merits of functional structures in frontier markets, they do make co-ordination across the firm more difficult. If this kind of internal structure is to be managed effectively, the areas where cross-functional co-ordination is most critical need to be identified and a facilitating structure put in place. Shanghai Mitsubishi Elevator Company have identified three such areas where co-ordination needs to be emphasised: quality, production scheduling and significant changes in the market environment. As a result, three cross-functional meetings dominate the managerial calendar.

1 A monthly quality meeting, presided over by the chief engineer and attended by all managers from the technical, production and installation functions. The meeting reviews quality performance, pinpoints the

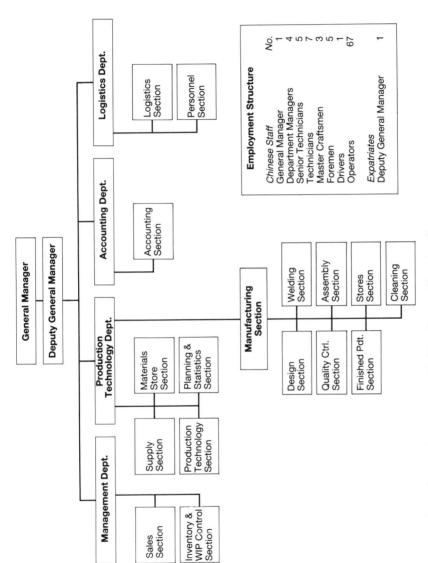

Employment Structure

Chinese Staff	No.
General Manager	1
Department Managers	4
Senior Technicians	5
Technicians	7
Master Craftsmen	3
Foremen	5
Drivers	1
Operators	67
Expatriates	
Deputy General Manager	1

Figure 8.5   Internal structure at Beijing Sanyo Electrics Co.

knock-on effects of quality failure in one area, on the performance and productivity in others and agrees an action plan.

2 A weekly production co-ordination meeting involving the set of managers whose responsibilities form the complete chain from sales, through installation, production and supply, under the chairmanship of the chief dispatcher. Its aim is to agree a schedule that smooths the production flow while maintaining customer service.

3 A weekly meeting of all section and workshop heads and their superiors, chaired by the managing director, that concentrates on developments in the market and the external environment. The objective is to make each function aware of external changes that may affect their activities and to gradually build increased market awareness in the organisation.

This last market awareness initiative has particular poignancy for frontier organisations. By their very nature frontier markets are undergoing rapid change. Yet historical circumstance means that most local managers and employees often fail to make a direct link between market developments and the success of the enterprise. Having an internal structure that includes mechanisms to progressively build this awareness is an essential, but often ignored, aspect of organisational design.

ABANDONING CONVENTIONAL WISDOM TO GET THE FRONTIER STRUCTURE RIGHT

To sum up: designing a structure that will work to support your strategy on the global frontier must begin with a shift in the basic premises on which organisational structures in the developed world are usually built. The problems a structure has to solve are peculiar to frontier markets and familiar structures often behave quite differently when transplanted to the global frontier.

So the right structure on the global frontier can require policies that contradict the prevailing orthodoxy at home. It could mean shunning a joint venture in favour of a processing contract; or allying with a small or medium-sized enterprise rather than a large state enterprise, despite the possible loss of political clout. It may require building a functional organisation with strong, even hierarchical lines of control; and investing in a large cadre of middle management – heresies in an age of de-layering and cross-functional teams. Such policies will test to the limit the receptivity of headquarters that we talked about in Chapter 2; so the benefits of adapting the structure to the realities of the global frontier often need to be sold hard at home.

Even when you have put a workable structure in place, it will have to be adapted over time, if not fundamentally restructured, as the business learns and new strategies emerge. And structure does not end within the bounds of the frontier organisation itself, it also needs to provide a framework for the way the local business interacts with its parents and affiliates back home.

Having sorted out the formal organisation structure, of course, the informal structure may still remain to be tackled: on the global frontier there is no guarantee that it will be moulded by your organisation chart. More than likely, the informal structure will be dominated by external pressures. That is one reason, among many others, it pays to have an organisation structure that allows the business to operate in harmony with the regulatory and institutional environment, rather than continually colliding with it. A way through these problems, including the issue of managing informal structure (and its sister, company culture), is to approach the task of building a frontier business as one of *managing an alliance, not a colony*. In our concluding chapter we begin by explaining the benefits to be gained by adopting this alliance philosophy.

References

1 A.D. Chandler, Jr., *Strategy and Structure: Chapters in the History of the American Industrial Enterprise*, The M.I.T Press, Cambridge, Massachusetts, 1962.
2 H. Mintzberg, Crafting Strategy, *Harvard Business Review*, July-August 1987.
3 S. Imai, A case study on Mabuchi Motor (Dalian) Co. Ltd, *China Newsletter*, No. 76, Japan External Trade Organisation, Tokyo.
4 Salgótaján Glass Wool, *East Europe Business Focus*, August-September 1990.

9

CONCLUSION – EXTENDING
THE GLOBAL FRONTIER

'The land was more than strange: it was incomprehensible to people from the other side of the world. In *The Endeavour* was Joseph Banks, one of Europe's most gifted natural scientists, but in his eight days ashore he had little hope of understanding even the seasons of this distant land. He and Cook saw freshwater creeks running into Botany Bay – creeks swift enough to turn the large waterwheel of a flour mill. They saw sweeping vistas of coarse grass and sent men to cut hay in what they thought were English meadows.'[1]

Whether we are eighteenth century explorers or 1990's business people, the sight of a new frontier evokes a vision of the future. And it isn't too surprising that this vision is usually dominated by the idea of reconstructing the best of what we already know. When Banks and Cook saw untapped torrents of running water in *Terra Australis*, they envisaged future watermills. The modern explorer would probably conceive of environmentally-friendly, hydroelectric power stations. But strategy based on cloning what we know often fails the test of market fit. That's one reason the World Bank now has a large department whose task is to 'restructure' the investments it made in third world industry a decade ago.

When faced with the bewilderment of an unfamiliar environment, we also tend to latch on to anything that is vaguely familiar and start applying practised techniques. Captain Cook sent his men to cut hay in what turned out to be a 'meadow' of resinous reeds and woody plants with razor-sharp leaves. Today, top managers would like to use their standard products and technologies to harvest what looks like untapped 'markets'. Superficially they *are* markets: they involve consumers, suppliers, exchange. But on closer inspection, these turn out to be a very different species from the information-rich, flexible and efficient markets which our standard business processes have been designed to profitably serve.

That doesn't mean a company should ditch its core competences and 'go native'. It would be foolish to set up a business so different that it was unable to benefit from a parent company's accumulated skills, systems and know-how. After all, the ability to lever off these capabilities is one of the few competitive advantages a foreign firm enjoys. To be successful a frontier strategy has to achieve the right mix of dogma and adaption living side by side. As we described in Chapter 7, for example, building a good frontier organisation can mean that quality control systems taken straight from the head office manual have to live comfortably with personnel policies that would be unthinkable at home. Frontier strategy involves much more than successfully cloning a mini-headquarters. Equally, to be competitive, foreign entrants have to offer more than an expensive imitation of the local act – where that exists – or a Disneyland creation, where it does not.

Knowing how and when to adapt is made more difficult by the fact that the best strategies for today's global frontier are often counter-intuitive. As we have found time and time again in this book, to be successful frontier strategies often have to turn the conventional wisdom of developed markets on its head.

Recognising the need for a rich cocktail of dogma, adaption and a healthy dose of counter-intuition, this chapter steps back to bring together the strategic threads. It draws out the principles that should guide those who are charged with developing a successful strategy for the global frontier (or who must ultimately carry the can for its performance). We begin by explaining a fundamental prerequisite that every frontier manager needs to accept: that the task on today's global frontier is to manage an alliance, not to build a colony.

MANAGING AN ALLIANCE, NOT A COLONY

The blueprints for today's frontier businesses cannot start with a clean slate. Unlike the Victorians' colonisation of Hong Kong, Lord Palmerston's 'barren island with hardly a house upon it', today's frontier businesses are not being built on virgin rock.[2] Instead, they face a set of institutions, infrastructures, skill concentrations and mindsets that are deeply embedded. The idea that all this will be swept away by the tide of change, however powerful, is a fallacy. Most of Eastern Europe may be moving toward a 'market economy'. But that term covers a multitude of sins; Eastern Europe is unlikely to build an exact replica of Western capitalism as we know it today; doing business in China in thirty years will not be the same as doing business in Japan now.

Of course there will be some convergence among different operating environments, especially since many frontier markets have been semi-isolated from outside influences for years. But like anywhere else in the world, today's global frontier will continue to have important idiosyncrasies. Anyone who doubts this should ask why, after unprecedented domination by America during the formative years of its postwar economy, the kind of business that succeeds in Japan today is far from a replica of that in Chicago or New York. So those who are planning to 'grin and bear it' until their frontier affiliates begin to 'act like Atlanta' (as one American manager put it) are in for a long wait. Distinctiveness is something that frontier strategies must face squarely and take on board. The days of trying to bulldoze everything out of the way so as to replace it with a 'proper' setup – one 'like ours' – are history.

Acting like the governor of a new colony is also sure to fall foul of another powerful obstacle: local pride. When we asked the foreman in a struggling Chinese joint venture why things weren't working smoothly he answered succinctly with a local proverb: 'better to be poor than to be bullied'. So even if some managers feel justified running their business like a reform school – because frontier nations' own methods and institutions have self-evidently failed – they will only make progress by approaching the task as *a partner in an alliance among equals*. To successfully manage such an alliance, two ingredients are essential.

1 A high degree of alignment between different parties' goals.
2 That as time unfolds, each party continues to have both something substantive to contribute and something substantive to gain.

Alignment of goals

Whether or not a frontier business involves an explicit joint venture, three main sets of goals need to be taken into account:

- private goals (of employees, customers, suppliers and possibly equity partners);
- national goals (which may be the responsibility of national governments, regional or local administrations or other institutions);
- international goals (including relationships between the national government of the frontier territory and those of a home country or other third country governments).

So far we have emphasised the role of private goals in shaping frontier strategy. Achieving a suitable fit with customer needs and objectives was considered in Chapter 5; with employees in Chapter 7; partners in Chapter 8; and suppliers in Chapter 4. Here we focus on alignment with national and international goals.

Success through understanding local expectations and needs

In an age of deregulation and privatisation, which has also spilled across into most of the world's frontier markets, business people might be forgiven for thinking that alignment with national, and particularly government goals was becoming less important. The rhetoric is that the foreign investors can enter a wide range of industries using a broad spectrum of strategies and structures with only the most general framework of restrictions. As far as *setting up* new ventures is concerned, this is largely true. But try to *run* a venture that is poorly aligned to national priorities and the importance of good alignment with national goals soon becomes obvious: investments that don't have a good fit with national priorities don't get quota allocations to enable them to import; they are first to be shut down when electricity or fuel is rationed; their railcars don't move; they can't secure raw materials; and demands for payment of taxes and levies seem to appear that others have never heard of.

In an economy with deep and well-developed markets, buyers are either anonymous (as is the case of markets for traded financial instruments, minerals or commodities, where brokers do not disclose the identity of the buyer) or customers who are willing to pay a given price are treated relatively equally. If there is a shortage in a developed market the price rises to ration supply to those who can afford to pay.

On the global frontier such efficient markets are the exception. Even where trading exchanges have been established (and both China and Eastern Europe have a number in financial instruments and some commodities), volumes tend to be low and trading is thin. Administrative rationing is still the primary way of dealing with scarcity on the global frontier (in other words a bureaucrat decides who gets priority); so it matters who you are and whether your *business is of national importance*.

Consumer products companies often have a hard time. Beijing Wacoal, the Sino-Japanese maker of lingerie mentioned in Chapter 7, for example, can't get a quota allocation for imported nylon or even to bring in vehicles for use in its business. Improving the design and quality of women's underwear, it seems, is not a matter of national importance. But innovative strategy can improve the position. The experience of Tambrands Inc. in the

Ukraine, provides a classic example.

On starting to explore the potential for their tampons in the mid-1980s, Tambrands were impressed by the lack of competitive offerings: the only available feminine hygiene products in the then USSR were packages of bleached cotton for fashioning home-made sanitary pads and, in some areas, non-adhesive manufactured pads. They also discovered that tampons were officially classified as a 'medical device', so the company decided to participate in a medical products trade exhibition in Moscow. Despite enthusiasm from crowds of people during times when the public were allowed in (one woman offered the equivalent of two-thirds of an average worker's monthly salary for a single box), the 'official' reaction was disinterest. One key government officer who did speak to the representatives offered a succinct piece of advice: 'Forget it; go home. Feminine hygiene issues are not exactly at the top of anyone's agenda at the Politburo.' Product quality and individual consumer need were not enough; it became obvious that Tambrands had to justify its existence in terms of the Soviet economy as a whole.

The breakthrough came when someone asked whether, when Soviet women made pads at home, they used more or less cotton than required to manufacture tampons. The answer turned out to be over five times as much. It was calculated that even if only 30 per cent of women switched to tampon use, a reasonable estimate based on Tambrand's experience in other markets, the cotton saved could earn almost $60 million annually for the government in hard cash; plus savings on the existing, heavy subsidy on each gram of bleached cotton sold domestically.[3]

Willingness to consider broader **community goals** also played an essential role when Tambrands made contact with the doctor who headed the organisation which would eventually become its partner in the Ukranian Republic who noted that:

> 'Most of the companies participating in the exhibition had only one thing on their mind: hard currency. The first things they wanted to know after I introduced myself was: "Does your department have access to foreign exchange?" Tambrands was different. Although there was a crowd of people around the exhibit, Mr Ohanian took the time to explain his product to me and then listened closely while I described to him the activities and needs of the Ukranian Central Pharmacy Department. At that point he proposed to meet for coffee. I was impressed. He wasn't pushy – he was willing to take time to get to know me. He didn't even mention hard currency.'

Fujian Hitachi Television Company (FHTC) has gone a step further in demonstrating its alignment with the Chinese national **goal of upgrading** the country's capabilities in the production of electronic components: the company formed a joint enterprise group with its 58 local suppliers. The group, a registered legal entity, co-ordinates production, quality assurance and technological innovation – using Hitachi's technical resources. Its aim: to bring local suppliers up to Japanese standards. Obviously FHTC benefits from an improved local supply base. And the company has also been rewarded for its contribution to helping Chinese companies develop: the government has given it special permission to make a proportion of its domestic sales in US$ – providing a source of foreign currency to meet the cost of the remaining imported content; its receives exemptions from normal customs inspections; priority in transport; simplified taxation procedures; continuity of electricity supply; and special immigration status to allow its expatriates to move in and out of China with minimum bureaucracy.[4]

Frontier ventures can also gain leverage by aligning with the **foreign policies** of various governments. China, for example, is of obvious strategic importance to Japan and the balance of political and military power in Asia. Not surprisingly the Japanese government has a programme of preferential loans to its neighbour; the third phase stretching from 1990–5 amounts to $8 billion. But Japan has no intention of writing blank cheques. In fact, China never sees any cash; instead the Japanese Overseas Economic Co-operation Fund makes payments for materials and equipment directly to suppliers (usually Japanese) for approved contracts. Most other countries also use their loans to promote their export sales. But under what the Japanese government calls 'combined economic co-operation' loans are not only linked with exports, but also with the needs of direct investment by Japanese companies as illustrated in Fig. 9.1.

The exchange of detailed information allows government and corporate strategies to be tightly bound together in mutual support. It is no accident that the loans underpin improved transport, power, communications and raw materials plants (such as chemical feedstocks) are located precisely where Japanese user companies need them in order to expand their own operations.

Governments around the world are keenly interested in developing their relationships with regions on today's global frontier: political alignments are up for grabs in the face of economic change; and these markets are destined to become more powerful as their wealth increases. So lobbying can pay dividends. And this need not be restricted to your 'home country' government: most multinationals have a wide network of relationships on which to build support. Even through Tambrands Inc. is an American company, Mrs Thatcher was one of the main champions of their cause in

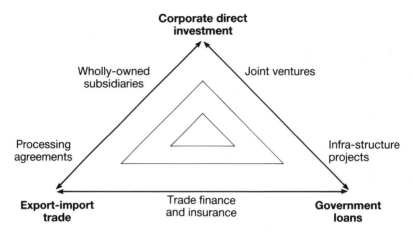

Figure 9.1   The trade/loan/investment triangle

the USSR: the British subsidiary was to provide the technical assistance and equipment to the project; besides, 'she would understand . . .'

Maintaining a balance of incentives

Many contracts on the global frontier are based on the principle of 'mutual distrust'. The result: agreements several inches thick that try to cover all eventualities. It is nice work for lawyers. But in a frontier environment with rapid change, expansion and learning, new situations and unrehearsed contingencies inevitably crop up. Agreements on the global frontier, be they with partners, suppliers, customers, local authorities or national governments are more like living organisms than fossils set in stone. As one Chinese municipal official put it: 'black and white is for printers; here we continually negotiate – that way everything that's unexpected can be sorted out'.

Nor it is possible to legislate for commitment and enthusiasm. When Otis Elevator Company decided it needed to expand its geographic coverage in China, as we discussed in Chapter 4, its partner Tianjin Elevator Company (TEC) agreed this was a good idea. But as one Otis executive remarked in 1988, after four years of working together: 'They have been willing to pay only lip service to any ventures they don't control.' On digging deeper, it turned out that the Tianjin partners were concerned that Otis might try to increase it share in TEC itself so as to gain control; that they felt Otis had been protective of a Chinese executive living in an extravagant manner and abusing his power; and that officials were concerned over high expense accounts and secrecy over salary and benefits associated with expatriate staff. Some local government officials had formed an even more negative view. At that time some reportedly felt that, with booming elevator demand, TEC could have prospered equally well without Otis's co-operation. And 'they felt that the joint venture had cost Tianjin in tax incentives provided to China Tianjin Otis Elevator Company (CTOEC), technology payments, dividends and expatriate expense reimbursements costs, and that Otis had exploited the venture through these payments, as well as by using CTOEC to promote sales of imported Otis products (on which they felt Otis made 'huge' profits). Promoting exports was done while Otis made little or no effort to live up to its export commitments.'[5]

Otis has since sorted these problems out. But similar strains between joint venture partners, local and national governments, suppliers and even customers are not uncommon. Under the banner of 'same bed, different dreams', Table 9.1 lists some of the many sources of disagreement the Japanese Nomura Research Institute found in a study of Japanese operations (including wholly-owned subsidiaries and processing agreements as well as joint ventures) in China. These range from equipment specification, employee numbers and an appropriate target return on sales (Japanese targets were considered too low!), to the term for which different agreements would run.

Some would say that on the global frontier these types of frictions are inevitable. The real issue is to solve them, rather than to pretend they won't occur. Solutions will only emerge if there are substantive incentives for continued co-operation on both sides.

The early experience of Western companies in alliances with their Japanese counterparts gives a clear demonstration of what happens when the local partner learns what it needs to know and the foreign firm finds it has run out of bargaining chips: co-operation comes painfully apart; one partner retreats feeling it been 'used'. In Japan's case, some put this down to a conspiracy to target key foreign competitors and vacuum out their proprietary competences; a sort of 'eat and run' strategy in which the package would be tossed aside.[6] But more reflective analysis found fault on both sides: Western firms often lacked a clear vision of the way the partnership would develop; they failed to control the flow information through the alliance membrane; many learned little because their own organisations were unreceptive to 'not invented here' ideas; and most importantly, many firms failed to keep on replenishing their own stock of skills, technologies and competences, so that they could continue to hold out the prospect that

Table 9.1 Same bed, different dreams

Point in contention	Chinese demand	Japanese demand
Type of product	Limited (several types)	Not limited (possibility of future expansion)
Ratio of exports to overall production	Large (70 per cent or more)	Medium to small (depending on product)
Foreign currency	Foreign currency surplus	Balance
Investment	Investment in kind and in RMB loans	Foreign currency and investment of own funds
Equity ratio	50 per cent or more	50 per cent or more
Total investment	As small as possible	Expand if necessary
Procurement of loans	Depends on foreign capital	Joint venture to procure funds by itself
Recovery of funds	Short-term (3 years)	Long-term (10 years)
Depreciation and internal holdings	As low as possible	As high as legally allowed
Profit-to-sales ratio (before tax)	High (35 per cent or more)	Low
Dividends	High dividends, in foreign currency	Suitable dividends according to monetary investments
Purchase of equipment	Low price and priority on domestic makes	Performance and priority on imports
Technical transfer	Advanced, and detailed in content	Suitable, and general in content
Technical royalties	As low as possible	International levels
Term of joint venture, co-operation, or independent investment	10 to 20 years	As long as possible (30 years)
End of term settlement	Liquidation by book value	Liquidation by market price
Arbitration of contract disputes	Arbitration commission of China International Trade Promotion Organization	Arbitration commission of Japan or third country

Table 9.1 Continued

Point in contention	Chinese demand	Japanese demand
• Prices of materials and parts	• Imported items low, domestic ones high	• Imported items high, domestic ones low
• Price of products	• Exports high, domestic low	• Exports low, domestic high
• Exchange rate	• Variable, $1=6.0 yuan RMB	• As much as possible $1=3.7 yuan (official rate)
• Number of employees	• Many Chinese and few foreigners	• As few as possible of either
• Salary to executives	• Equal work, equal pay	• Based on salary of company dispatching
• Housing for executives	• Borne by company dispatching same (foreigner)	• Borne by joint venture
• Position on land cost (including development costs)	• Suitable (according to regulations)	• 'Too high'
• Position on factory costs (including construction costs)	• Suitable	• 'Too high and quality poor'
• Status of proposal and feasibility study	• Official with binding force	• Unofficial, and with no binding force
• Overall negotiations	• Following Chinese procedures	• 'Too complicated and time consuming'
• State of legal regulations	• Being worked out	• Not yet in place, not standardised, too many 'internal' (*neibuc*, not public) documents

Source: *Chigoku toshikankyo joho* [Information on China's Investment Environment], Nomura Securities, August 1988, special issue

the alliance would be of benefit to both parties in the future – rather than simply making a one-off investment and hoping to collect the dividends thereafter.[7]

The final point is especially pertinent to relationships on the global frontier. Alliances with equity partners, customers, suppliers or governments will run aground if one party sees a future where it will simply be carrying the other. This is largely true even if the foreign participant made a large investment of cash, resources, know-how and management time near the start; memories fade with time. So it is essential to maintain substantial *future incentives* for continued co-operation from *all* parties on which a frontier business depends. This means building a shared vision with each of the other stakeholders of the path of future development a frontier business will follow. Each of the main parties a frontier business interacts with need to have a 'strategic staircase' in mind; including an understanding of what benefits might accrue to them as the business climbs with their help.

Advancing your strategy whilst building trust

There are a number of ways to operationalise this concept of Utopia. These include:

- sketching out a path for progressively upgrading technology as the frontier business proves it has mastered simpler techniques;
- implementing plans for the frontier business to continually move to more complex and sophisticated products and models within the overall product line as its capabilities develop;
- developing plans to grow the volume and value-added of exports and enter new export markets as the business demonstrates it can meet world standards of quality and delivery;
- continually exploring the viability of new investment projects, contingent on the performance of the existing operation.

Of course there are always competitive risks of too much openness. But secrecy on the global frontier is not without severe downsides (quite apart from the fact that it is usually futile): it breeds destructive mistrust and forgoes the powerful motivational impact for future plans in everyone from customers to employees and governments. People on the global frontier know that many boats will sink in the sea of restructuring and often erratic change; they want be convinced they are giving their backing to a seaworthy vessel that knows its future course and the ports at where it will call. Numerous companies, like Beijing Matsushita Color CRT Company and

Omron's medical instruments subsidiary in Dalian, to name just two, have successfully deployed these **progressive upgrade strategies** to maintain the incentive of local stakeholders to extend and improve co-operation on a broad front.

Nothing but the best in technology

The right mix of incentives varies with both the type of business and the particular stakeholder. Government's concerns, for example, may not be identical to those of suppliers, employees or customers. Technology, how-ever, is usually the most sensitive point. Unaware venturers often assume the global frontier is the perfect dumping ground for obsolete technology and equipment. But customers who buy components or intermediate pro-ducts from a frontier venture, or suppliers who hope to upgrade their technical knowledge and systems by working closely with it, know that they will never be able to compete in a more open world market with second-rate technology – no matter how low their costs. They have tried that approach and demonstrably failed. Employees become uncertain of their future, local authorities lose face, and the 'antennae' of national governments become suspicious if they think they are being palmed off with the technological cast-offs.

That doesn't mean that investors on the global frontier have to arrive with

Industry sector of sample venture	Estimated Vintage of Technology*			
	State of Art	< 5 years	5–10 years	> 10 years
Colour CRTs	●			
Elevators	●			
Pharmaceuticals		●		
Soya bean processing		●		
Garment making			●	
Automobile maintenance			●	

*Estimated on the basis of interview with management

Figure 9.2   *Technological vintage in a sample of Sino-Japanese joint ventures*

the latest technological concept straight from their research labs. As the examples in Fig. 9.2 illustrate, entry into frontier markets is possible with technology which spans a range of different vintages. The argument about learning to crawl before you walk does hold some sway.

A recipe for suicide, however, is to arrive with an 'appropriate' technology that you have no prospect of upgrading in the foreseeable future, or perhaps even in the short to medium term. That may have worked in the days of colonies, but in today's world of alliances the whole range of people whose support you need to make things work can smell this particular rat at a hundred paces. Appropriate technology may be a useful stepping-stone, but today's global frontier aspires to match world-class technology – and not in the thirty- or fifty-year cycle it originally took to develop.

Broadening the benefits

Of course if an alliance with the global frontier is going to work, there have to be substantial benefits for the foreign participant too. As we argued in Chapter 3, the key again lies in understanding how the venture is going to develop along its strategic staircase and exactly what kind of benefits will be thrown off. As with any alliance, limiting the upside to an annual cash dividend is too restrictive; potential opportunities will be missed. Other channels through which the returns can flow include:

- using the frontier operation as a source of cost-competitive, intermediate products or components for other sister operations around the world;
- accessing raw materials from partners or other frontier contacts to supply the worldwide system;
- using a frontier nation's preferential supplier status to bypass tariffs and trade restrictions faced by other supply bases (an especially important consideration in industries boxed in by trade restrictions, like textiles);
- utilising the frontier venture's customer contacts, local brands loyalty or distribution network to promote sales of complementary imports from other subsidiaries or affiliated companies;
- earning royalties, technical and licence fees both from a joint venture, but also from other, independent operations within a partner's group or those of third parties;
- strengthening relationships with existing international customers and suppliers by using a venture to help support the development of these firms' own business initiatives on the global frontier (as Japanese suppliers and service providers have done as their major customers moved into the USA, Europe and South East Asia).

Extending the global frontier, then, is not about establishing colonies on a virgin, if foreign, soil. The philosophy of managing a multifaceted alliance with numerous stakeholders needs to become pervasive. But managing a complex network of alliances is a lot more difficult than planting the flag on a fort. Our final task is to summarise how the strategies described in this book can help.

MANAGING ON THE GLOBAL FRONTIER

Whoever said 'life wasn't meant to be easy', must have had managing on frontier markets in mind. Managers charged with the task of extending the global frontier face a barrage of day-to-day problems; and in the heat of battle it is easy to lose sight of the fundamental, strategic issues that need to be addressed if all this energy is to be directed at more than fighting a lost cause. Boiled down to the bare essentials, this book has identified the following eight major obstacles in the way of building a frontier business that can successfully contribute profits and growth:

- *The information void*: quite simply, its difficult to work out what to do when its so hard to know what's going on in a frontier market;
- *The cluster bomb*: that you inevitably find yourself fighting on too many fronts at once;
- *Locational drag*: the fact that every option for locating the business is an uneasy compromise where one or more of the activities at the core of the business will be disadvantaged;
- *The locust plague*: that hordes of new competition seem to appear from nowhere, just when you seem to have a clear run at growth;
- *The leaking bucket*: that the organisation never seems to be up to the job – it lacks the right staff, enough skills and any managers who are willing to take responsibility instead of only power;
- *Brand ignorance*: the lack of established brand awareness – most consumers don't know you from Adam (or worse, the competition);
- *The 'black hole' of distribution*: that products disappear into local distribution channels that focus on volume, not on timeliness or providing information or service, its never clear when, and if, they will re-emerge;
- *The malevolent structure*: the organisational structure seems be designed to thwart each new initiative.

Faced with this litany of problems, it is tempting to rush off and do a few good (short-term) deals. After all, that's a sure way of keeping headquarters off your back. But this approach has an important downside: you're only as good as your next deal. And deals on the global frontier have a habit of going sour. As competitors build a network of strong and stable relationships with customers, suppliers, and various tiers of government, and the organisational capabilities to go on delivering time after time, the flood of deals that characterises the early days of a new market also tends to dry up.

The challenge of frontier strategy is not only to face the problems listed above, head-on, but to turn them to your advantage. The schema in Fig. 9.3 outlines how. Each of these ideas for building competitive advantages that will last merits some concluding remarks.

Superior information

Every strategy depends on information. The problem is that frontier markets are far from transparent; there is a world of currents and streams running below the surface. And people on today's global frontier know that knowledge is power, so they tend to play the cards close to their chest. The huge information industries that now account for a significant amount of total economic activity in developed markets hardly exist on the global frontier.

Worse still, information is a difficult commodity to buy. Since it's hard to judge the quality of what you have bought until its too late, transactions in information are subject to 'moral hazard' – or more bluntly, people selling you well-packaged dross with a smile. Many third party sources have their own axes to grind. And because we bring to any new market unquestioned assumptions in our baggage, we usually don't even try to buy either enough information, or information of the right sort.

So relying solely on asking the right questions of others and using the answers they provide, is a dangerous frontier game. There is no substitute for learning from experience. The issue is how to learn before making too many expensive mistakes and building more local overhead than you can cover. Chapter 2 sets out some ways forward: the strategic use of representative offices, local service centres, leasing arrangements and technical support agreements as relatively low-cost 'vacuum cleaners' to get behind closed doors and suck up information about what is really going on.

In Chapter 2, we saw that these approaches, which have served wily firms well, also have other positive spin-offs: they can ensure the reputation products and equipment exported to the global frontier are preserved by quality maintenance, user support and after sales service; they can turn a modest profit; and because the information is based on the actual experience

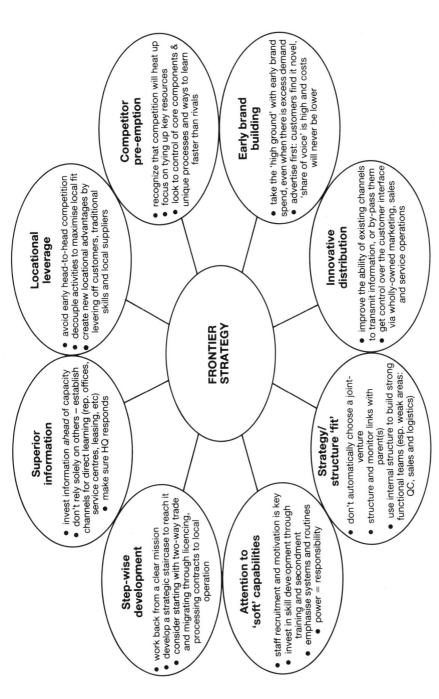

Figure 9.3   Winning on the global frontier

of your own staff, it may carry more weight back at headquarters.

To make such an information strategy work, however, things back at the home base also need to change. Traditional performance measures need to be adjusted to value outputs with less immediate benefit to the bottom line – like quality of information and an expanding knowledge base. But precisely because the benefits are less intangible, senior managers need to press hard to ensure progress is actually being achieved (especially since, in many frontier markets, it can be more comfortable to hide behind a desk). Measures also need to be taken to increase receptivity at home. The news from the frontier is often just what managers at headquarters don't want to hear (the product or process needs adaption, you can't use the standard sales approach, etc). Quality information is of little use if headquarters isn't set up to take it on board and respond.

Of course there is no such thing as perfect information. Fortunately perfect information isn't what you need: it only needs to be superior to what competitors have been able to glean. To get this advantage requires putting people on the ground and involving them in activities where they enter *the bloodstream of a frontier market* so as to build relationships and learn – passively collecting sanitised data is by no means good enough. Involvement in servicing, leasing and technical advice have the advantage of taking them close to the heart of changing operations in frontier markets. Locating these activities in the thick of things is also to be preferred: people don't find out much in a bell-jar or perhaps even the kind of special development zone which we referred to in Chapter 2 as a 'golden cage'.

Step-wise development

The second major problem we identified was that of fighting on too many fronts at once. With the many potential opportunities the pace of development in frontier markets throw up, and the severe shortage of resources to devote to them, setting strategic priorities is even more important than elsewhere.

If a frontier business is to do more than be buffeted by the waves of frontier chaos it needs clarity of mission. And not just any strategic intent will do – it's easy to dream up a folly – the mission needs to be firmly grounded in local market behaviour. That's the first sort of leverage a strategy to build up superior information can provide.

If a frontier business is also to avoid sinking into what can seem like an impossible gulf between current reality and future aspirations, the task of closing this gap must be broken down into manageable steps. The venture needs what we have called a 'strategic staircase': a logical sequence of steps through which it can build the capabilities required for success.

As Chapter 3 pointed out, trade transactions are often a good first step. The trade capacity of frontier markets usually runs ahead of their domestic economic development. A number of the key frontier markets today are major traders (China, for example, now ranks tenth in the list of world trading nations). And in building a platform of trade on which to build, it's often better to begin as a buyer. You will receive an assured reception; as a buyer, doors open which would otherwise be bolted shut. We saw that finding an exportable product also helps provide a source of foreign currency to underpin the operation of a subsequent manufacturing base (which often requires hard currency to import materials, components or spare parts). Foreign currency balance is often essential to operations on the global frontier. And people who say there is nothing in frontier markets to buy should remember that some of these regions in fact run a trade surplus with the rest of the world, and even with the USA.

From a trade platform, the path of migration can sensibly proceed through equipment deals and processing contracts: each step builds securely on the knowledge and relationship base established by its predecessor which can also provide seed-corn staff with the skills to get the next initiative up and running quickly; over-commitment to partners whose real intentions and foibles are unknown can be avoided. This approach may seem unduly cautious and downright slow. But in the experience of a number of the companies we discussed, it has proven to be a case of less haste, more speed – progress was steady and continuous and they spent less time sliding backwards than some of their more reckless cousins.

Locational leverage

One of the other key decisions that needs to be taken early in the life of any frontier business is location. There are two basic problems: no single location is ever ideal; and once a firm puts down roots, it's often difficult to move. Locational 'magnets' that attract some activities repel others: sales and service want to be near customers and growth, but they don't want to find themselves in a siege for the 'walled cities' of competitors; manufacturing want to be away from congestion and near traditional skills bases (many of which are not in the major centres due to the distortions of former central planning throughout much of today's global frontier), and so on. Compromise risks end up with the worst of all worlds.

The peculiar nature of dispersed geographic development on the global frontier (and this heritage is very slow to change) may therefore necessitate that the concept of a single, integrated headquarters needs to be abandoned in order to succeed in a frontier market. Successful frontier strategy often means activities within the organisation need to be decoupled: so manufacturing should migrate to a location that suits it, while the centre of sales and service is elsewhere, and logistics is run out of a major transport node.

This has two further strategic implications. First, companies need to pay particular attention to intra-firm communications across considerable distances. This often means setting up a private network – like the Hungarian insurance company that runs its business with mini satellite discs – until the public infrastructure catches up. Second, to take full advantage of decoupling, each unit needs to proactively build on the local resources its location offers.

The last point is true, to a greater or lesser extent, for all frontier businesses: gaining locational leverage means creating new sorts of local advantages, not just passively choosing a promising site. That means working closely with local customers to test new product ideas, getting close to local educational institutions who train scarce staff, and developing cost-competitive local sources by working with suppliers, to recap just some of the initiatives for which we gave examples in Chapters 4 and 7 of this book.

Strategies for locational leverage, then, go far beyond identifying a favourable place to set up: they go to the heart of how a successful frontier business should structure its activities, draw strength from local clusters of customers, suppliers and other institutions, and decide if and what it should make versus buy.

Competitor pre-emption

Because the global frontier offers obvious growth potential, it's tempting to believe that you have thrown the competition off. And it is true that you may have escaped the trench warfare for half of one point of market share that is so common in many saturated markets today. But as soon as you have taken your eye off the competitive ball, competition on the global frontier, like Chingiz Khan, appears out of 'nowhere' behind your line.

A more realistic working hypothesis would be that once a new market opportunity is proven, it will attract new competition as sure as night follows day. With it will come many of the cash traps associated with competition in developed markets like investment stalemate, unprofitable attempts at differentiation, costs of complexity, and the prospect of becoming caught behind barriers to mobility. In fact, as we saw in Chapter 6, they may come sooner and in a more virulent form. The advantage of doing business on the global frontier is that you get a chance to do something to head off these destructive spirals *before* they take root. The challenge of frontier strategy is to use this time window wisely; too many companies simply fritter it away under the pressure of getting the organisation to deliver.

Frontier strategy therefore needs to use the grace period of muted rivalry that frontier markets offer to pre-empt future competitors. The key weapons of pre-emption are threefold:

- tying up prime sources of supply and channels of distribution;
- becoming the major local supplier of certain core components or inter-mediate products (so the competition is dependent on buying from you);
- finding ways to build your local capabilities faster than both the existing competition and future entrants can.

Recall the example of Beijing Matsushita Color CRT Company in Chapter 6: they now virtually control China's massive colour TV set manufacturing industry by dominating local production of the picture tubes that form the core of other's products. But any single competitive advantage seldom lasts for ever, so the ideal pre-emption strategy involves using an initial period of muted frontier rivalry to build the kind of organisation which can go on developing its local capabilities and absorbing foreign technology and skills faster than its competitors can. Against a business that has developed a superior capacity for learning, rivals have little hope of ever catching up.

Attention to 'soft' capabilities

Building such an organisation isn't easy in the most conducive of environ-ments. On the global frontier it is the process of building the 'soft' capabilities: quality of staff, skills, systems, embedding the right decision-making style, that managers find the toughest challenge. The local organisa-tion never seems to be up to the tasks a frontier market presents. There is a shortage of good staff; no one to train recruits; when they are trained they auction their skills elsewhere and resign; the managerial ranks, bred on risk aversion, grab power, but eschew responsibility.

An important reason for these problems, as we saw in Chapter 7, is that investment in hardware often runs ahead of softer organisation capabilities. And it's hard to focus on recruiting and training people when $100 million of shiny, new plant is plagued by breakdowns, quality problems and shortages because the organisation can't cope.

One solution has its roots back in our staircase of step-wise development:

people trained and systems developed in a previous local activity can provide the seed-corn for the organisation to underpin the next initiative. This provides a way of building up a stock of soft capabilities ahead of the next hardware investment: 'soft before hard'. A similar result can be achieved by seconding staff back to home base or sister subsidiaries elsewhere to be trained before they are needed on a new, frontier line.

This basic approach to developing organisational capabilities can be bolstered by other initiatives we detailed in Chapter 7: careful design of the reward and penalty systems aimed at shaking out unsuitable individuals and motivating others to stay; painting a clear vision of future development which staff can rally around; by embedding detailed systems and routines designed to eliminate bad work habits and make the task of control easier by increasing transparency; and through tightly defined job descriptions and chains of command to ensure power and responsibility are glued together.

Early brand building

Early investment in brands is another important means of pre-empting competitors. Faced with initial excess demand for their products, many frontier investors pass up what is, in fact, a unique opportunity. They feel marketing is a waste of money at a time when they can't supply enough. As we saw in Chapter 5, they are often wrong: there are important arguments for taking the high ground in a frontier market while it is available.

Recall that one important reason lies in what we called the 'paradox of up-market consumerism' on the global frontier. Disposable income levels need to be judged against other outlets for spending: since governments still tend to play a large role in life on today's global frontier, the proportion of income spent on education, transport and health care tends to be low. There are often few opportunities to invest in real estate in contrast to many developed markets where bigger and more luxurious housing is a major sink for personal cash. Items considered mundane in many developed markets are still status symbols on the global frontier. Many people on the global frontier also resent having to make do with the world's third class offering. All of these forces act to favour up-market brands of many types of goods. And things initially get better for these brands as frontier market consumers get richer: more people can satisfy their aspiration to buy the top ranking brands. It therefore pays to build volume from the base of an initial perception of quality – not the kind of low-end product people can't wait to abandon.

At the same time, the early years in the life of a frontier market is often the most cost efficient time to build a brand: customers are impressionable, you don't have to break down loyalty to existing brands; since there are often few competing advertisements, you can achieve a high 'share of voice'; and advertising rates are often lower than they will ever be again.

So while a cheap and cheerful strategy may be the way to maximise initial sales volumes, this is often not the best way to build the future potential of a frontier business. Indeed, a number of the companies emerging as frontier successes today started marketing their brands to prepare the ground and take advantage of a never-to-be repeated opportunity even before they had more than a trickle of products to sell.

You only get one chance to enter a frontier market completely afresh. And once you establish a product positioning it is usually difficult and costly to change it – history is difficult to throw off, especially in a frontier market where first impressions can count for a lot. So it's important to get the initial positioning right. In Chapter 5 we showed how a tool like the value line can help you decide where to position your brand on the price/quality spectrum – a choice that also impacts other fundamental decisions like what technology to deploy and how much capacity to install.

Innovative distribution

As we noted at the start of this section, a constant frustration of frontier markets is that so little of what is there already ever works. Distribution is no exception; it can be a 'black hole'. Chapter 5 also pointed out one of the main reasons: existing distribution systems in most of today's frontier markets were designed with one performance measure in mind – volume. Time in the guise of speed and certainty was immaterial. And distribution didn't take much of a role in marketing the product, advising customers how to use it, or servicing it after sale. Its main role was as a pipe from plant to customer.

For most frontier businesses, that kind of distribution support won't do. There are three basic alternative strategies: to invest in existing distribution channels with the aim of improving their capability to act as a conduit for marketing information, technical advice and service; to abandon existing channels and go direct; or some of each.

The last of these approaches which involves partial forward integration, usually into marketing and service, leaving physical distribution to existing channels, is often the most fruitful. It seeks to strike a balance between the major advantages of using an existing third party channel: avoiding an additional lump of fixed costs and levering off existing customer relationships; and the advantages of going direct: better control of the customer interface and improved flow of information to and from the market.

Ultimately, where exactly the best tradeoff lies, will vary product by product, case by case. But the important strategic point is this: distribution can make or break a frontier business, and yet, because it is out of sight of the executive office, or 'too difficult' in many of today's sprawling frontier markets, it seldom gets the innovative management it deserves.

Strategy/structure fit

The final bane of the frontier manager, as we saw in Chapter 8, is a structure that brawls continually with its brother, strategy. This insolent structure has often been imposed from above: a standard subsidiary organisation chart; or 'a joint venture where we have equity not less than 50.1 per cent'.

The first point is that if strategies are to respond to the frontier environment, they should differ from the standard template; so in order to fit, and support, the strategy, structure needs the flexibility to adjust.

The latest organisation chart deigned by head office is unlikely to be ideal. One of the counter-intuitive points we noted, for example, is that while many organisations in developed markets are trying to break the power and rigidities of functional organisations, on the global frontier a functional structure may be just the ticket. Functional baronies do have their problems. But they do make a contribution. And on the global frontier building functional strength is more often the problem than limiting the function's power. Notably weak areas in many frontier organisations are quality control, sales and logistics. Putting them under a direct reporting line to the managing director is one way that structure can be used to build up and fulfil the frontier strategy.

Similarly, while the fashion for flat organisations in the developed world is making middle management an endangered species, a strong cadre of middle managers can be exactly what a frontier business needs to function smoothly and to help it grow. Frontier workers often lack a shared vision of success, they frequently need a great deal of on-the-job traning and close hour-by-hour supervision, the kind of support that only a strong middle management team can provide.

The other strategic lesson was not to automatically choose an equity joint venture. Other structures, like processing agreements or wholly-owned subsidiaries can have powerful advantages for the right kinds of strategies on today's global frontier. The basic point is straightforward: consider the spectrum of options and the kinds of pros and cons we outlined in Chapter 8.

HARNESSING THE GLOBAL FRONTIER FOR GROWTH

This book began with a fundamental problem facing the top management of today's corporations: the fact that economic growth in developed markets is insuffient to meet the demands of their shareholders and their organisations for consistent expansion at double-digit rates. A long string of initiatives have been launched to fight market saturation in North America, Europe and even Japan: driving costs down along scale and experience curves; product differentiation; diversification; a massive expansion in variety within each product line; increased responsiveness and service; and even mass customisation. Each makes a contribuion; it staves off saturation for a few more years; it squeezes out a little more growth from a consumer base often overwhelmed by products and choices. Yet each initiative eventually reaches its natural plateau: it continues to make a contribution to total sales, but not the substantial kick of new growth that is necessary to make any real difference to the overall results of a large corporation.

So the boards of large corporations are taking another look at world maps; geographic expansion is back on the agenda. But most of the easy markets have already been claimed, by these corporations themselves, their competitors, or both. The maps are already awash with pins. The next phase of geographic expansion will have to come by extending the global frontier.

From the comfort of the boardroom on the 82nd floor it can look deceptively simple: a map with empty white spaces just waiting to be filled; millions of potential customers, hungry for Western products; world-class competitors not yet entrenched. And while these white spaces used to be politically hostile, they are moving rapidly in our direction – towards 'market economies' (just like ours); the time for extending our global frontier looks ripe. So it's tempting to clone the kind of operation that has served us well elsewhere; safety with the devil you know; besides; that's what 'they' need (if they know what's good for them). There are a few 'little local difficulties', but these peculiarities are nothing money can't bulldoze out of the way, or a well-connected partner can't fix. And we must move fast, the opportunity won't wait; let's not dabble – big companies need to make big, decisive moves right from the first day.

This is a caricature, of course. But these are cruel delusions and they are more common than we would like to admit. What we have demonstrated in this book is that rushing off to replicate the kind of businesses we know, clones of our headquarters on the empty steppes of the global frontier, cannot be expected to produce the desired results. Assuming that all our tried and tested formulae will work on the global frontier has all the same problems of forecasting the future on the basis of a straight-line projection of the past. The reason is that in many respects, today's global frontier is the world we know turned upside down.

Sometimes we need to discipline this topsy-turvy frontier with dogmatic application of our corporate systems, technologies and work practices – quality control and stock management systems are classic examples. But at other times, successful frontier strategy has to overturn corporate orthodoxy, flatly contradict the conventional wisdom of management in the developed world; in short, it has to break all the rules. Recall just a few examples from earlier chapters of this book:

- Toyota filling the information void by starting with after-sales service before setting up manufacturing;
- ICL building one of eastern Europe's most successful computer operations on the basis of a joint venture manufacturing furniture for export;
- Shanghai Mitsubishi Elevator decoupling manufacturing, sales, installation and service across 36 sites;
- McDonald's buying paper from one Russian supplier and shipping it to another Russian manufacturer in order to develop a local source of take-out bags;
- Hitachi spending heavily on advertising its TV sets at a time that it couldn't hope to supply enough units to meet demand;
- Mars Inc. filling Russian billboards and airwaves with advertisements for chocolate in order to pre-empt competition that didn't yet exist;
- Wacoal setting up a network of – demonstration counters to sell women's underwear in Chinese retail stores;
- Ryan International becoming the first Western company to gain a share of Poland's huge coal industry, and exporting 111,000 tonnes of coal per year from a facility it built to reclaim coal by cleaning up an existing discard tip;
- Beijing Matsushita becoming a dominant force in the Chinese market for TV's by setting up an operation to manufacture picture tubes and sell them to its local competitors rather than concentrating solely on selling sets, and by building a cadre of 250 Chinese staff training in Matsushita systems before it even built a local TV plant;
- Shanghai Mitsubishi Elevator building its success on a structure based on tight functional divisions with middle management at its core – in an era where most companies at home are breaking down functional structures and shedding middle management through delayering;
- Tambrands Inc. obtaining its initial approval to manufacture and sell its

products in the Ukraine on the basis that, by converting women to tampons, the country would have more cotton available to export.

In navigating through the minefield the global frontier presents, the need for dogma and heresy side by side should be obvious. The difficult problem is which of these stances to take at any particular juncture. And because pushing back the global frontier is something *you can do only once*, it's important to *get it right first time*. Most frazzled frontier managers are not, in fact, struggling with inherent problems of frontier markets, but fighting fires they, or their predecessors ignited (often under pressure from headquarters) earlier on.

Extending the global frontier is the next source of corporate growth. The tasks of this book have been to show, in practical terms, where the traps are; how to improve the odds; and why conventional strategy often needs to be turned on its head in order to make the next phase of globalisation a profitable reality.

References

1 G. Blainey, *The Tyranny of Distance: How Distance Shaped Australia's History*, Sun Books, Sydney, Revised Edition, 1985, p 11.
2 N. Cameron, *The Cultural Pearl*, Oxford University Press, Hong Kong, 1978.
3 Tambrands, Inc. The Femtech Soviet Joint Venture (A), Harvard Business School, case No. 9-390-159, Publishing Division, Harvard Business School, Boston, Massachuetts.
4 S. Imai, Case Study Three – Fujian Hitachi Television Company, Ltd, *China Newsletter*, No. 75, Japan External Trade Organisation, Tokyo, 1988.
5 Otis Elevator Company (B-1): China Joint Venture, Harvard Business School case No. 9-393-006, Publishing Division, Harvard Business School, Boston, Massachusetts, p 8.
6 See, for example, R.B. Reich and E.D. Mankin, Joint Ventures with Japan Give Away Our Future, *Harvard Business Review*, March-April, 1986.
7 Many of these points are discussed more fully in G. Hamel and C.K. Prahalad, Collaborate with your competitors – and win, *Harvard Business Review*, January-February, 1989.

INDEX